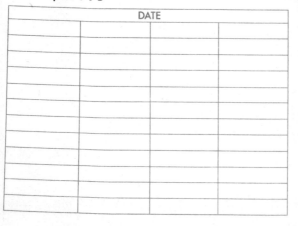

Bashing Chicago Traditions

Bashing Chicago Traditions

HAROLD WASHINGTON'S LAST CAMPAIGN: CHICAGO, 1987

MELVIN G. HOLLI and PAUL M. GREEN

GRAND RAPIDS, MICHIGAN

WILLIAM B. EERDMANS PUBLISHING COMPANY

For
SIDNEY FINE
scholar, mentor, friend

Copyright © 1989 by William B. Eerdmans Publishing Company
255 Jefferson Ave. S.E., Grand Rapids, Michigan 49503

Library of Congress Cataloging-in-Publication Data

Holli, Melvin G.
Bashing Chicago traditions.

Includes index.
1. Washington, Harold, 1922–1987. 2. Mayors—
Illinois—Chicago—Biography. 3. Chicago (Ill.)—
Politics and government—1951–
I. Green, Paul Michael. II. Title.
F548.54.W36H65   1989   977.3′11043′0924 [B]   89–1381
ISBN 0–8028–7052–X

Contents

Preface

HAROLD WASHINGTON was the most colorful, charismatic, and articulate urban politician in the memory of most Chicagoans. Robust and handsome, he could speak the king's English or engage in funky down-home banter on the streets; he could switch easily from a speech to the proletarians to a speech to the patricians. A yarn spinner, especially in the black community, he could paint vivid word pictures that would express defiance or ask for sympathy. As a political wordsmith and campaigner on the hustings, Mayor Washington had few peers in contemporary Chicago. His election in 1983 would lead to a revolutionizing of the city's politics and bring about permanent and lasting change.

This study of Washington's mayoral years is intended neither as a paean of praise nor a critical jeremiad. We hope, rather, to render an objective analysis by examining both the positives and the negatives in the Washington story. The paradoxes of Washington's public career make that imperative: he was a superb and consummate politician who galvanized the black electorate unlike any leader in Chicago's history; at the same time, he was a below-average and sometimes mediocre administrator and chief for the whole city. The political promise was greater than the mayoral performance. The paradox between the performance and promise became most apparent in that last shining month of his mayoralty, when Washington made a grand gesture of reconciling Chicago's multiethnic, multireligious, and multiracial people. Unfortunately, the grand gesture was too late to be put into operation as a governing philosophy for the mayor.

He died on November 25, 1987, before the "mayor-of-all-the-people" could be fully unveiled. The last act was truly as creative and courageous as the first three years were stalemated and stumbling. The challenge we accepted was to paint the "warts-and-all" picture but not to mistake blemishes for the whole picture. We have sought to achieve a balanced assessment that is thoroughly grounded in the events of history—although we do address the mythic proportions of the man in the closing chapter.

Our book is divided into two sections: the first five chapters deal with political events evolving out of Harold Washington's first election, including "Council Wars," the aldermanic redistricting elections, "Operation Incubator," the Richard M. Daley-inspired nonpartisan mayor petition drive, the preprimary and primary maneuvering, and finally the feverish four-way battle in March and April of 1987 that resulted in Washington's last election. Part II focuses on the meaning of the Washington years by examining the "hollow prize" thesis, the Chicago political traditions that Chicago's first black mayor affirmed and denied, the public measures of Mayor Washington's successes and failures; and we end with a look at the pageantry of the Washington funeral and the chaos of installing an acting mayor in City Hall after his death.

We are indebted to a large number of people for both information and insights into the Washington campaigns and administration, and we would like to discharge at least a token of that debt by publicly thanking some of them for their assistance. Dr. Robert Mier, commissioner of economic development, Samuel Ackerman, deputy commissioner of personnel, Ularse Manar and McNair Grant of the city's Department of Purchasing, and Kirstin Svare of Streets and Sanitation provided us with vital data by following the spirit and letter of Mayor Washington's freedom-of-information executive order. Laura Washington of the mayor's press office often steered us in the right direction. Raymond Scannel of the Construction Employers' Association, and Michael Thom, then with the Association of Commerce and Industry, gave us the private sector's angle of vision on the city administration (as did some others who prefer to remain unnamed). John McDermott of Operation CONDUCT and Jerry Harris, a keen labor history researcher, helped us to zero in on some of the key issues in the book. We would also like to acknowledge the assistance of many elected and appointed officials and candiates who submitted patiently to our interviews and sometimes thorny questions, including Jane Byrne, Donald Haider, Cecil Partee, Charles Pounian, and Aldermen Edward Burke, Keith Caldwell, Burton Natarus, Martin Oberman, Edward Smith, and Bernard Stone. For their critical reading of various parts of this book, we would like to thank professors William J. Adelman, Barry R. Chiswick, Edward Marciniak; and for critical discussion raised by some of the issues in this book, we are indebted to Professors Robert Starks, Charles Branham, Pierre DeVise, and to Thomas Roeser of the City Club. We would also like to express our appreciation to the Campus Research Board of the University of Illinois at Chicago for granting one of the present authors a one-term research leave, which expedited the completion of the final phase of this book. Special thanks also go out to the University of Chicago's Professor Arthur Mann for encouragement, constructive criticism, and unfailing collegiality. All, of course, are absolved of any responsibility for any errors of fact or interpretation.

I.

The Event

WASHINGTON'S LAST ELECTION

CHAPTER ONE

Harold Washington's First Election

HAROLD WASHINGTON rushed upon the Chicago political scene like an angry burning ember on tinder-dry prairie grass, and he ignited a political prairie fire that burned fiercely in 1983, profoundly altering the "natural order" of things and changing the political ecology of power. The guiding light of the old-time power brokers flickered and dimmed. With the help of a black power movement, Harold Washington had mounted the most powerful populist, grassroots challenge to the political establishment since Kelly-Nash put together the modern machine in 1933.

Only twice in the twentieth century had political progressives or maverick reformers been able to knock over the established political machine: in 1905, when lifelong reformer Edward Dunne won the mayoralty, and again in 1923, when an oddly puritanical Catholic, William E. Dever, succeeded. (Jane Byrne's 1979 upset is not counted as a reform win.)[1] Both Dunne and Dever served but one term before old-guard machines reasserted themselves and took back power. Ironically, the outsider challenger who in 1983 caused all of the fuss was neither an oddly puritanical Catholic nor a lifelong reformer. Instead, Harold Washington was a lifelong patronage employee and a machine minion who had spent most of his career working for the Democratic organization and alternately representing a single-race district and advancing mostly its single-race concerns.

3

Harold Washington, the maverick seeking to beat City Hall in 1983, was born in Chicago in 1922, the son of an itinerant preacher and precinct captain, Roy Washington. Harold attended the local public schools and was also sent to Milwaukee's St. Benedict the Moor Catholic School, which he disliked so intensely that he ran away three times. In high school he showed some spark playing softball, running track, and boxing. But he quit before he graduated and did a stint in the Civilian Conservation Corp (a New Deal relief program for youth) planting trees and quarrying stone. Drafted into the service during World War II, Washington became a soil technician who checked ground samples for hardness for potential airfield runways in the Pacific. Then it was back to Chicago as a G.I. Bill student for an undergraduate degree at Roosevelt University, where he was a "big man on campus," and after graduation to a more demanding Northwestern University Law School, where he was not a big man on campus. In fact, Washington's law professors could not remember anything about him, nor could his student peers recall much of his law school days. But he did plug through for a degree in 1952, and then he took over his father Roy's precinct when the latter died in 1953. For the next decade and a half he held a series of patronage jobs and was described by one critic as the "original ghost payroller." Washington was elected to the state legislature in 1965, where he served through 1978, when he went to the U.S. Congress for two terms. He absented himself from Congress to enter the Chicago Democratic mayoral primary in 1983.[2] There was very little in Washington's career to suggest a reformer in the making or a political maverick who would rebel against his political machine sponsors.

Although Washington was the first plausible black mayoral candidate in the city's history, his run was not completely *sui generis*, as so many of his supporters thought at the time. Washington's candidacy was part of an ongoing stream of political history in which mavericks and outsiders from time to time have used the primaries to defeat the political establishment's candidates. Primaries have historically served the "outs" against the "ins," and in time-honored fashion Washington entered the George Washington-day primary of 1983 to bring the "outs" in and to overturn the decisions of the Democratic slatemakers. No challenger in the post-Daley era had such a powerful, well-organized community movement behind him. It was different

4

from Jane Byrne's spontaneous and unorganized grassroots up-
rising in 1979. The Byrne insurrection was, as it developed, a
multiracial, citywide, one-shot howl of protest. The Washington
movement, by contrast, had legions of "true believers" behind
it—mostly black—and was part of a historical protest becoming
a crusade.

The Chicago primary election campaign ran from December
to election day, February 22, 1983. The Republican party, long
since reduced to cipher status and political impotence by twenty-
one years of the Daley machine, often ran a no-name candidate
in their own primary, to which no one paid any attention. These
uncontested primaries generally produced a vague-sounding reform candidate who was expected to pay his own way and go
the distance in the general election, which had become a hope-
less kamikaze mission. The GOP's pick in 1983 was a northside
Chicago millionaire insurance lawyer and former state legislator
named Bernard Epton. The Democratic candidates, all seasoned
politicians, included Jane Byrne, the incumbent mayor, who was
elected in 1979 and was now seeking renomination; young Richard M. Daley, son of "Boss," the Cook County state's attorney;
and 61-year-old black congressman Harold Washington, whose
maiden run for the Democratic mayoral nomination in 1977 had
produced a poor showing of only 11 percent of the vote.

Although the incumbent Byrne was a woman, the Chicago
newspapers—the *Tribune*, the *Sun Times*, and the *Defender*—refrained from attacking her simply as a woman, subject to her
"raging hormones," female proclivities, and changes of mind.
There had been some of that early in her first term; but by
renomination time the news media had become more circum-
spect and avoided treating her as some caricature of a female.
Even so, Byrne did not enjoy a favorable press. She was called
"Calamity Jane" and "Attila the Hen" by the news columnists and
by her opponents, who tried to create the impression among
Chicago's citywide electorate that she had destabilized government, business, and labor relations in the city.[3]

When the campaign began in December, Mayor Byrne saw
young Rich Daley as her principal opponent. Born in the blue-
collar 11th Ward, young Daley was proud of his dad, the ex-
mayor, and of having been raised in a ward that Chicagoans
called the "neighborhood of mayors." Four of the last five had
come from the district known as Bridgeport, the nesting place
of their Irish forebears. Young Daley was determined to make it

five out of six. Rich Daley campaigned on the theme of the unsteadiness of Byrne, implying that she had disrupted the orderliness of Chicago business-labor-political community and turned Chicago into a "Chaos-fest" instead of a Chicagofest (a weeklong series of rock and pop concerts with food bazaars and exhibits paid for by the city). Daley reached for a citywide electorate with promises that, if nominated, he would bring "stability, predictability, and calm" back to the city.

Harold Washington, the former machine politician, had presumably become a reformer. When he spoke to white audiences of lakeshore liberals, yuppies and citywide groups, he charged that the Byrne administration was shot through with corruption, family favoritism, waste, and contract awards to political cronies, and that the mayor was bankrupting the city. (In the last charge Washington was suggesting to citywide audiences that Chicago, like New York, might be teetering on the brink of bankruptcy— even though very little factual evidence existed to support that claim.) Washington promised these predominantly white audiences that if he was elected mayor, he would clean out the "corruption" and give the city's contracts only to the best and most qualified bidder, regardless of race; fire hundreds of unneeded and wasteful city employees; and bring honesty, probity, and good government to Chicago.

Washington aimed his message at two or possibly three different audiences: he assured the black community, which got three-fourths of his campaign visits, that it would become the major power player in Chicago if he won; he told the citywide white community (and some upper-income blacks) that he would end corruption, open up city government to everyone, improve street repairs and cleaning, divert downtown resources to the neighborhoods, and bring jobs to the city; and finally, he assured the liberal lakeshore yuppie community that he would reform government, bring in a "clean-as-a-hound's-tooth" administration, open up city records, and run a no-nonsense, businesslike administration.[4]

The incumbent, Mayor Jane Byrne, faced a difficult uphill communication battle. She had committed costly blunders by turning former supporters, the black voters, against her by replacing black appointees on the Chicago Housing Authority and the Chicago Board of Education with whites, and by petulantly attacking a popular black alderman and targeting him for defeat. Her negatives had grown. She had to persuade Chicagoans that

6

she was not a "Calamity Jane" who "shot from the lip" and kept Chicago politics in a state of turmoil with her helter-skelter firing and hiring policies, which had become known as the "revolving door" policy. This was how Washington, Daley, and some of the news media had come to portray her.

Her first move toward changing that unflattering public image was the hiring of a New York public relations consultant, David Sawyer. Sawyer mounted a million-dollar television advertising campaign (beginning in December 1982 and extending through February 1983) that portrayed a different Jane Byrne. Instead of flashy, brightly colored outfits, she appeared in the television ads wearing two-piece oxford grey business suits, looking more like a staid English banker than a Chicago politician. The pitch of her voice also dropped noticeably in those ads—to a low-keyed, modulated, steady purr. Gone was the excitable, "shoot-from-the-lip" Jane; gone too were the scowl and the furrowed brow. Instead, viewers saw a steady in-control administrator who said nothing derogatory about her opponents but intoned about the achievements of her administration. She recounted what she had done for the city at large, for the neighborhoods and the schools, and for the "minority" communities.[5]

When her opponents and newsmen continued to harp on the old "Bad Jane" image and asked where the abrasive and combative—the "fighting Jane"—had gone, Byrne's answer in TV commercials was that "Chicago was a tough and feisty town" and needed a "tough and feisty mayor" like her to make it run. She also occasionally used clichés like "when the going gets tough, the tough get going." Yet for most of the campaign the incumbent mayor stayed in character with the "new Jane": cool and calm, saying little disparaging about her opponents. It was a masterful transformation—but not masterful enough.

In a series of candidate television debates beginning on January 18, 1983, Harold Washington looked good. Photogenic and ruggedly handsome, the black challenger was crisp and articulate, and he zeroed in with surgical skill on the incumbent mayor's weak spots. Dropping such blockbusters as "Mayor Byrne is destroying our city," he was a hit in the first debate. Most observers conceded the event to Washington. Part of the reason was that his opponents, chipping away timorously with dry and wooden prose, appeared to be zombies. Byrne, almost catatonically tuned down by her media advisor for all four of the debates, recited a dull litany of achievement. Daley, who, it was said, could not stand on his feet and debate at the same time, occasionally interrupted his low-key droning with short, monosyllabic attacks on Byrne, referring to some unclear future should he be nominated. Some of the dullness of the debates can be attributed to the two white candidates' hesitation to attack the black challenger for fear of losing some of the all-important black vote. "The thing we feared most was the race issue. That's why we couldn't attack Washington," said Byrne's media advisor afterwards.[6] Faced with a feeble opposition, Washington scored big not only in debate points but with a larger public.

With an outsider's critical advantage, Washington unloaded indictment after indictment of the incumbent for ignoring the neighborhoods, souring the business climate, wasting taxpayers' money, and general incompetence. Washington ignored young Daley as though he were merely sideshow entertainment. The black challenger was tough and articulate; he established himself as a viable candidate and a realistic alternative. Above all, he looked the most mayoral of the three.

Only during the closing week of the campaign, when Mayor Byrne realized from her private pollster that her "new Jane" campaign was not working well enough to win her renomination, did she take the gloves off. Her polls showed that she was slowly losing black voters to Washington, and that white voters alienated by Washington were not moving to her side of the column. Persuaded that she could only win by enticing white Daley voters to her side, she had one of her campaign advisors, Alderman Edward R. Vrdolyak, make a desperate plea for white voters by telling an audience of precinct captains: "Don't kid yourself. . . a vote for Daley is a vote for Washington." This "has become a racial thing. . . we are fighting to keep the city the way it is."[7]

This last-ditch gamble was widely interpreted as a blatant appeal to racism, and it had an unanticipated and paradoxical effect. It hurt Daley only slightly, helped Washington enormously, and probably lost for Byrne her black vote and the election. Mayor Byrne's dwindling black support nose-dived about seven percentage points after Vrdolyak's remarks, as registered in the Dressner-Sykes nightly tracking polls.[8] Blacks who had been intending to stick with Byrne to the end deserted her in droves and moved over to Washington; white voters who were strongly committed to Daley, on the other hand, went unmoved by the last-minute racial plea. When the votes were counted,

Byrne had lost renomination as the Democratic mayoral candidate by a razor-thin margin. Out of more than a million votes cast, Byrne was a mere 36,000 behind Washington, who took 36 percent of the vote, to Byrne's 34 percent, to Daley's 30 percent. Losing the 1983 primary election was clearly no fun for Jane Byrne, as she reminisced later: "I went to the polling place sixteen points ahead and woke up three points behind. . . . It was like we were all in the intensive care unit of a hospital watching the machine. It was like when the doctor calls you aside. I felt like a member of the family had died."

The General Election for Mayor, 1983

In the aftermath of the primary election, one of the biggest vote-swapping binges in Chicago history was in the making. During the general election campaign, which ran through March and culminated on April 12, a vast reshuffling of people from one banner to another was taking place – mostly by race. It had already been foreshadowed in the Democratic primary when blacks overwhelmingly ignored the advice of the Democratic party leadership and voted not for the party's choice but for a maverick and an outsider, black candidate Harold Washington. Now it was the whites' turn to do something similar. Anticipating the rapidly approaching general election, whites flocked toward another maverick and outsider, Bernard Epton, as they prepared to vote Republican. (Defenders of black political apostasy would later argue that ignoring the party's advice in the primary to vote for a black man was politically less "treasonous" than whites' crossing the party line to vote for a white man who was a Republican. There is something to be said for that argument, but not much. Both races were mainly voting on the race of the candidate and not his qualifications for high office.)

Defecting Democrats flocked into Epton's headquarters during the two weeks following the primary, overburdening and incapacitating the ability of Epton's people to absorb them or even record the names of individuals and organizations. Vowing to do their damnedest to elect Chicago's first Republican mayor since 1927, former Daley and Byrne supporters set up campaign offices, printed fliers, passed out buttons and handbills, manned telephones and distributed huge Epton posters. Epton offices popped up on the ethnic Eastern European Northwest and Southwest sides like mushrooms after a spring rain. Lifelong card-carrying Democratic party members were deserting to the other side: Aldermen Vito Marzullo, Roman Pucinski, and William Banks, park district boss Edmund Kelly, and at least a half dozen committeemen were openly hosting and sponsoring pep rallies, fund raisers, and "Bernie" rousers for a Republican! In the first two weeks of the general election campaign, Epton doubtless drew more volunteers and support from ex-Democrats than from lifetime Republicans.[9]

In defecting, however, they were not plowing virgin soil. The plow that broke the Democratic plain was a group of city Democrats, including Marzullo, who deserted the party over a liberal-left presidential nominee in 1972, George McGovern, and voted for Republican Richard Nixon. Furthermore, the growing conservatism of voters in the ethnic neighborhoods had resulted in a large Reagan vote in 1980. The vote harvest for the Democrats was thin that election. The old ethnic-urban coalition was becoming a dustbowl for Democratic presidential candidates. Now in 1983, when ethnics were deserting a Democratic mayoral nominee, critics charged that somehow the act was more invidious and politically "treasonous" because he was black. Yet historical perspective suggests that white ethnic fallout had at least some ideological base and was not completely based on race.

With new volunteers flooding their offices and new organizations springing up daily, the Epton people simply lost control of their own campaign. Such a groundswell of unexpected white grassroots support was bound to spell trouble for a patrician progressive Republican. Uneasy about the racial feelings of some of his more feverish supporters, Epton disavowed in advance the use of racial appeals, saying early in March that he did not want people supporting him who were merely antiblack. He asked candidate Washington to join him in a joint pledge to renounce white and black racism, but Washington declined to join Epton in such an appeal. Politics being a game of addition and not subtraction, Washington did not want to cool down the red-hot Afro-nationalist and problack elements who were using such appeals to stir up black neighborhoods to a fever pitch in order to get out the vote. Votes, after all, are votes.[10]

Slow to react to the implications of Washington's nomination, the state GOP finally moved in with promises of assistance to the mayoral candidate. In the past the Grand Old Party had generally left the Chicago mayoral nominee to his own slender resources in slogging uphill against a Democratic avalanche. But now it was different. Republicans smelled the possibility of victory in the air. Campaign help and endorsements came from prominent Republicans (many of whom had formerly endorsed Democrat Boss Richard J. Daley, or at least not opposed him).

The Epton Campaign

Under the direction of two newly hired top guns, Jim Fletcher, former aide to Gov. James R. Thompson, and John Deardourff, noted Republican media adviser, Epton went directly after the anti-Washington primary voters. A vast majority of these voters were white ethnics who had split fairly evenly between Byrne and Daley. Unlike those candidates, Epton had little expectation of gaining much support in the black wards, and thus he had little to lose by attacking Washington. In the now-famous tagline at the end of his TV commercials, he trumpeted: "Epton for Mayor—Before It's Too Late."

Critics condemned Epton for injecting race into the campaign and for turning the contest into a simple white-black struggle. But given the political movement sweeping the black community and the results of the primary, Epton took the only real road open to him if he hoped to win the election. Indeed, it is difficult to figure how Epton could have appealed to the 700,000 anti-Washington primary voters without having race crop up in the campaign. Perhaps his attacks on Washington could have been more delicate or discreet, but it is unlikely that the media or Washington would have responded to any Epton campaign charge without discussing its racial overtones.

As the campaign lurched along, Epton unleashed a brutal barrage of accusations against Washington. Unlike Washington's primary opponents, Epton brought up Washington's past legal and financial problems—early and often. Using a caustic wit that sometimes went too far, Epton chastised the congressman for failing to file his tax returns. At a northside rally he told a cheering crowd that "he would be happy to reveal his income tax returns" for the last twenty years if Washington "could find his," and that it was "sheer idiocy to support a man who had been sentenced to jail." In one ethnic neighborhood after another on the Northwest and Southwest sides, the liberal Jewish Republican received resounding screams of "Ber-nee, Ber-nee" from conservative, heavily Catholic Democrats.[11]

Washington's Campaign

Following the euphoric aftermath of his brilliant upset victory in the primary, Washington and his staff developed a conciliatory campaign strategy for the April election. Put on ice was showboater Jesse Jackson, whose "media bites" broadcast on Chicago television during Washington's primary victory night included such calls as "It's our turn now. Our time has come. We want it all."[12] Jackson's exuberance was scaring the "bejesus" out of white voters, most of whom thought he sounded like an out-of-control ghetto demagogue that night. Damage control was necessary. Washington, no admirer of the showbiz Jackson anyway, repeatedly told Chicagoans in the days following that the reverend would play no role in his administration. Fortunately for Washington, Jackson got a case of "Potomac fever" and began his long-term quest for the White House, thinking perhaps that what Washington was doing in Chicago he could do at the national level. With the Jackson distraction out of the way, candidate Washington could return to trying out his new role as political healer.

Running as if he were already mayor, the Democratic nominee spoke of his coming programs that would enable "all Chicago to move forward under [his] regime." He deftly sidestepped a verbal fistfight with the city's top cop. The overwhelming Democratic numbers in the city suggested that the obvious winning Washington strategy rested on a simple premise: encourage Democrats to vote for the party's nominee.

By early March it had become apparent that the healing strategy was not working and that Washington was not going to have an easy reconciliation with various white Democratic ward committeemen. In the large vote-producing ethnic wards, powerful organization leaders balked at endorsing Washington or refused outright to recognize him as the party's nominee. Unlike the Epton campaign, which had a single-minded direction, the Washington postprimary efforts swirled like a whirlpool caught up in the contradiction of its own political parts.

Washington was the Democratic mayoral nominee, and he demanded that he be treated and supported by the party in the same political fashion as had previous white candidates. At the same time, the so-called "movement in the black community" was cresting into a political tidal wave demanding that he not bend to the city's white power brokers. The candidate, by nature a cautious and careful politician, pondered his campaign alternative. If he were to run as an antipatronage political reformer, he would give his party foes a nonracial issue on which they could hang their support for Epton; yet if he moved too close to the party regulars, he might alienate some of his black and many of his liberal lakefront supporters, who would see him pulling a "Byrne-like" doublecross on reform. Moreover, deep in his heart Washington could never be sure of how sincere regular party endorsements would be to his campaign and whether powerful white ward committeemen could even deliver a sizable vote to him on election day. Thus Washington's campaign stalled in the limelight of the national media.

The Byrne write-in, write-out

Then came a blast from the past. Mayor Byrne flung herself back into the mayoral picture by announcing her write-in candidacy on St. Patrick's eve. Calling herself the "unity candidate," Byrne attacked both Washington and Epton, claiming that "as mayor I've concluded that neither of their candidacies represents the best interest of the city." If Mayor Byrne was looking for a political groundswell to her write-in campaign, she was greatly disappointed. The annual St. Patrick's Day Parade was not a "Byrne-fest." Her political foes, County Board President George Dunne and Rich Daley, denounced her actions. Moreover, her former close allies, Democratic County Chairman Edward Vrdolyak and Park Superintendent Edmund Kelly, called the move "political suicide." The city's black leaders cried "racism," while Washington and Epton, interrupted in their preparations for their first political debate, mouthed astonishment at the sudden turn of events. Stripped of political support, unable to raise the sizable amounts of money needed for her unorthodox campaign, and facing uncertain court action on her efforts to clarify legal write-in procedures, Byrne meekly withdrew from the battle a little over one week after her entrance. In the end she left most Chicagoans gasping at her chutzpah, while she evoked the words of G. K. Chesterton for others:[13]

> For the great Gaels of Ireland
> Are the men that god made mad,
> For all their wars are merry,
> And all their songs are sad.

13

The Debate

With the fallout of Byrne's surprise write-in campaign still settling around them, Washington and Epton squared off in their first and only debate. The Republican challenger was clearly the aggressor, and he flailed away at Washington's tax return problems and his suspension from practicing law for taking clients' money and then failing to represent them. For his part, Washington attempted to remain on his "high road strategy," though Epton's barbs provoked the congressman to say of him: "He's been saying he was going to take off the gloves. What he took off were his shoes, and we found he didn't wash his feet and he didn't wash his socks." Post-debate analysts praised neither performance, claiming that Epton overused his satiric wit in an effort to attack Washington's character, while the latter voiced few specifics about his future programs and policies. *Sun-Times* columnist Roger Simon summed up the debate as "two decent men in a dirty war," though many Chicagoans were tickled by the Hyde Park-style sarcasm used by both men.

The St. Pascal episode

Newspapers and radio and TV stations were nearly unanimous in their endorsement of Washington's candidacy. Yet Epton's campaign was unmistakably gaining momentum as the contest began to turn more and more on the race issue. Ugly comments and racial slurs were picked up for widespread dissemination; some local and most national reporters and commentators acted as social and political leeches sucking as much bigotry and racism out of the campaign as possible. On Palm Sunday, March 27, the national news media found an incident that graphically portrayed their view of the campaign. Washington and former Vice President Walter Mondale were jeered and told to go home by a group congregated at St. Pascal's Church. Both men refrained from entering the church, where a mass was well underway, and, with cameras grinding, they retreated to their car under a barrage of words and shouts. That event that was televised and broadcast around the world as emblematic of "Chicago's Ugly Racial Election," as a sensational flaming-red cover story in *Newsweek* magazine put it. Later in the day Washington blamed Epton for the incident, as he told a massive crowd at the University of Illinois at Chicago Pavilion: "What manner of people would ever remotely consider such a dastardly thing?" Epton disavowed any part in the episode and criticized Washington for blaming him, but the final parameters of the campaign had been set. It was now a street fight.[14]

Down and dirty at the end

The Washington-Epton campaign deteriorated to the gutter and below in the closing weeks. Neither man exhibited much wit, charm, or polish as he tore into the other, leaving no aspect of the other's character or record unexamined. Washington questioned Epton's mental health and demanded that he release his medical records before a second debate could be scheduled. Epton had undergone psychiatric evaluations at Michael Reese Hospital during 1975 and 1978. The Republican candidate, infuriated by the release of these records, claimed that he had been in a state of depression because doctors were unable to find the cause of his severe abdominal pains (later diagnosed as ulcers). Washington also tried to paint his opponent as a Reagan Republican on social issues, even though Epton had a voting record fairly similar to his own. The heat of Washington's attacks and the persistent questions on race by reporters unnerved Epton; more than once during the campaign's closing weeks the GOP candidate engaged in temper tantrums directed at his perceived enemies.

Epton and his staff counterattacked Washington from every conceivable direction. They intensified their charges that "Washington is unfit to be mayor because of his historic disregard of the law." Every day new accusations against the congressman hit the front pages and the air waves. Epton claimed that: 1) Washington did not pay property tax on a building whose tenants were evicted by the city for safety reasons; 2) that the Democratic nominee avoided paying his various utility bills; and 3) and (in a final radio commercial) that Washington was a convicted felon who had been disbarred. (In reality, Washington was convicted of a misdemeanor, his law license was suspended, and he spent a month in jail for not paying his federal income taxes.) But it was a later piece of literature, totally disavowed by Epton, alleging that Washington was a child molester that truly shook the heretofore unflappable congressman. On the Thursday before the election Washington's campaign seemed in disarray. He missed a scheduled appearance on WGN Radio's Wally Phillips' Morning Show, blew up at a student heckler at Northeastern Illinois University, and seemed out of control answering reporters' questions.

15

Going into the campaign's last weekend, Washington needed desperately to regain the political momentum. The candidates had virtually written off each other's racial strongholds, and both camps agreed that only two contestable blocs of voters were left in the city: white lakefront liberals and Hispanics. Pollsters differed only slightly on how many of these voters Washington had to win, and they all concurred that if the expected turnout reached 80 percent or above, the Democratic nominee needed a sizable chunk of this vote. Pulling himself together, Washington poured himself into the crucial last weekend of campaigning. On the other hand—and for reasons yet unexplained—his opponent did not match his effort: Epton's run for city hall cooled down to a walk during the campaign's waning hours.

Washington dominated the media during the campaign's final push as he geared his remarks directly to the undecided lakefront liberals. At rallies up and down Lake Shore Drive, the Democratic nominee bellowed out, "The battle cry is reform." He openly attacked the turncoat Democratic ward committeemen who backed Epton, calling them "greed merchants," and he downplayed his own legal financial problems, claiming "he was slow in paying bills because he spent his money campaigning against the Democratic machine." Washington had little alternative to becoming a robust reformer during the campaign's last days. He never had the easy-win option of running as the endorsed Democratic mayoral nominee and receiving a traditional organization landslide plurality. What was left would have to be a sweep of the heavily turned-on black electorate and significant support from lakefront liberals and Hispanics. However, if the turnout went over 1.3 million votes, Washington would need some white ethnic Democratic voters in order to become the city's first black mayor.[15]

Conclusion

Harold Washington beat Bernard Epton in 1983 because he carried all of the black vote and some of the white vote; Bernard Epton lost because he carried almost all of the white vote and none of the black vote. Only 46,000 votes out of about 1.3 million cast separated the winner from the loser. The narrowness of Washington's victory made it possible for several different voting groups to claim that they had provided the vital 46,000 vote margin that put him over the top. Hispanic spokesmen pointed to their 75,000 votes, of which two thirds went to

Washington. Similar claims were made for white ethnics in the neighborhoods, as well as for lakefront liberal voters (40 percent of the latter group supported Washington). All of these groups could come up with the vital 46,000 votes, or even about half that number – 24,000 votes – which is all that it would have taken to swing the election in the opposite direction.

Yet none of these parlor games that voter interest groups and political scientists play would have been possible without a solid black vote for Washington. Above all, it was the massive, unprecedented, and crusade-like folk movement led by charismatics and "race" men that swept Washington into office. The base for Washington's victory was simply the overwhelming black vote. So massive was the black champion's appeal that he received an unbelievable 99 percent of ten almost-all-black wards, and in six others he did better than 90 percent. But since no ward is composed 100 percent of a single race, other measures, such as election-day exit polls, become important: they go beyond *inferring* individual and racial voting patterns from the dominant race in the ward and actually link the race of the voter to the candidate. The exit polls showed a citywide 98 percent black vote for Washington. Harold Washington also scraped together enough white votes to win: the exit polls and an examination of district returns indicated a range of about 12 to 18 percent.

A rising tide of black protest, race consciousness, and vigorous campaigning, along with a thin slice of the white vote, had put into power Chicago's first black mayor.[16] The election, a real barnburner, was a record setter in other ways as well. An astonishing 43,000 voters who cast ballots in the general election did not vote for the office of mayor. About 100,000 more voted in the general election than did in the primary, and the citywide turnout reached a high of nearly 75 percent.

The Republican loser Epton garnered about 200,000 more votes than the *combined* totals of the last three GOP mayoral candidates. Not since 1927, when Republican William "Big Bill" Thompson won the mayoralty, had a Republican won as many wards as Epton did. On the other side of the coin, Washington's mayoral victory was the smallest since 1919, when Big Bill won a squeaker in a hotly contested four-way race. And the two spellbinders, Big Bill and Harold, were alike in other ways, as Harold Washington's first term would show.

Chicago's political winds blew briskly during the first three years following Washington's victory. The politics of race and of new executive leadership collided with the city's existing political framework and political structures to produce a whirlwind of antagonism and excitement. For most black Chicagoans, Washington was a messiah, with thousands of apostles ready to do his bidding; while to most white Chicagoans, the city's first black mayor was an aberration, and his time in power merely a painful interlude to be endured. The 1987 mayoral election was to resolve some of those conflicting views of Mayor Washington and the future direction of Chicago politics. We turn in the next chapter to pick up the preliminary sparring in 1986— the preparation for the main event the following year.

CHAPTER TWO

A Year of Tribulation and Triumph: 1986

A S THE NEW YEAR of 1986 dawned, the Washington administration was plagued by unraveling scandals. A federal investigation was digging up evidence of suspected widespread payoffs, bribery, and corruption in the city council and in several city departments, including the mayor's office. One week before, the first shot had been fired on Christmas Day, when the Chicago *Sun-Times* revealed that the FBI had an undercover investigation underway.

Operation Incubator

"Operation Incubator" had "wired" an informer, Michael Raymond, and the "mole" had video machines and recorders whirring away, capturing the sights and sounds of Chicago public servants anxiously soliciting bribes, taking bribes, and otherwise corrupting themselves.[1]

It was later observed that friendly aldermen no longer patted each other on the back but rather "patted each other down" to detect wired listening devices.

As public knowledge of the probe spread, the mayor was forced on January 1 to fire John Adams, second in command in the city's revenue department, for wrongfully accepting an alleged payoff of $10,000. Washington also had to suspend the head of that scandal-ridden department for being a conduit for "tainted" cash on the way to his brother, then Alderman Eugene Sawyer. Adams was a political appointee whom Washington had placed in the revenue department as an apparent reward for having run a losing race against one of the mayor's fiercest enemies at the time, black legislator Larry Bullock. Four aldermen from the mayor's bloc were being investigated for possible solicitation of bribes, and the mayor's chief fiscal advisor, Ira Edelson, was alleging that appointees in both the Revenue Department and the mayor's office and participated in what appeared to be a "cover-up" of corruption.[2] The mayor's inner circle was being hit hard by a federal corruption investigation led by the U.S. district attorney for Northern Illinois, Anton Valukas. Like his illustrious predecessor of the 1970s, James R. Thompson, who had cleaned house during the Daley years, Valukas hoped to clean up graft in City Hall during the 1980s.

Revelations of alleged wrongdoing struck especially close to home when the mayor's chief of staff, James Montgomery, was accused of trying to cover up evidence of wrongdoing in the revenue department. This was added to the burden of earlier charges that Montgomery had secretly and illegally opened up sealed bids on a multimillion dollar "people mover" project for O'Hare Airport. And Montgomery had created other problems for himself. A Chicago judge had upbraided corporation counsel Montgomery as the city's chief legal officer for switching sides in a public interest case and switching in favor of the owners of a chicken franchise after the franchiser hired the son of Montgomery's former law partner, which created the impression that the public interest had been subordinated to cronyism.

Finally, the telling blow came when it was revealed that the lobbyist wanting favors for his waste management company had paid for a $4,000 luxury vacation to Acapulco for Montgomery, his wife, and his two children. Montgomery claimed that he had thought all along that Chicago Alderman Clifford Kelley had picked up the bill, which Kelley said emphatically was "totally untrue." Kelley, in fact, insisted that the mayor's chief of staff had been soliciting a free vacation and had asked Kelley whether he knew of anyone who could pay the bill. Strengthening the alderman's version was the story of the travel agent who had sold the Mexican vacation package: he confirmed that the waste management company's lobbyist had arranged the trip for Montgomery and his family in "deluxe accommodations." What the company apparently sought in return was the right to build a waste transfer station for the city on the South Side.

Montgomery resigned on February 19. His timely resignation as corporation counsel and chief of staff, critics pointed out, freed him from having to testify or cooperate with a City Hall-sponsored internal investigation then underway.[3] Earlier, on February 6, another top mayoral advisor on intergovernmental affairs, Thomas Coffey, though not implicated in the scandal, submitted his resignation. Finally, the mayor's chief financial advisor and former revenue director, Ira Edelson, was frozen out by the mayor because of their dispute over who was responsible for the alleged cover-up.

The widening probe netted others outside the administration's inner circle, including Circuit Court Clerk Morgan Finley for allegedly taking payoffs from the "mole," and his chief investigator, Michael Lambesis, for selling an Uzi machine gun and silencer to a convicted felon, the "mole" Michael Raymond. In an interesting twist, the last big federal probe of the 1970s had also picked up the circuit court clerk who had been a close friend of then Mayor Richard J. Daley. Finley was not a member of Washington's team.

February brought more ill tidings for the mayor when Clarence McClain, his friend and former patronage chief, was back in the news. McClain, an influence peddler with a "sleazy" reputation derived from a string of vice convictions which included pimping and keeping a house of prostitution, had been forced out of the Washington administration by public outrage late in 1983. The FBI's "Operation Incubator" showed that long after his official departure McClain continued to exercise insider influence and had stopped the award of a multimillion-dollar collections contract. Demonstrations of such powerful influence—which Chicagoans call "clout"—gave credence to McClain's description of himself as the mayor's "best friend." In late February McClain had tried to sequester in excess of $400,000 in several Milwaukee banks; but the U.S. Internal Revenue Service had those accounts frozen to collect unpaid back taxes. The feds seized $47,000 in delinquent taxes; Cook County laid claim to a sizable sum for unpaid property taxes; the City of Chicago was looking for $24,000 for unpaid sewer and water bills, and for demolition of McClain's slum properties; People's Gas was seeking $46,000 for unpaid bills. The U.S. Small Business Administration also wanted its share, the repayment of a $40,000 loan.[4]

The mayor, embarrassed by revelations of influence peddling and the shady behavior of a person he once called "a fine, fine

21

gentleman," now turned on his erstwhile friend, saying, "Mr. McClain, shut up! Don't throw my name around." Yet public interest in McClain failed to abate. Early in March, McClain was arrested on drunken driving charges, when it was also discovered that his driver's license had expired some two years earlier and that the car he drove lacked a city vehicle sticker. Toward the end of the month, McClain again hit the news, this time alleging that two women he had invited to his motel room in Milwaukee had taken $1,600 from his pants pockets while he was in the bathroom. Throughout the ordeal McClain continued to insist that he was the mayor's best friend. In April, when a judge ordered McClain to deliver $113,000 in unpaid taxes to Cook County State's Attorney Richard M. Daley, McClain claimed that prosecutor Daley "went after me because I'm black...."[5]

Washington's Response

During the first four months of revelations in 1986, Mayor Washington issued several sputtering defenses of his besieged administration. On January 2 the mayor accused the federal investigators of racism for focusing on crooked black aldermen. But during the week of January 23 he blamed the corruption on sloppy administrators inherited from his predecessor, Jane Byrne. In early February Washington complained that the FBI had "set up" his people and also attacked the character of FBI informant Michael Raymond. Later in the month, while trying to explain away his administration's fall from grace, Washington—in almost a paraphrase of the way Mayor Daley used to defend himself—began with: "Let's talk about institutional corruption: where did it come from? It came from the city council. Tom Keane [Daley's council leader] was the epitome of it."[6] Missing from this remarkable series of explanations was any hint that the mayor accepted responsibility for the misconduct of his administration.

Harold Washington's "red herring" allusion to Tom Keane as the "epitome" of corruption was meant to remind reporters of the 1972-74 scandals of the Daley administration, which had some striking parallels. In that earlier housecleaning two Daley allies—Keane, Daley's council floor leader, and the mayor's speech writer, Earl Bush—had been convicted and jailed for extortion, tax evasion, and mail fraud. In addition, the mayor's old friend Matt Danaher, then clerk of the circuit court, was indicted for income tax evasion but died before coming to trial.

Loyal Democrat Edward Barrett, Cook County clerk, was found guilty in 1973 of soliciting bribes for a voting machine contract, and Illinois's former governor, Otto Kerner, Jr., then a federal judge, was sent to jail for income tax evasion and perjury in 1974. During this time of trouble for Daley, Leon Despres, a reform alderman, argued that Daley's friends were pillaging the city. Another leading voice of reform, one-time mayoral candidate William Singer, asserted that the "mayor had to be held responsible in these convictions."[7]

During Mayor Washington's first administration, the federal government's "Operation Incubator" uncovered what came close to matching the corruption and sleaze record of the Daley years. Three members of the Daley council had been indicted, compared to four members of the Washington council bloc; Daley's speech writer and aide, Earle Bush, went to jail, while Washington's chief of staff, James Montgomery, had to resign along with the director of intergovernmental affairs; Daley's friend Matt Danaher had descended into an alcoholic stupor and got himself involved in zoning bribes and income tax evasion, while Washington's sleazy friend Clarence McClain had a string of vice convictions and was being sued for back taxes and fees by all four units of government—city, county, state, and federal. In addition, Washington's revenue director and his deputy had to be removed from office, one for accepting bribes and the other for being a conduit for tainted cash—as had Daley loyalist Edward Barrett for soliciting bribes from a voting machine company. It could be argued that former governor Otto Kerner should be tallied up as a negative on the Daley side of the ledger. So if one were to accept Kerner, along with more than fifty policemen named for wrongdoing, then the Washington scandal (1985-87), by any kind of objective body-count measure, is less debauched than the Daley mess. But only somewhat less so. Beyond dispute is the fact that the Washington administration's corruption scandal of 1985-87 was the biggest since the Daley federal blowout in the early 1970s.

Conspicuously missing from public response to the "Operation Incubator" scandals of the Washington administration was any expression of moral outrage by the reformers, liberals, and those outsiders who had so long been critical of Daley administration misdeeds. Former Alderman Leon Despres, when interviewed, dismissed any comparison, saying that corruption under Washington was "petty" and not systematic as it was under Daley.

Aldermen William Singer and Dick Simpson had long since left politics, but their apostolic successors, Aldermen Lawrence Bloom and Martin Oberman offered only silence. Once, when Oberman was asked why he seldom drew public attention to the Washington administration's venality, the dean of the council reformers said that criticism would have "lent aid and comfort to the enemy," a reference to the Vrdolyak-Burke bloc that opposed the mayor.[8]

Unfortunately, the old "outsiders" had now become the "insiders"; the critics of the establishment had become the establishment. Some, it is true, had "burned out" on Chicago politics, but others had been flattered by attention and recognition or had been given jobs in city administration. Erstwhile nay-sayer Alderman David Orr had now become a yea-sayer as deputy mayor; Kristin Svare, formerly of LEAP, a fierce opponent of vote fraud and a thorn in the side of previous administrations, had now leaped onto the city payroll and was turning out favorable press copy for the administration. Lakeshore liberals such as Oberman and Bloom had found themselves on the winning side and were suddenly the "ins." In short, the natural protest voices of the former watchdogs of public probity had been stilled.[9]

The powerful, vibrant, and morally outraged protests of the past had been reduced to a feeble, almost inaudible squeak. It was mostly the press and the prosecutors who grumbled about the incompetence, sloppiness, and crude corruption within the administration. One echo from the past was the voice of Rev. Don Benedict, an unpaid advisor for a proposed ethics ordinance and a former director of a conscience-raising group called the Community Renewal Society. Benedict called for a local "summit meeting on corruption" to enact a new ten commandments for Chicago politics. He said that "it would lift the cloud of cynicism that hangs over efforts to raise the level of political honesty in Chicago." Benedict ended his peroration with a bow to liberal prejudices by gratuitously slamming the federal "Operation Incubator": "We have been humiliated long enough by having the FBI spy on us."[10] Rev. Benedict failed to recognize that without the "feds" neither Daley's barnboss, Thomas Keane, nor Washington's ally, Clifford Kelly, would have been caught. Benedict's call for a moral summit was ignored by yesterday's reformers and the outsiders who were now part of the system. Besides, at the time of Benedict's appeal, April 8, 1986, Washington partisans and erstwhile reformers were gearing up for the runoff aldermanic elections looming at the end of the month, which promised to change the balance of power in Chicago.

At the height of the corruption exposé the mayor used a time-tested Chicago strategem: on February 5 he appointed a blue- ribbon crime fighter, former U.S. Attorney Thomas Sullivan, to investigate the mess in City Hall. At the same time the mayor promised that the investigative report would be released when completed, which turned out to be October. Later the mayor changed his mind and refused to release it. Nonetheless, the report leaked out to the press in bits and snippets. It showed that Washington and his top aides had run a slipshod administration in several departments and that they were more concerned about bad publicity coming from "Operation Incubator" than in public accountability. The report also revealed that, at the very time the mayor was accusing the FBI of a racially motivated investigation, he was learning that his aides had indeed taken questionable payoffs. Furthermore, the report painted a tawdry picture of mismanagement by Washington and his aides, who were scurrying around holding late-night meetings trying to minimize damage to the mayor's "reform" image. One of the wrongdoers, John Adams, had continued to work for the city even after his acceptance of questionable payoffs was known, and he was soliciting campaign contributions for Washington's re-election campaign from city vendors and contractors. The Sullivan Report also confirmed, in the words of the *Tribune* editor, that "Mr. Washington's creepy friend Clarence McClain was a corrupting force around City Hall long after the mayor said he had banished him."[11]

The silence of Chicago's self-appointed guardians of public morality was depressing enough; but even more frustrating for the anticorruptionist was the fact that "Operation Incubator" did not have much demonstrable electoral effect. The city's "remap" special elections for seven council seats could have been run on Mars or the moon as far as any "Operation Incubator" influence was concerned. These local elections were decided on local issues, the hottest of which was the race or ethnicity of the candidates and their pro- or antiadministration sympathies. Ethnic, race, and proadministration candidates won most of the elections. As always in Chicago, blood is not only thicker than water but a more powerful force in determining election outcomes than reform or ideology. Politically astute, the mayor refrained from endorsing those under the corruption cloud; on the other hand, he neither condemned them nor supported their challengers. The two indicted councilmen who lost their races were defeated for reasons other than their indictments. None of the taint of corruption rubbed off on the mayor's choices for the council. Scandal seems to run off Chicago politicians like water off a duck's back; it seldom penetrates the oily plumage.

Polls

What impact did "Operation Incubator" have on the mayor's standing with the public? A citywide poll of Chicago voters conducted for Alderman Edward Burke in March 1986 indicated that the mayor's claim to be a "reformer" was in dispute. Some 44 percent of those interviewed said that he was a reformer, but a larger 51 percent said he was not. Washington's base was still primarily in the black community, where 78 percent accepted the mayor as a "reformer"; 80 percent of whites rejected that notion. When asked what impact the payoff investigation might have on Washington's re-election campaign, which was nearly a year off, about two-thirds guessed that it would hurt his chances, whereas 28 percent foresaw little impact. (That 28 percent would eventually turn out to be correct.) At the same time, the Burke poll showed challenger Jane Byrne leading Washington 46 to 42 percent in a one-on-one match-up. In a trial contest pitting Washington against a larger field of four candidates, the mayor emerged with a lead of 36 percent to 31 percent for Byrne, and a scattering for the others. Although the sample size of the poll was a small 500 – with a 5 percent plus or minus margin of error – it suggested that the mayor had not suffered greatly from " Operation Incubator." Polls conducted later that year, by Gallup in August and Penn-Shoen Associates in October, would show a two-candidate Byrne-Washington race tightening, with Washington in the lead. Although the mayor had lost some support as the poll question on corruption-honesty revealed, on the other side of the coin he had surged ahead strongly in the leadership dimension, probably because he had a working majority in the council and had won several political fights with his opponents.[12] Just as Daley had survived the 1973-74 breakup of the Democratic council "gang of boodlers," so would Mayor Washington not only survive the wrongdoing of four of his council bloc but actually increase his edge of control even while under the cloud of corruption.

Redistricting Elections for the City Council, 1986

The biggest single political event of 1986 was not the corruption probe but the court-ordered remap elections in seven wards. The outcome of the remap elections was the kind of political breakthrough that had eluded the mayor for three years. What the mayor was unable to achieve through conventional politics he was able to achieve through the judicial system.

The key to Harold Washington's belated takeover of the city council was court-ordered redistricting, which gerrymandered several white opposition wards into "supermajority" black and minority wards. The remappers and the appellate court correctly guessed that this would change the balance of power in Chicago. From 1982 through December 1985 the federal courts issued a series of substantive and procedural decisions that redistricted wards, ordered special elections, and intervened even to the point of determining the validity of candidate petitions—all decisions that favored Mayor Washington over the opposition "29 bloc" led by Councilmen Edward Vrdolyak and Edward Burke.

The council remap story had begun under Mayor Jane Byrne in 1981, when, in compliance with election laws, Chicago began its decennial redistricting of aldermanic wards. A 1981 remap of the wards resulted two years later in the election of seventeen black and one Hispanic aldermen, which diminished the number of black aldermen by two from the pre-remap period. The new ward map was the work of planner Martin Murphy and the foxy old machine strategist Thomas Keane, the former council floor leader for Mayor Richard Daley. The Murphy-Keane remap went too far in assuring white dominance, for it cut out two black-majority wards—which vigorously protested. Black activists argued that their electoral strength had been legally "diluted" and their council power diminished, which was a violation of their civil rights.

The remap was thrown out in December 1982 by U.S. District Judge Thomas McMillen, who ordered the number of black and Hispanic-majority wards increased from 17 to 19 and 2 to 4 respectively. A new map was drawn with black majorities of 50 percent plus in the disputed districts and in place for the 1983 elections, but the results proved unsatisfactory to minority spokesmen, and they appealed again. The 1983 mayoral and city elections had not significantly changed the racial and ethnic composition of the city council, which remained in white hands and which in May 1983, after Washington's election, formed a solid "29 bloc" majority opposed to the newly elected black mayor.[13]

The unsatisfactory results from the McMillen map (in the view of blacks) and the new ethno-racial division in the council heated up the remap issue, for upon the success of such an appeal lay the only hope Washington had of asserting anything like the power of his predecessors over the council. The critical court decision that "turned the world upside down" for the opposition "29 bloc" was handed down on May 17, 1984. A three-judge federal appeals court rapped District Judge McMillen for an "abuse of discretion" for not going far enough to correct past discrimination and assuring minority representation in the future. Justices Richard Cudahy, Robert J. Keller, and Harlington Woods, Jr., in a daring move, ordered that racially and ethnically disputed black-and-white wards be gerrymandered into 65 and 70 percent black and Hispanic majorities. The choice of the 65 percent "supermajority" was not totally arbitrary, because the Appeals Court asserted that that figure had been used by the Washington-based Justice Department and apparently was the magic number that resolved all minority election disputes. The judges also said that a 65 percent "supermajority" would give minority candidates a "reasonable" chance to elect candidates of "their choice." The 65 percent figure is arrived at by beginning with a simple plurality of 50 percent and adding 5 points because minority populations are normally younger and have fewer voters than do majority populations; adding another 5 points because black and Hispanic populations have fewer voter registrations than do whites; and adding yet another 5 points because blacks and Hispanics traditionally have lower voter turnouts than do whites.[14]

Finally, in handicapping the elections in favor of minorities, the appeals court added a new wrinkle by throwing in yet another 5 percent for Hispanics—to compensate for the large proportion of Hispanics (mostly Mexicans) who were not citizens, which presumably counted illegals who were in Chicago in violation of the immigration laws. The opposition bloc's lawyer, William Harte, argued that the court had gone beyond previous cases in which "supermajorities" had been invoked to assure minority representation. Harte also pointed out that one of the court's 5 percent add-ons was unnecessary because the 1982 Judge McMillen remap had taken voting-age population and not general population into account already. The appeals court was unmoved by criticism, and the election remap process clanked forward, which augured well for the Washington administration. Harte also protested that the 1982 Voting Rights Act did not require that the courts "guarantee" the election of minority candidates. But as a practical matter, the Appeals Court-ordered remap would do precisely that—something many observers recognized long before the new elections.[15] Washington campaign consultant David Axelrod read the outcome almost a year before the event when he said that a 65 percent "supermajority" has "historically meant victory for black candidates." The Chicago Tribune editor called this "packing," the technical term for stacking electoral districts against one race or another, "preposterous," grumbling that "it is not the court's duty to insure election results."[16]

What practical reasons had prompted the appeals court to set upon the 65 and 70 percent figures to cure Chicago's minority problem? If one looks beyond the court's language, the primary reason was that the McMillen map had not produced and would not produce the desired result of electing black and Hispanic aldermen in proportion to their numbers in the population. For example, a 60 percent black majority population in white Alderman Frank Brady's 15th Ward had not been sufficient to defeat him and replace him with a black in 1983. The later minority remappers also remapped Brady out of his ward, but the resourceful council survivor moved back in and prevailed over a gang-scene primary and won re-election. Although the appeals court's reasoning is not fully spelled out, it seems obvious that the survival of white candidates like Brady in black-majority wards was the problem.

The court's solution was to raise the bar for the political high-jumpers like Brady; he would be forced to face a 75 percent black-majority ward on his next political outing, and that did the job. Not even the resourceful, bullet-dodging Brady could survive those numbers in the increasingly racially heated political climate of Chicago. Brady was defeated in the judge-called special election of 1986 and replaced by Marlene Carter, a black. Reflecting on his odyssey of inner-city survival against heavy odds, Brady told newsmen: "I've been shot, and I've been burglarized, and that didn't move me out. But a federal judge did it with the stroke of a pen."[17]

The remapping handiwork created a field day for political cynics, who hooted at what appeared to be the capricious, irregular, and cavalier changes approved by the court. Alderman Edward M. Burke, one of the opposition leaders, was first mapped out in the draconian version and later remapped back into his ward. Brady found himself not only in a three-quarters black ward but one drawn with ragged lines and jagged edges that physically resembled the classic textbook illustration of gerrymandering. Some racially and ethnically disputed wards had their black majorities raised to comfortable simple majorities, whereas others were jacked up as high as 77 percent black. No uniformity prevailed in the process. One grizzled machine veteran, Alderman Vito Marzullo, saw the Hispanic population of his ward leap upward from 57 to 66 percent, ruling out the likelihood of his re-election. Marzullo retired from the council. On the other hand, the 31st Ward, which had produced the city's only Hispanic councilman (but who lined up with the opposition white bloc against Washington) had its minority population dropped downward from 55 to 52 percent. This crazy-quilt pattern of super and not-so-super majorities, cynics argued, seemed to be saying that those minorities loyal to the mayor's bloc would be rewarded, and those disloyal, like the 31st Ward, would not.[18]

Even so, no amount of grumbling or fulminating could stay the result, which was enormously pleasing to Mayor Washington and the minority bloc in the city council. In the court-ordered special council election, the mayor's candidates won most of the seats, giving the mayor control over nearly one-half, or twenty-four of fifty aldermen (assuming in advance an easy runoff win of a black over hapless white incumbent Brady in the 15th Ward). Yet it was not enough to declare a victory in Council wars; the mayor was still one vote short of a takeover.

Aldermanic Run-off Election — Spring 1986

Ironically, the key ward victory that gave Washington's council control would not come from his black community base; rather, the voters in the heavily Hispanic near-northwest-side 26th Ward decided the outcome of "Council Wars." The March 18, 1986 special aldermanic election had been inconclusive as to who would control the council. The mayor increased the administration's allies to twenty-four (counting the expected Carter win in the 15th Ward), but that was still not enough to overcome the Vrdolyak bloc, which, though reduced in power, was still holding twenty-five seats. A runoff election was slated for April to decide which side would win control of the lone, hotly contested alderman's seat.

What had happened was that in the March 18 special aldermanic election, Washington's candidate, Luis Gutierrez, an energetic community organizer, was forced into an April aldermanic runoff with the Vrdolyak-backed Manuel Torres, a former Cook County board member and 26th Ward Democratic committeeman. In a photo finish, Gutierrez was denied a majority victory due to a handful of write-in votes for a third candidate. Controversy raged for days as Washington supporters of Gutierrez charged Chicago election board chairman Michael Lavelle with pro-Torres hanky-panky. Yet, despite numerous accusations, the real election spoiler was a little-known independent candidate, James Blasinski, who had garnered twenty-one write-in votes, thereby setting up a Gutierrez-Torres run-off rematch that was really a Washington-Vrdolyak showdown.[19]

There was another aldermanic run-off in Brady's racially gerrymandered southwest-side 15th Ward, but Washington's candidate, with a 75 percent black electorate, was a shoo-in. All political eyes and energy centered on the 26th Ward. Washington loyalists from all over the city converged on this formerly rather insignificant ward. City-sponsored public works projects began popping up throughout the ward, and many top mayoral aides in City Hall found their nightly journey home detoured and delayed as they "volunteered" to help Gutierrez in the precincts.

The Cook County Democratic chairman, Vrdolyak, responded to the mayoral challenge by sending his top lieutenants to run the opposition Torres campaign. However, critical to the Torres effort was the position of the aging former ward boss, county board member Matt Bieszczat. Vrdolyak had pressured Bieszczat out of politics when he saw the once predominantly Polish ward turn Hispanic. Still feisty, Bieszczat had influence in several remaining ethnic precincts in the ward, and it was questionable whether or not the former Democratic organization ward kingpin would actively support Torres.

Election day in the 26th Ward was a Chicago political junky's dream come true: bright sunshine, each of the ward's 44 precincts inundated with rival workers from across the city, and a political intensity not seen since the Bridgeport/Stockyard Irish ward battles two generations earlier. Every polling place had at least ten to fifteen workers hovering outside its premises. The beleaguered 26th Ward constituents had to run a human gauntlet to get inside the polls, and, once at the election judge's table, they faced several poll watchers who checked or challenged all voters before they finally had the opportunity to punch their ballot for their aldermanic favorite.

The final results saw Gutierrez defeating Torres by 880 votes (53% to 47%); the Washington-backed candidate carried twenty-nine of forty-four precincts. Three factors gave Gutierrez victory. First, at Washington's urging, the few black precincts in the 26th Ward dramatically increased their support for Gutierrez in comparison to the first contest. Second, Gutierrez received a significantly higher share of the dominant Puerto Rican vote. Third, Bieszczat and his white ethnics were either unable or unwilling to increase their effort for Torres. In the end, the 26th Ward contest became an old-fashioned organization precinct captain's election—where turnout, not issues, decide the outcome. And as in the glory machine days of former Mayor Richard J. Daley, the fifth floor at City Hall had more resources and workers to prevail in a local contest. However, unlike in past races, this time the mayor was black, the campaign theme was reform, and the goal was the destruction of Ed Vrdolyak's council control, though many of the winning tactics remained the same: money, people, and organization.[20]

Gutierrez's aldermanic victory also drove home the point of how new city demographics and new philosophical outlooks had altered Chicago's political landscape since the death of Daley. White flight, the council remap, and an aroused black and Hispanic political consciousness gave Mayor Washington's forces enough winable wards to take council control. It is doubtful that even a political wizard like former Mayor Daley could have withstood the new realities of Chicago politics.

Washington's Second Big Victory

By May 1986 the remap elections had given the mayor a 25-to-25 split in the council, with the mayor casting the tie-breaking vote and emerging in control. Once again, just as he did during his victory of 1983, the mayor returned to an old bad habit of flaunting victory and rubbing the noses of vanquished Democrats in the ashes of defeat. Speaking to reporters, he arrogantly lashed out at the Cook County Democratic Committee: "I don't need it. It needs me." Some of the mayor's friends shuddered and feared that a fit of hubris had seized the mayor once again. In 1983 the mayor's nonstop vitriolic attacks on anyone and everyone who disagreed with him had played a major role in creating the "29 bloc" that hampered him for most of his first term. Was the bombast in May 1986 the beginning of a second uncontrolled "I danced on patronage's grave . . . thieves in the night" name-calling contest that might turn a second victory into a Pyrrhic one or even defeat?

The mayor had clearly shown in the wake of the 1983 win that he was capable, with his rhetorical excesses and political maladroitness, of snatching defeat from the jaws of victory.[21] Was history about to repeat itself? The answer was no. The mayor did an abrupt about-face, pulled in his rhetorical big guns, put some of his hottest *ad hominem* on ice, passed out some favors, and worked out a rapprochement with some of his former enemies, who how joined the new victors. Some of his first-term foes offered the mayor support on key issues. The most important political battle of the first term had been won and, even more remarkably, it had been won under the cloud of the largest corruption scandal the city had seen for a decade. After three and a half years of ferocious battle, Harold the lion had also learned how to play the role of the fox.

The Takeover: Summer 1986

It did not take Mayor Washington long, however, to flex his new council muscles. At the next Chicago City Council meeting, the mayor unleashed his newly won aldermanic clout and began consolidating his control over city administrative boards and agencies. It was Washington's interpretation that under council procedures a tie vote could be broken by the mayor. During "Council Wars" the "Vrdolyak 29" had prevented the mayor from appointing or replacing members of critical boards (e.g., Chicago Transit Authority, Park District, City College, etc.) by using their council control to keep his nominees locked up in the appropriate council committees. By refusing to act, the Vrdolyak-controlled council effectively limited Washington's administrative power while saving important jobs for their allies. But in seven days in May 1986, Washington freed his hostage appointments by breaking down council barriers and routing their former captors.

On May 9th the jam-packed city council chambers, filled with cheering Washington supporters, saw the mayor begin to take charge. First, his council allies approved twenty-five long-standing appointments to fourteen different boards and departments. Second, in personal verbal confrontations with his two bitterest aldermanic foes, Vrdolyak and 14th Ward Alderman Edward Burke, the council finance committee chairman, Washington put down with style all their political protestations and parliamentary maneuvers. A good example is the following duel between Washington and Burke over the latter's objections to the mayor's authority in breaking tie votes:

> Burke: "Same point of order."
> Washington: "Same ruling."
> Burke: "Same appeal."
> Washington: "Same result."

And third, the mayor and his council allies scoffed openly at warnings from Vrdolyak and Burke about legal action over the day's council proceedings. (Nothing ever came of the lawsuit.) After three years of being on the short end of Council Wars, the mayor, bolstered by his new troops, was counterattacking with a clear purpose.[22]

In early June, Washington and his allies slashed the number of city council committees from thirty-seven to twenty-eight. Proadministration aldermen were given chairmanships of most of the newly reorganized committees. After much internal debate with his advisors, the mayor decided to leave his "council enemy number two," Alderman Burke, as chairman of the finance committee; however, he stripped away most of this important committee's critical powers over the city budget by establishing a new council budget committee, headed by his council floor leader, Alderman Timothy Evans (4th Ward).

Despite cries of "legislative piracy" by Vrdolyak and renewed threats of legal action by Burke, the mayor gloried in giving his two rivals their "comeuppance." Basil Talbott, Chicago *Sun-Times* political editor and one of the city's shrewdest observers, depicted Washington's council confrontations with Vrdolyak and Burke as a "Cheshire cat eyeing mice." Politics and issues aside, the duel between the "two Eddies" and the mayor had become personal. For three years it had been crucial to each man's respective citywide supporters that he display the verbal dexterity and quickness to taunt, defame, and, if necessary, vocally brutalize his rival. Chicago politics during Council Wars had become similar to the black ghetto game of "Playing the Dozens," a contest in which adolescents exchange fast-paced insults, often in rhyme, with their rivals. All three men had won and lost past verbal jousts, though the "two Eddies," with their 29-to-21 council majority, had usually ended up at least split-decision victors. With his tie-breaking vote giving him a legislative upper hand, Mayor Washington was enjoying the prospects of verbally beating on the weak points of his two long- time adversaries.[23]

Washington's plan to consolidate council and administrative boards under his command had one ultimate target: "another Eddie," Edmund Kelly, 61, the powerful superintendent of the Chicago Park District. Ed Kelly personified the halcyon days of machine domination under Richard J. Daley. Appointed park superintendent by Daley in 1972, Kelly had parlayed his governmental position (the park post gave him vast patronage, about 5,000 jobs) with his political position as Democratic committeeman of the northside "Fighting 47th" Ward into a major position in city and party affairs. Kelly's influence was so great that his name was mentioned constantly as a leading candidate for mayor or Democratic party chairman – or both.

It became clear to Kelly that his job was in jeopardy as Washington's council allies began passing out mayoral appointments to the various governmental boards and agencies. He told *Sun-Times* columnist Tom Fitzpatrick that "Washington [is] the biggest racist I've ever seen. I think he perpetuates the fuel and the fire that's constant here in the city." A little more than a month after making that statement, Ed Kelly came face to face with its political consequences: Washington came after him with all his mayoral guns blazing.[24]

At the mid-June park board meeting two new Washington board members, Walter Netsch (a well-known architect and "limousine liberal") and Margaret Burroughs joined former Kelly ally William C. Bartholomay (a prominent businessman) to strip Kelly of most of his powers. The mayor and his new park board majority circumvented the problem of Kelly's three remaining years on his superintendent's contract by simply creating a new chief administrative position for the board. Former westside state representative Jesse Madison, a long-time participant in black independent politics, was given both the title of park district executive vice-president and most of the responsibilities of running the board. Kelly countered with a lawsuit claiming that Madison's new position "was not authorized by any statute and was created for the purpose of attempting to depose and humiliate the plaintiff [Kelly]." But like almost every other lawsuit brought by the anti-Washington forces against the mayor during his first term in office, this one also ultimately proved unsuccessful.[25]

In late June the Kelly melodrama shifted suddenly to the state capital in Springfield and to the cutthroat politics of the closing days of the general assembly's regular legislative session. All during Council Wars, the Democratic legislative leaders, Senate President Philip Rock and House Speaker Michael Madigan, had prevented a second front from opening up in Springfield between Washington and Vrdolyak loyalists. But the mayor's park board takeover ended the Springfield calm.

A strange coalition of Republicans, some downstate Democrats, and anti-Washington Chicago Democrats attempted to push through legislation to save Kelly's park district position. Key to Republican support for Kelly was their demand that legislation be approved giving the GOP-dominated suburbs a substantial voice in the running and control of Chicago's O'Hare International Airport. Because of the huge stakes and the likelihood of black voter revenge against any major state or Cook County elected Democratic official who would support this political tradeoff, most influential Democratic party leaders decided to line up with Washington against Kelly. The legislation died.

A few weeks later—exactly three months after the critical 26th Ward aldermanic run-off election—Ed Kelly quit his job as park superintendent. The man who was once considered nearly impregnable within Chicago's governmental system was toppled by the very system that gave him power in the first place—political clout. In an emotional farewell speech Kelly told his supporters that he was leaving "without bitterness" because according to him, "If you lose...you got to be a good loser." But for most of his political life Kelly had been a winner, and seeing Kelly humbled by Washington was a jolt to many old-line Chicago pols. To them it was also the clearest evidence yet that if Washington were not defeated in 1987, no traditional Democratic power base in the city or county would be safe.[26]

Nonpartisan Mayoral Elections for Chicago: Summer-Fall 1986

As in 1983, Washington's mostly white opponents were split among themselves about who would be the most effective candidate to beat a man who was now holding more political "aces" then he had four years earlier—when he was first victorious.

Complicating the strategy of the anti-Washington forces was the declared candidacy of former mayor Jane Byrne. In the summer of 1985, Byrne had "jump started" the field by announcing her bid to run in the 1987 Democratic mayoral primary. Those Democrats loyal to State's Attorney Richard M. Daley, who was shown by several early polls to be Washington's toughest potential mayoral challenger, had to find a way for their champion to run against the mayor without falling into the same 1983 trap – a three-way (Daley-Washington-Byrne) primary race that had resulted in defeat for Byrne and Daley.

One political fact was certain: nothing was going to force Byrne out of the Democratic primary contest. Thus Daleyites needed an optional electoral method to get their man in but circumvent Byrne's candidacy. They had to avoid at all costs having their candidate labeled a "spoiler," a term that nearly cost him his political career following Washington's 1983 primary win. The state's attorney's ethnic voter base would not stand for a replay of a black victory caused by a split of the white vote.

The answer to Daley's political predicament was simple: make the election of Chicago's mayor a nonpartisan contest. The vehicle would be a citywide referendum on the November 1986 general election ballot. If approved, this referendum would turn the 1987 mayoral race into a "primaryless" free-for-all contest between candidates running without party labels. A run-off election between the two highest vote-getters would take place if no candidate received a majority of the total vote cast.

The efforts to place a nonpartisan mayoral referendum on the November ballot would dominate Chicago's political scene throughout the fading summer of 1986. Unlike the successful move for the nonpartisan election of Chicago aldermen in the early 1920s, neither proponents nor opponents would call this proposed electoral change a reform. Everyone clearly perceived it as a political move to create a path for Daley to challenge Washington while taking on Byrne at the same time. Daleyites were convinced of the following scenario in a nonpartisan election: 1) their man could prevent Washington from winning a majority; 2) Daley would come in a strong second, thereby knocking Byrne out of the picture; and 3) in a one-on-one mayoral run-off Daley would defeat Washington.

Daleyites started a petition drive to garner the necessary quota of referendum signatures (over 142,000) in pro-Daley northwest- and southwest-side wards. All petitions had to be filed with the Chicago Board of Elections office by August 18th. As the filing date approached and reports of successful petition efforts mounted, the nonpartisan referendum issue grew as hot as Chicago's summer sun.

Washington, who at first either ignored or scoffed at the nonpartisan advocates, reacted vigorously to the petition drive's apparent continuing momentum. He called the electoral change "badly timed and foolhardy." The mayor warned referendum proponents that his "forces in the city would not sit idly by and let this [action] be perpetrated." He also put Democratic party leaders on notice, as well as 1986 state and county candidates, that if the referendum were put on the ballot, "they would see a tremendous political backlash among his black, white, and Hispanic constituents." [27]

In late July, Mayor Washington's aldermanic allies stunned referendum supporters by implementing a political strategy that would have brought a smile to the face of every past machine hack in Chicago history. Without warning, Washington's city council majority approved the placement of three separate *nonbinding* referendums on the November ballot, thereby knocking out any chance for a nonpartisan mayoral referendum in November. How was that possible? According to state law, no jurisdiction could submit more than three binding or nonbinding referendum questions to the voters at one time. Moreover, the law also stated that these referendums could be referred to the ballot by petition or by council action. Washington's council action was a legal manipulation of the system to prevent a potential grassroots people's movement from pursuing an alternative to the current governmental process. In short, Washington the reformer had made a move that former Mayor Richard Daley, the machine boss and father of Washington's opponent, would have applauded and admired.

The reaction to the council's action was instant and sharp. Washington supporters, barely hiding huge smirks, claimed that the three referendum issues (expansion of the Chicago Board of Education from eleven to fifteen members, the desirability of legalized gambling, and the possibilities of lowering natural gas bills) were all critical council issues that warranted in immediate voter opinion response. Anti-Washington aldermen, led by Vrdolyak and Burke, were angered by the maneuver but were also hard pressed to hide their professional admiration for the deftness of the action. Burke summed up the views of this group by asking the mayor in open council: "Who's kidding who?. . . Why are you so afraid of having the people vote–this is only a clever ploy." But he added with a smile, "I must compliment whoever thought of it." [28]

Both Chicago major newspapers were shocked by Washington's power play. The *Sun-Times* labeled the mayoral move "pathetic" and "smacking of legal trickery," while the *Tribune* suggested that the mayor was copying the political tactics of those he pledged to oppose and eventually bury. For the first time in Chicago's political history, the "who" (the candidates and their respective party affiliations) were being challenged by the "how" (the procedures of the electoral process) for political coverage by the print and electronic media. Each potential candidate would create various alternative campaign scenarios based on how the race would be contested as much as who would be running against him or her. Chicago was entering a new stage of "cutthroat poker" politics.

Nonpartisan mayoral proponents, shaken but not deterred by Washington's action, appealed the council decision to the three-member Chicago Board of Elections while they continued collecting more referendum signatures. In mid-August they submitted more than 200,000 names on several thousand petitions to the election board. At the same time, State's Attorney Daley publicly declared himself a leader in the drive for the nonpartisan referendum. Daley claimed that his full support for the referendum was based on his belief that "a nonpartisan election would benefit Chicago. . . it would require a majority of people to vote for a mayor." Washington's response was simple and direct: "His father [former Mayor Richard J. Daley] would be rolling over in his grave with his son trying to destroy the Democratic primary for mayor."[29]

One week after the petitions were submitted, the controversy surrounding the referendum struggle reached a new level of intensity. The Chicago Board of Elections voted two to one that the nonpartisan mayoral question was qualified for the November ballot–thereby negating the three-referendum Washington council gambit. Alderman Tim Evans, the mayor's council spokesman, immediately declared that the Washington forces would challenge the election board's decision. Both Washington and Evans singled out the election board chairman, Michael Lavelle, as the villain in the process. On the evening of the board's decision, Washington told the congregation of a southside black

39

church that "Lavelle was ramrodding the people of Chicago, [for] the law says whoever gets there first with the most gets on the ballot. We got there first and put three referendums on the ballot." The mayor was no longer hiding behind the facade of a good government, because this referendum struggle was now an all-out political battle; and the mayor recognized that a loss here might cost him the entire war–his re-election.

As the legal wheels began to deal quickly with Washington's challenge of the election board's decision, another front opened up in this bizarre but critical procedural ballot battle. If the petitions gathered by the nonpartisan advocates were found to contain an insufficient number of legal signatures, then the entire referendum issue would become moot. So the Washington forces amassed a small army of "volunteers" to scrutinize each of the 8,100 petition sheets containing the submitted signatures.

It was now role reversal time in Chicago politics: the former "ins," who were now the "outs," were petitioning to open up the mayoral electoral process by eliminating partisan politics, while the former "outs" and self-styled reformers, now the "ins," were intent on shortcircuiting this move by using the old-fashioned machine tactic of petition examination to throw the issue off the ballot.[30]

The election board established an elaborate set of rules Washington's volunteers had to adhere to in examining the non-partisan referendum petitions. The mayor's people were given one week to go through the huge stack of submitted sheets; badges were required to enter the "controlled area" (the examination room); the maximum number of examiners working at one time was 100; and the 8:00 A.M. to 7:00 P.M. workday would have designated break and lunch periods.

On August 19th the examination process began, and, even in a city famous for its unique brand of politics, this event was special. Room 402 at City Hall was the scene of the petition check. Throughout the entire day all available seats were filled by volunteers going through the petitions sheet by sheet and name by name, looking for forgeries, nonregistered voter signatures, circulators' (those who obtained the signatures) procedural mistakes, or any other irregularity–big or small–that would put the number of submitted signatures below the legal target.

Who were these volunteers? Given the political stakes and media attention, the mayor's people made certain that no volunteers were current city workers. Instead, Washington's forces fielded an examination team that had racial and gender balance and a single-minded game plan to prevent the referendum from getting on the ballot. For the white checkers, the one-week exam process turned into a mini-reunion of old Independent Voters of Illinois members. For years this organization had fought former Mayor Daley in its advocating of open, reform-minded, grassroots, citizen-oriented, and democratized city politics. It was a somewhat surrealistic sight to see these graying and wrinkled veterans of countless civil rights marches and lettuce boycotts now attempting to use technical deficiencies to stifle the voice of the people as expressed in popular petitions. As for the black examiners, they were considerably younger than their white counterparts; and though they did have strong views on many social and economic issues, the driving force behind their actions was the man – their unflinching belief in Harold Washington.

It did not take long for Washington's volunteers to find indisputable and blatant signature discrepancies in the referendum petitions. Congressman William Lipinski, a Daley ally and petition point man, defended the referendum effort, claiming that in Chicago "normally petitions are 10 to 15 percent forged...maybe this, since it is so large, will go 20 percent." Even to veteran Chicago political observers, Lipinski's unorthodox defense of the petition drive was astounding. More and more participants on both sides of the issue were becoming convinced of a strong likelihood that enough illegal signatures could be found to deny the referendum ballot access.[31]

The issue of flawed petitions pointed out the painful reality of Chicago in the 1980s to the remaining regular city Democrats. In the old days of Mayor Daley, obtaining petition signatures had been a mere machine formality. It was done with precision and efficiency. The troops (precinct captains and loyalists) were brought together under the leadership of knowledgeable and bright ward committeemen and young organization lawyers. They handed out clear instructions, gave assignments, and completed the signature process with crisp swiftness. The petition follies of 1986 reflected the decay of the machine. The regular Democratic organization army had been reduced from brigades to platoons; leadership was mainly geriatric and ineffective (only a few ward organizations of the Daley-era style remain in the entire city); and a major effort like the nonpartisan drive was

41

simply too great a task for most of those aging ward leaders who were left. Undoubtedly, many people worked hard and honestly to collect a huge number of signatures; others simply did not have the energy or the will to do likewise.

As charges of referendum signature improprieties made daily headlines, the Washington forces went before the Chicago Election Board to 1) challenge the validity of the petitions and 2) restate their views that the "rule of 3" (allowing only three referendums on the ballot) should be enforced. In early September the election board ruled by a two-to-one vote in favor of the mayor on the latter point, thereby knocking the nonpartisan referendum off the November ballot. (The board did rule that the referendum was eligible for the February 1987 ballot.) However, the board refused to address the allegations of petition fraud.

The political fallout was remarkable. Both sides were disappointed with one-half of the decision, and thus they united in displaying open contempt for the board—for different reasons. Washington allies pointed to board chairman Michael Lavelle as their main culprit, while the nonpartisan referendum supporters leveled strong criticism at James Nolan, the board's lone Republican.[32] The autumn political season in Chicago found Illinois statewide candidates playing a weak "second fiddle" to the city's ongoing mayoral referendum brawl. Mayor Washington and Representative Lipinski exchanged daily charges and political threats as the entire issue moved into the court system. On September 16, Circuit Court Judge Joseph Schneider decided in favor of Washington by upholding the Board of Election's decision to prevent the referendum from being placed on the November ballot. And Schneider simultaneously overruled the board on its position that the referendum could be placed on the February 1987 ballot. The judge ordered that such a move could only take place after a thorough inspection of the petitions.[33]

Judge Schneider's ruling was a technical knockout for the mayor. The judge argued that under Chicago's home-rule powers the city had "maximum flexibility" to determine ballot referendum procedures. Anti-Washington political insiders claimed that Schneider's decision was expected because he had long been friendly with many current independent and liberal-minded mayoral advisors. Others suggested that Schneider's decision was influenced by the political fact that he was "up for retention" in the November election (under Illinois law, sitting judges, after a specified number of years, must receive a 60 percent ballot retention vote to remain on the bench) and that he was fearful of antagonizing Washington's huge bloc of black voters. Whatever the rationale, Schneider's ruling left the referendum forces with one final hope: the Illinois Supreme Court.

In early October, nearly two and a half months after the entire issue had become headline news, the state's highest court ended the petition controversy in favor of Harold Washington. The Supreme Court's decision was more than a legal victory for the mayor; it was a "mercy killing" for the referendum movement. The high court, in upholding Judge Schneider's ruling, called the nonpartisan petitions "totally defective." In almost brutal language Justice Seymour Simon (a former Chicago alderman and Democratic ward committeeman), writing for the court, beat down the citizen nonpartisan referendum, stating: 1) the wording was too vague; 2) it did not fit the existing election calendar; 3) it called for a 50 percent majority vote (which Simon called self-contradictory because a majority is more than 50 percent; and 4) it did not promote a coherent electoral scheme to replace the existing one.

William Lipinski, a shrewd and articulate political operative, responded to the expected high court verdict with a sigh of relief, saying, "This is like being shot after you're already dead." Alderman Tim Evans, Washington's top political advisor, was naturally ecstatic. "This is," said Evans, "an overwhelming victory for those of us who suggested that attempting to change the rules in the middle of the game is unfair, unreasonable, and unconstitutional." What Evans did not say was that, by winning Chicago's legal summer-fall spectacular on mayoral election procedures, Harold Washington had become an overwhelming re-election favorite. The mayor was now in control of the process. He could tease foes and reporters alike with such potentially tantalizing moves as an independent candidacy, which would bypass the now-guaranteed February primary battles, thereby giving him a three-way (two white opponents) general election battle in April. Whatever the game plan, the mayor was in command and was assured that under no circumstances would he have to face young Rich Daley one on one.[34]

43

CHAPTER THREE

A Cast of Candidates at the Starting Gate

A T THE TURN OF THE TWENTIETH century, Chicago's legend-ary saloonkeeper-philosopher Martin J. Dooley said: "Pol-itics ain't beanbag. This is a man's game; and women, children, and prohibitionists do well to keep out of it." Mr. Dooley did not envision Margaret Jane Byrne. As Chicago's only woman mayor had proved, her gender did not prevent her from being "pound for pound the toughest mayor in the city's history." She was also the first candidate into the starting gate for the 1987 mayoralty race.

Jane Byrne's path to city hall had been unique. She had held no previous elective office, she had no geographic or ethnic power base in the city, and she benefited from no clever political or governmental alliances to propel her into office. In short, Jane Byrne was the ultimate "pop-up" candidate who had suddenly emerged at the opportune moment to win it all. Any analysis of Byrne, either as a candidate or as mayor, is difficult; for in order to understand her, one must come to grips with the demons and dreams that drive this amazing woman.

On the campaign trail in 1979, Byrne was a relentless pursuer who attacked incumbent mayor Michael Bilandic, while in 1983 she defended her tumultuous mayoral record by calling herself a professional public manager. Yet it is Byrne the administrator who confounds any meaningful interpretation of her as a poli-cymaker or politician. As mayor she could never accept victory: she saw enemies all around her (especially young Rich Daley)

45

and had a difficult time living in political peace. Still, she never lost her dreams of herself and the city basking in glory, excitement, and greatness. At best, Jane Byrne was a walking contradiction of idealistic governmental vision and backroom political pettiness; at worst, she mirrored the person described by the Irish poet William Butler Yeats:

> I sing what was lost and dread what was won,
> I walk in a battle fought over again.

Byrne's 1987 mayoral strategy was a simple one: "Declare and Accuse." This meant that she would be the first to announce and would then proceed to accuse any other potential white mayoral candidate who attempted to challenge her in the Democratic primary of being a spoiler. As a political tactic it was brilliant. But in the end she would fall short of her ultimate goal—reclaiming the fifth floor of City Hall.

The Chicago *Sun-Times* headlined Byrne's mayoral candidacy announcement with three words: "See Jane Run."[1] Her July 16, 1985 move surprised no one because she had been leaking her mayoral intentions for months. What was interesting was how Byrne, isolated from big-name political support and lacking a large campaign war chest, was able to use free media exposure for her political purposes. Aided only by her campaign manager press secretary, the amiable and effective Joseph Pecor, Byrne played the print and electronic media like a maestro. Her most noteworthy innovation was to peddle her limited paid advertising as news stories. Byrne previewed her political commercials to all Chicago television stations, who then excerpted them on the evening news.

Once the flurry over her announcement abated, Byrne settled down to a slow and deliberate campaign for the primary, which was still more than eighteen months away. She played down her once-mercurial reputation with a new low-profile, "cool Jane" image. In military terms, she hoped to challenge Harold Washington by adopting the strategy of another Washington—a fellow named George. Like America's revolutionary war commander, Byrne avoided major confrontations with her main enemy. Instead, she conducted a guerilla war campaign by selectively striking certain targets and thereby forcing her opponents to recognize a political fact of life: her forces were already in the field. In short, Byrne's greatest accomplishment between July 1985 and November 1986 (the actual beginning of the mayoral campaign) was to maintain a powerful presence without winning a political battle.

How did she do it? Byrne used the eighteen-month interim period to work the political coffee circuit, meeting with small groups of Chicagoans in various neighborhoods (usually white or Hispanic). She discussed topics such as crime and police protection, taxes, patronage, and the general cleanliness of the city. She called Washington a poor leader and his leading council nemesis, Alderman Vrdolyak, "a loser." Byrne told reporters that she had a solid "three-phase" political campaign timetable that she would follow all the way to victory in the general election in April 1987. So convincing were Byrne's private and public efforts with voters and the media that in late October 1986, Ed Vrdolyak announced that he would not run in the Democratic mayoral primary – if Washington and Byrne were also candidates.

Given her opposition and the political stakes, Jane Byrne had a marvel of a year in 1986: she did more with less than has any Chicago politician in recent history.

Edward Vrdolyak

Edward Vrdolyak is the quintessential practitioner of the Chicago political tradition. He is both tough and charming, devious and loyal, moneymaker and favor provider. But above all, this man, who is known as "Fast Eddie" by friends and foes alike, is in the game for one overriding reason – power. Observing him running a Democratic central committee meeting or strutting around the city council floor, sartorially resplendent in his tailored suits and gleaming gold cufflinks, one sees a man relishing the acquisition and dispensation of political and governmental power – "clout," as Chicagoans call it.

No matter what the situation or audience, Ed Vrdolyak seems at ease and in control. This command of his public personality is even more remarkable considering the steep political ladder Vrdolyak has had to climb to prominence. No one gave Vrdolyak a free ride to the top. His neighborhood base is the 10th Ward in Chicago's working-class and smokestack-filled Southeast Side, an area that is geographically isolated from the rest of the city. Over the years, residents of this ward (heavily eastern European in background) have exhibited a "chip-on-the-shoulder attitude" concerning the amount of services and respect they have received from city government. Ed Vrdolyak recognized and reflected his community's perception of being underdogs in Chicago's political and social structure; and among the many factors that have altered and directed his career and lifestyle, Vrdolyak has never lost his identification with his belligerently proud constituents.

The Climb Up

In the late 1960s, Vrdolyak, a young neighborhood lawyer (he had graduated from the University of Chicago Law School) with a reputation for not being afraid of a fight, successfully challenged the incumbent Democratic ward committeeman. A few years later (in 1971) he completed his ward takeover by ousting Alderman John Buchanan in a bitter contest. It did not take Alderman Vrdolyak long to indirectly challenge the ultimate city leader, Mayor Daley. In the council Vrdolyak rebelled at the tightly run political system, and he soon became the leader of a group of organization aldermen known as the "Young Turks." These individuals wanted greater input into the government process, and, according to one "Turk" veteran, "we also wanted a greater share of the output."[2]

In 1974 the rebel Vrdolyak surprised even his most ardent supporters when he challenged the Daley machine in the Democratic primary by running for Cook County assessor. Though he was soundly beaten by the organization candidate, Thomas Tully, Vrdolyak gained citywide party respect both for the guts of his spirited challenge and for his ability to easily rejoin the organization after his loss. Daley's death in 1976 meant a push further up the ladder, but he still was not in command of either the government or the party. Leadership would finally come to him in 1982, when Mayor Byrne dumped party chairman George Dunne (a man whom she disliked personally and whose relationship with her likely 1983 challenger, young Rich Daley, frightened and angered her) in favor of Vrdolyak.

With the chip still squarely on his shoulder, Vrdolyak became Byrne's muscle in the heated 1983 Democratic mayoral primary. "They were," said one machine veteran, "a perfect political match, like fire and fire." But it was no secret that the alliance between these two fierce competitors was one of temporary convenience and no long-lasting friendship.

Vrdolyak parlayed his new political power into a governmental role of opposition spokesman during most of Washington's first term. His 29-21 aldermanic majority created more than

Chicago's "Council Wars" and citywide political chaos; it also fanned the fires of ambition deep within his own breast. Out front on almost every issue, challenging Washington in the council and in the media, and by sheer force of personality and some intimidation boosting timid and potentially wavering ethnic aldermen and Democratic politicians – Vrdolyak was the glue that held the mayoral opposition together. Vrdolyak knew that he alone could generate the emotional support to challenge Washington's people politically for control of the streets.

He also realized that his high negatives, which appeared in every public and private poll, would frighten off most potential mainline Democratic support for any Vrdolyak mayoral candidacy. Yet, as he would say often during the 1987 campaign about his rival anti-Washington mayoral aspirants, "For four years they never took a card." By this he meant that he was the only candidate who had been a major player in the mayoral political game, and now that the big hand was about to be played they wanted to deal him out. His opponents and many Chicagoans did not realize that Vrdolyak the rebel still carried that southeast-side chip, and he was not about to step aside for anybody.

As Vrdolyak prepared for the intense, high-level mayoral political maneuvering that would dominate the Chicago political scene in November and December of 1986, his relationships with both major political parties was of special interest.

The Democrats

Though he was the Cook County Democratic party chairman, Vrdolyak's power in the party hierarchy was hardly dominant. As expected, black ward committeemen publicly separated themselves from the chairman; but he also had his problems with State's Attorney Daley's white ethnic loyalists, prominent statewide Democratic officeholders, and almost anyone in the party associated with the man he deposed as chairman, the county board president, George Dunne.

For example, in late 1985 the old Democratic warhorse, U.S. Congressman Daniel Rostenkowski, chairman of the House Ways and Means Committee and 32nd Ward committeeman, refused to endorse Vrdolyak's re-election candidacy for party chairman. "It all depends," Rostenkowski said, "on who is running against [him]."[3] In March 1986, George Dunne hinted broadly at a major challenge to Vrdolyak's party leadership, and though it never came off, the continued hard feelings between the two were open and obvious.

Through all the intrigues and disasters of the 1986 primary (in which the state Democratic ticket was rocked by victories in the lieutenant governor and secretary of state races by two Lyndon LaRouche disciples and by the flagrant break of party unity of several top ward committeemen who pushed their own countywide candidates against the endorsed slate) Vrdolyak persevered. In simple Machiavellian terms, most white committeemen did not love him; they feared him. They could chip away at his power and occasionally finagle around his authority, but no one had the guts or desire to go one on one with Vrdolyak for party leadership. As one committeeman suggested, "Given the racial situation in the city, there is no way anyone can 'outwhite' Eddie." [4]

The Republicans

Not since the late 1920s, when Democrat Anton Cermak allied with factions within the Republican party, had a local Democratic party chairman like Vrdolyak been so open in his relationship with the GOP opposition. In late 1985, Vrdolyak told a local radio show audience that he preferred two Republicans, former Gov. Richard Ogilvie and former U.S. Attorney Daniel Webb, to Harold Washington in the 1987 mayoral election. Vrdolyak's bombshell was a blatant—but not surprising—statement of current Chicago political reality: race had overtaken party as an organizing weapon. It also demonstrated Vrdolyak's weariness in leading a party whose core supporters (black voters) viewed their chairman as a devil.

As expected, rival Democrats jumped all over Vrdolyak. Byrne called him "a poor Democrat and a poor sportsman"; Washington chimed in that "only in Chicago is there a Democratic party chairman who is a Republican"; while long-time Democratic stalwart Michael Howlett expressed the historical view: "If Mayor Daley was to come back . . . he wouldn't believe it."

Yet Vrdolyak continued his GOP courting throughout 1986. There were stories of Vrdolyak meeting with GOP Gov. Jim Thompson, a candidate for re-election, and with the Republican contender for county board president (Dunne's opponent), Joseph Mathewson. Noted downstate journalist Mike Lawerence labeled Vrdolyak's allies "Eddiecrats," comparing them to the

Dixiecrats of the late 1940s in their disloyalty to the Democratic party and its statewide candidates. Nationally known columnist George Will captured, perhaps unknowingly, the essence of the split in Chicago and Democratic party in an interview with Vrdolyak. Will wrote that Vrdolyak called his typical Chicago voter "Barney Bungalow." "This guy," Vrdolyak argued, wants the government to "get out of my face, make the streets safe, pick up my garbage; otherwise, get away from me." A good quote, but Will missed a critical point. Unfortunately for Vrdolyak, both the Barneys and the bungalows in Chicago were being replaced by nonwhite, nonhomeowning voters. Moreover, a sizable portion of Vrdolyak's Barneys, most of whom had voted Democratic all their life, had moved philosophically closer to the GOP and in recent elections were willing to assert this new identification by voting for certain Republican candidates—like Ronald Reagan and 1983 GOP mayoral candidate Bernard Epton. Will's column, written forty years earlier, would have been no big deal because Chairman Vrdolyak would have fit nicely the socioeconomic demographic mix of Chicago Democrats. But in 1986 these hardcore ethnics were no longer dominant, and Vrdolyak's GOP courting could be summarized as "a leader following his people."

Washington's Preparations

Washington prepared for his 1987 re-election campaign by putting his political operation on cruise control. His Council Wars victory, coupled with his successful blockage of the nonpartisan referendum effort, solidified and elevated his political standing. A second mayoral term was not totally assured; but given recent events, his unified black support, and his splintered opposition, the mayor could afford the luxury of allowing his potential opponents to gain publicity by attacking each other.

To be sure, Washington and his political operatives did not remain completely mute. The mayor continued his calls for the ouster of Michael Lavelle as chairman of the Chicago Board of Election Commissioners. Lavelle, a cagy and shrewd political insider, was one of the few remaining big-time citywide "players" who had the power and the guts to cause Washington political problems. Washington also became a key team player in the ill-fated gubernatorial campaign of Adlai Stevenson's Democratic-Solidarity party ticket. (As would be the case through his entire mayoral career, Harold Washington would always end up

51

supporting his party despite early warnings from him and his aides that he might not.)

Through a long-time political associate, David Canter, then serving as an assistant commissioner of Streets and Sanitation, the mayor began publishing his own political newspaper, aptly named *Second Term*. The paper's tone and purpose was totally pro-Washington, as it praised his friends and pilloried his enemies while raising Washington to near political sainthood. To old-time Chicago political observers, Washington's *Second Term* publication was similar to former mayor and machine creator Anton J. Cermak's personal propaganda newsheet of the 1930s, *The Public Service Leader*. By these actions and other subtle political moves, Washington informed his pals and foes alike of his plan to continue using the winning reform rhetoric of 1983 while his associates on the inside would use old-fashioned mayoral muscle to win again in 1987.

On August 13, 1986, Washington held the biggest fundraiser of his life to launch his re-election campaign. He announced his campaign slogan, "Chicago Working Better Than Ever for Everyone," at a giant Palmer House hotel reception. An overflow crowd heard Washington call himself the "most productive" mayor in Chicago history. The mayor boasted about his major administrative accomplishments, made fun of his political opponents, and rattled off a long list of citywide accomplishments (*Sun-Times* reporter Donald Schwartz, covering the event, suggested that on the final point the mayor's approach was "very much in the style of former Mayor Daley").⁵ At the end of the evening the city's first black mayor, who had been elected on a shoestring campaign budget less than four years before, walked away with a gross take of almost one million dollars.

Looming on the sidelines during the political jockeying were two potentially powerful forces. First, the Daley faction— those Chicagoans who were mainly ethnic and centered on the city's Southwest Side but aligned with a growing smattering of lakefront yuppie types—was an odd coalition that existed because the Daley name represented the golden power days of Richard J. to the neighborhood ethnics, while the young professionals who lived along the lake, many of them also ethnics, saw the son Richard M. as a new-generation leader who combined administrative competence with old-fashioned organization building. As mentioned above, the Daleyites were centering most of their political efforts on pushing the ill-fated nonpartisan issue. The other force gathering its troops was the Chicago Republican party. James O'Grady's victory in the 1986 race for Cook County sheriff, along with Gov. James Thompson's strong re-election performance in Chicago's ethnic wards, had partially mended the long-broken hearts of the city's GOP. It seemed apparent to Republican leaders that Bernard Epton's narrow mayoral loss of 1983 was not a political aberration but, in fact, could be a harbinger of a renewed and reinvigorated GOP effort in 1987.

Small political boomlets exploded almost weekly for potential 1987 Republican mayoral nominees like former governor Richard Ogilvie and former U.S. Attorney Dan Webb. Both men played hide-and-seek with a possible run for City Hall throughout the late summer and early fall of 1986. In keeping their illustrious names on the GOP mayoral front burner, they effectively closed out any organized attempt by any other potential major Republican challenger from establishing an early political base. Their eventual and predictable refusal to run for mayor would leave the party in its usual mayoral electoral disarray by late autumn, the time for slating the candidates.

The opening battle of the 1987 Chicago mayoral campaign took place on September 24, 1986, on the hallowed floor of the city council. The issue was taxes, with the Washington administration demanding an increase and the Vrdolyak aldermanic bloc firmly opposing one. Whether the city truly needed the requested $80 million property tax increase and other new taxes was difficult to determine: obtaining reliable statistics on Chicago tax revenue is like sticking one's hand in a bowl of oatmeal – a lot goes through your fingers. But what was apparent to all were the political implications for 1987.

The mayor needed a firm aldermanic majority (twenty-six votes) to pass the tax increase. Because of a quirk in the state law, the mayor could vote on a tax increase bill if one more vote was needed for it to pass. Washington's council supporters, following the spring special aldermanic elections, numbered twenty-five. Thus, in order for the mayor to cast the deciding vote, he had to have unanimous support from his council faction. And, as often happens in such cases, one man held the balance of power: Alderman Burton Natarus of the 42nd Ward.

Natarus' ward stretched from expensive highrises and townhomes on the lakefront west to the infamous Cabrini-Green public housing projects. His mentor and patron, Cook County Board President George Dunne, was one of the few mainline white Democratic pols who had openly supported Washington's candidacy against Epton in 1983. Throughout Council Wars, Natarus had voted with the Washington faction; but on this issue the alderman saw an enraged constituency from the east part of his ward demanding no more tax increases.

The floor fight on the issue was a Chicago classic. Everyone knew Natarus held the key vote. He was lobbied by both sides, had chats with Vrdolyak and Washington, and when the council session was called to order, the 42nd Ward alderman looked like a rumpled suit at a garage sale – all worn out. As the debate over the tax increase ebbed and flowed, Natarus began to waver from his pro-Washington stance. He called for a vote delay, then a recess, then a new meeting date. He told his colleagues that "both sides want to see me dead," and that his indecision "had nothing to do with politics." A packed council audience, many of them pro-Washington community leaders and city employees, acted and sounded like they were at a bullfight as they cheered and booed the spectacle.

Finally the moment of truth came. Mayor Washington told the council to be at ease for five minutes, and then he called Natarus to the rostrum. In front of the assembled multitude the mayor handed the alderman the phone, and for a few minutes Natarus listened to someone on the other end. Who's on the phone with Natarus? was the question racing through the council chambers. Alderman Wallace Davis (a westside black alderman and Washington supporter) captured the moment when he said: "Ha! it's George Dunne, who else? It [certainly] ain't his wife. Dunne's telling him how to vote. Hell! Ray Charles can tell you who he's talking to."[6] A thoroughly deflated Natarus eased back to his seat and eventually cast the deciding vote for a tax increase (which also included a new gasoline tax). Roars of protest came from antiadministration council members. Alderman Roman Pucinski, a far northwest-side Polish leader, claimed that from this day on the mayor would be known as "High Tax Harold." Alderman Michael Sheahan, from the city's far Southwest Side, charged, "This administration takes our tax dollars and doesn't give us service." And Alderman Ed Burke, the former council finance chairman, sounding like anti-Mayor Daley aldermen from bygone council clashes, chimed in, "This entire tax hike procedure is out of order . . . there has been no public testimony or committee hearings."

At the end, Washington's council floor leader, Alderman Tim Evans, summed up the entire proceedings with words reminiscent of past administration defenders: "This tax package is not a surprise—it's a solution." What had happened? The council under Washington's direction had passed its second major tax hike in under five months (there had been another one in May following Washington's winning control of the council). The September property tax hike was bulled through by the administration to prevent threatened layoffs in areas of vital city service, for example, among police and firemen. Washington's forces attempted to soften this second big hit on the property owner by arguing that if the gas tax produced expected revenues (they were hoping it would be around $27 million), some of the property tax increase would be rolled back. Leading budget experts outside the administration, such as Donald Haider, a Northwestern University professor and budget director under Mayor Byrne, had been warning Washington's City Hall financial people that before considering another tax hike, the administration had to be sure that "the city's fiscal house [was] . . . in order and that all major efficiencies and economies in the city spending [had] been taken."[7] Despite these warnings, despite the traditional "no tax fever" before a pending election campaign, and despite outrage from the city's white ethnics, Harold Washington had the political confidence to move ahead with the tax increase.

The Battle is Joined?

After the midterm fall 1986 elections for state, county, and congressional office were over, Chicagoans returned to their first political passion—mayoral politics and the horse race that would precede the February Democratic primary. First out of the gate was Jane Byrne. Liberated from months of low-key personal campaigning and political organizing, the former mayor—as she had in her previous primary battles four and eight years before—dominated the city's written and electronic media. She paraded endorsements of past political allies before the voters. Former park district superintendent Ed Kelly, still a 47th Ward committeeman, claimed that Byrne was the city's real mayor. Aldermen Thomas Cullerton, Roman Pucinski, and Richard Mell quickly followed with strong pro-Byrne endorsements. Byrne's stated strategy was to go one on one with Washington in the Democratic primary. By announcing early and campaigning immediately, Byrne not only played out that strategy but also reminded any other potential Democratic white challengers that if they joined the fray, they and not she would be labeled "spoilers."

Most noteworthy of Byrne's early campaign moves was her intensified use of paid TV advertising. Byrne hit the airwaves first with a spot on the property tax increases suffered by Chicago homeowners during the Washington administration. It became clear that she had drawn blood when the mayor threatened to ask the city's major television stations to pull the ads because, in his opinion, they were "totally and completely misleading, false and phony."[8] He never went through with his threat, but Byrne had clearly landed a solid punch. However, whatever momentum she had built with this salvo soon vanished when events outside her control pushed her campaign off the front pages and forced her to go to a neutral political corner as new players began to enter the mayoral ring.

On November 4, 1986, Cook County Assessor Thomas Hynes led the Democratic county ticket against another helpless GOP challenger and was re-elected for a third term. Hynes was recognized throughout the city and suburbs as a man of integrity and intelligence. He had parlayed his administrative professionalism with political cautiousness to move slowly into the front ranks of the Democratic power brokers. A former state senator, he was named "best freshman senator" after being first elected in 1970 and ended his legislative career by serving as president of the Illinois State Senate. A thorough political organizer, Hynes had also built a strong Democratic organization in his own southwest-side 19th Ward, where he was the Democratic committeeman. His political loyalties rested squarely with the Daley faction, but his friendships and relationships were spread throughout the party. A careful and thoughtful man, Hynes was not one to make impetuous or risky political moves—unless they involved the political ambitions of Jane Byrne.

Byrne and Hynes hated each other. The former mayor saw Hynes as the alter ego of Rich Daley. It was Hynes who had stood against her when, late in 1979, she had attempted to steamroll a Chicago Democratic organizational endorsement of Sen. Edward M. Kennedy's presidential candidacy against incumbent Jimmy Carter. It was Hynes's acting as a high coconspirator and strategic planner in Daley's 1983 mayoral primary push that had denied Byrne renomination and re-election. And it was Hynes who had blocked her acceptance by the one community Byrne coveted more than anyplace else in Chicago: the upper-income southwest-side Beverly neighborhood with its heavily politicized and influential Irish residents.

From Hynes's perspective, Byrne was unpredictable, unacceptable, and untrustworthy. As mayor she had played "Wheel of Fortune" with long-time 19th Ward city workers, spinning them all over Chicago, disregarding geographic location (proximity between home and job), and demoting and punishing several others. It had been Byrne who refused to let Chicago police patrol a Hynes-supported "South Side Irish St. Patrick's Day Parade." Regular school crossing guards were sent in their place, thereby forcing parade organizers to request state police officers to maintain traffic control on city streets. It was the ill will between Byrne and Hynes that had first spurred southwest-siders into setting up their own St. Patrick's Day parade (held on the Sunday before St. Patrick's Day), separate from the traditional downtown parade. Finally, Hynes was a close friend of Rich Daley, and, given the Daley-Byrne feud, this meant that he would not compromise in his course of preventing Byrne from ever regaining political power.

In view of all the above, why did Hynes want to run for mayor? The answer is one of the unsolved riddles of the entire 1987 mayoral picture. In some ways Hynes's fumbled decision to run demonstrated the chaos that has befallen regular Democrats in Chicago since the death of Richard J. Daley. Splintered leadership plus demographic change has rewritten the unwritten rules concerning political power-grabbing of city or party offices. This is what Hynes faced in early November: Washington was mum on whether he would run in the February 1987 Democratic mayoral primary or skip the primary and run as an independent in the April general election, thereby guaranteeing him another three-way (two whites against one black) 1983-style primary. Byrne was in the primary, and no one—especially not Hynes—was going to force her out of the race. Yet Hynes found himself being pushed forward by a powerful but nonmajority faction within the Democratic party.

Congressmen Daniel Rostenkowski and William Lipinski (long- time Daley stalwarts) claimed that Hynes could beat both Washington and Byrne in a three-way 1983 rerun. Vrdolyak, pondering his own candidacy and basking in the victories on most of the state and county Democratic tickets—despite the LaRouche primary fiasco—suggested that "Hynes would be a great mayor."[9]

Appreciative of the party chairman's fine words (he knew that Vrdolyak's own burning ambition to run for mayor matched Byrne's), Hynes nevertheless balked. One thing was certain: the 1987 mayoral race would not be governed by Marquis of Queensbury rules. He had never been a political alley fighter, and since he did not have the mayoral hunger burning in his gut, stopping Byrne was simply not worth the price of getting into the Democratic campaign meat grinder. He figured that she probably could not beat Washington anyway.

Less than one week after the Hynes talk surfaced, his reluctance to enter the fray seemed like sound strategy. Vrdolyak announced his upcoming mayoral candidacy with his typical bravado: "It's going to be a war out there." Reacting to Vrdolyak's announcement, Hynes told the press: "I have been urged by many people in and out of politics to run for mayor of Chicago.... I have looked carefully at the situation and have decided not to be a candidate, since to do so would be politically unrealistic in an already overcrowded field."[10] Shrewd words, shrewd reasoning, and shrewd advice. It was unfortunate for Hynes that he did not listen to himself one month later.

"Vrdolyak's on the Loose." The word rushed through the inner leadership circles of Chicago's political and business community. Preparing for his formal mayoral announcement, Vrdolyak flooded selected white ethnic precincts with his petition circulators. As would be the case for the next two months, reporters read the petition's small print carefully to see whether Vrdolyak was preparing to run in the Democratic or the Republican mayoral primary—or in the general election as an independent. Disregarding Washington's stated glee over his scrambling potential opponents—observing his growing number of challengers, the mayor said, "I'm having the splittin' time of my life right now"—Vrdolyak plunged forward to remake his image.

Appearing before the Publicity Club of Chicago, Vrdolyak unveiled his battle plan for the upcoming campaign. He told the audience and a full complement of Chicago newspapermen that Harold Washington was an incompetent who "doesn't have a clue about the job [mayor]." He pledged not to use race as a weapon in the campaign but complained that the mayor should be forced to make the same commitment. "Harold says when he hears I might run," Vrdolyak told the overflow crowd, "that he feels just like Joe Louis waiting for the next White Hope. I never said I was Rocky Marciano...race is not an issue with me."

The audience loved the performance, the press clamored for quotes, and Byrne supporters held their breath. Neither Vrdolyak nor Bryne were blinkers, and in an eyeball-to-eyeball confrontation neither would take a step back. For the rest of the month of November, Chicago politics made Machiavelli's city of Florence look like a pre-serpent Garden of Eden. Rumors flew. Hynes was reconsidering his decision not to run for mayor. Washington was leaving all options open: would he eventually run for re-election as a Democrat, an Independent, or as a separate new-party candidate? Byrne was moving deftly to guarantee that no white candidate would contest her in the Democratic mayoral primary. And Vrdolyak, the supreme political manipulator, was turning on the charm as Vrdolyak the mayoral candidate—though, like Washington, he was not revealing his campaign plans.

As the political pot bubbled and boiled, a new ingredient emerged to complicate an already mixed-up electoral stew. Chicago Republicans realized that time was running short and that they needed a real candidate, not just an unwilling prominent name, to run for mayor. Unfortunately for the GOP, their party bigwigs quickly proved that they were just as confused as their Democratic counterparts were in finding agreement on a single candidate. The Republicans set up a mayoral search committee during the second week of November. Daniel Webb, one of the two unwilling dream GOP mayoral hopefuls (Ogilvie was the other), was selected by Cook County Republican leader Donald Totten to chair the committee. As the GOP searchers began their deliberations, the defeated 1983 Republican candidate, Bernard Epton, announced his mayoral intentions. Epton denounced the Webb committee, attacked Ogilvie for his open support of Byrne in the 1983 Democratic mayoral primary, and paraded support from a handful of GOP ward committeemen. He told Chicago columnist Tom Fitzpatrick that one of his main reasons for running again was "to leave my family a good name . . . [because] I was portrayed as a racist SOB during the last campaign against Harold Washington."[11]

As the Webb committee sifted through potential mayoral choices, one fact became perfectly clear: there were not many options. With Epton already playing the role of a rebel and committed to run in the primary, GOP party regulars needed to find someone with enough name recognition to at least beat the now-unwanted 1983 standard bearer. Incredibly, the name of

State Senator Jeremiah Joyce, a Democrat from the Southwest Side and a 19th Ward ally of Tom Hynes, emerged as a leading Republican contender. Webb told the press of his high regard for Joyce, and the only two Chicago Republican state legislators, Walter Dudycz and Roger McAuliffe, openly backed a proposed Joyce candidacy.

The ramifications of a Joyce party switch and possible mayoral run were staggering to Chicago political observers. In Springfield it would narrow the Democrat's senate majority to one vote; it would split one of the few remaining deliverable Democratic ethnic wards in the city, the 19th; and it would be yet another party raid for office-hungry Republicans, following the successful sheriff candidacy of another former Democrat, James O'Grady.

While Joyce and his close friends pondered the advisability of his crossing over to the Republican party, the Webb committee continued its search process. Stalling for time and trying to find some respectable back-up if Joyce declined to make the switch, Webb and Totten announced their intention to find a "blue-ribbon candidate." (Historically, any candidate labeled "blue-ribbon" was someone who party leaders had found to run for an office they did not think they could win.) Two eminent Northwestern University professors, Donald Haider and Louis Masotti, suddenly emerged as potential leading mayoral contenders. Friends and office mates, Haider and Masotti taught in the university's prestigous Kellogg Graduate School of Management. Though both were respected academics, neither was a Chicago political novice, since Byrne had appointed both of them to highly visible city positions: Haider to budget director and Masotti to transition chief.

Not convinced of Joyce's sincerity about switching parties and fearful of possible Epton political momentum, the Webb committee settled on Haider. In a close Republican central committee endorsement vote, Haider beat back a spirited Epton challenge. However, Haider's committee victory was overshadowed by a simultaneous surprise announcement by Joyce that he would run for mayor as a Republican. A shocked Webb, losing his usual legalistic cool, angrily denounced Joyce's move and speculated that he was "trying to hijack the primary."

Even for a city that prides itself on blindside and back-alley politics, the situation in both parties was becoming nearly incomprehensible. Insiders mumbled that Webb was angry at Joyce because he thought that the latter might be fronting for Hynes or Daley. Perhaps only in Chicago could the following political scenario be considered understandable, let alone possible: 1) Joyce enters the GOP primary; 2) due to solid southwest-side ethnic support and the paucity of citywide GOP voters, he wins the Republican mayoral primary; 3) Washington beats Byrne in the Democratic primary, partly because Joyce siphons off considerable ethnic support; 4) Joyce drops out of the general election showdown with Washington and either Hynes or Daley takes his place; 5) either Hynes or Daley, running as a Republican, now gets the mayor one on one, with Byrne defeated and out of the picture and with Vrdolyak having no place to go. As bizarre as this scenario is to ponder, many observers believed it to be plausible and even workable. One local commentator simply dubbed the Joyce move a possible "Daley Double."

Thanksgiving 1986 saw the final political piece appear in Chicago's most confused electoral mayoral puzzle. Assessor Hynes, who for sound and logical reasons had taken himself out of the mayoral sweepstakes a few weeks earlier, suddenly began to reassess his 1987 options. For reasons known only to him and a few advisors, Hynes, at first quietly and then boldly, re-entered the mayoral game. Few observers, then or now, could understand what or who changed his mind; but a Hynes candidacy depended on the occurrence of certain events that were completely out of his control. His plan was to skip the February party primary and run as an independent in the April general election against the Democratic winner, Byrne or Washington. But key to this longshot gambit was his ability to persuade Vrdolyak to drop his own independent candidacy and, if possible, convince Haider, a long-time friend, to do the same if the latter won the Republican primary.

Hynes loyalists at the time—and even today—claim that if this double drop would have taken place, their man would be the city's mayor. Unfortunately, then and now they did not have a firm game plan as to *how* this Machiavellian process could have been accomplished. The only potential mayoral candidate to drop out of the picture was Hynes' 19th Ward ally, Sen. Jeremiah Joyce.

Considering its basic faulty reasoning and an unworkable campaign premise, the Hynes candidacy was doomed from the start, and there was little of a positive nature the assessor could have done in his upcoming campaign to turn it around. The great irony, almost tragicomedy, of these events was that, of all the potential candidates, Hynes had the best track record as a professional administrator and practical politician. Yet it was Hynes alone who embarked on a mayoral campaign that was a "kamikaze trip" from the start.

An insider's view of the situation reveals that the Hynes people could not even frighten a management professor out of the race. According to Haider, "Prior to Thanksgiving, Hynes informed me that he wasn't going to run, saying 'The numbers are not there for me.' " Uplifted by Hynes's words, Haider saw himself as the so-called final option of the anti-Washington crowd: if he would win the GOP primary, then he would most likely be able to challenge the mayor one on one in the April general.

Haider's dreams ended with another Hynes phone call a few days after Thanksgiving. The assessor told the professor that he had reconsidered his mayoral plans and that he hoped Haider had not drawn the wrong conclusions from the previous conversation. "I was shocked back to reality," reflects Haider about his emotions following the second Hynes conversation. "The moment Hynes re-entered the mayoral sweepstakes, my campaign contributions dried up." However, it was a phone call from a close Hynes advisor that irked Haider the most and reflected the lack of strategic planning behind the assessor's futile campaign. Haider's recollection of the conversation went as follows: "I was asked if I was going to do the right thing [drop out]. . . . I responded, 'What is the right thing?'. . .The caller said, 'You know.' "[12] In the clout and pressure chronicles of Chicago political history, this call ranks below the bottom. Haider disregarded the call, plowed on with his longshot campaign, realizing that there was indeed a new day in Chicago politics.

In the remaining days of 1986, the following political events set the mayoral menu for 1987. After much feinting and bluffing, Washington filed to run against Byrne in the February Democratic mayoral primary. Of all the major Democratic candidates Byrne was the only candidate who had never hinted at deviating from an announced game plan, even though the Joyce-Hynes-Vrdolyak late maneuverings had pushed her off the front pages. Hynes, fearful of being labeled a spoiler in the Byrne-Washington primary race, announced the formation of a new party – the Chicago First party. By forming a new party instead of running as an independent in the April general election, Hynes gave his petition signers the opportunity to vote in the February Democratic primary. Haider and Epton were set to go at each other in the February Republican primary. Yet it was Vrdolyak who dominated the media and set the tone for Chicago politics in the final days of the mayoral maneuvering derby.

In mid-December, Vrdolyak filed as a mayoral candidate of the Solidarity party. This party existed because the 1986 Democratic gubernatorial candidate, Adlai Stevenson, had refused to run with two Lyndon Larouche supporters who had captured the Democratic nominations for lieutenant governor and secretary of state. In desperation, Stevenson formed a separate party, Solidarity, and even though he was overwhelmed by the GOP candidate, Jim Thompson, Solidarity remained an established party in Illinois (at least for two years).

Vrdolyak's move, like Hynes's, left Byrne one on one with the mayor in the Democratic primary. But in the eyes of more future-oriented pols, it made the April election look like an incomprehensible free-for-all. Vrdolyak's move was greeted with derision from Hynes's supporters. Rostenkowski questioned Vrdolyak's continuation as party chairman, saying, "I can't even recall another situation where the chairman of the Cook County Democratic party ignored his own party and ran in another party . . . [we need] a reappraisal of Vrdolyak's leadership role in the party."[13] Alderman Richard Mell, a Byrne backer, also questioned Vrdolyak's Solidarity mayoral move, saying simply, "I don't think he can do both."[14]

Vrdolyak held firm and then did what he does best: he attacked. To further assure anti-Washington forces that his candidacy would not take primary votes away from Byrne, Vrdolyak promised 2000 workers for Byrne's race. (Vrdolyak would have his own Solidarity primary on the same day as the Democratic primary, and insiders were predicting that the mayor's people would put up a token Solidarity candidate to pressure the 10th Ward alderman into deflecting substantial votes from Byrne to his own candidacy so that he would be assured of winning his own primary.) Vrdolyak charged that Haider and Hynes had worked up a deal that Haider would drop out of the race in favor of Hynes if both he and Washington won their respective primaries. Vrdolyak further claimed that Hynes and not he would be the "spoiler" in 1987. Finally, he scoffed at a Washington move to strip him of his party chairmanship in favor of county board member John Stroger, a black 8th Ward committeeman.

"I'm not gonna participate in their charade or games," said a defiant Vrdolyak. "I'm the chairman. I've been the chairman. And I still am the chairman."[15]

Vrdolyak's efforts were not limited to internal party politics. He began issuing a series of personal letters and mini-position papers, which were addressed to important groups and people (always with copies to the editorial boards of the *Tribune*, *Sun-Times* and *Defender*). He wanted the Committee on Decent, Unbiased Campaign Tactics (later to be known as the CONDUCT Committee) to monitor and examine possible racist campaign speeches and political tactics of the Washington campaign. In the area of crime, he claimed that under Washington "the fear factor for the average Chicagoan [had] skyrocketed...." If elected mayor, he promised, "we'll take control of our streets back from the criminals." He attacked the Chicago Housing Authority and the Chicago Police Department for supporting pro-Washington political activities. In sum, Vrdolyak was working overtime to make himself the "real" mayoral alternative to a second Washington administration—even though, at the same time, he had to pledge all-out support for Byrne in the primary. Even for Chicago, Vrdolyak's moves were breathtaking for their timing and unmitigated gall.

For years the late Pat Piper was the Wrigley Field announcer for home games of the Cubs. His famous opening line was "Attention, attention please, the batting order and line-ups for today's game." On New Year's Day, 1987, a resurrected Piper would have had a wonderful time announcing the cast of candidates for the 1987 Chicago mayoral contest. In the February Democratic primary: Washington against Byrne; in the February Republican primary: Haider against Epton. In the April general election the two primary winners would be joined by Hynes of the Chicago First party and Vrdolyak of the Solidarity party.

It was Alice-in-Wonderland politics at its best. A Haider GOP primary victory would mean that four Democrats would be running for mayor, representing four different political parties. Moreover, in perhaps the most ironic and telling shocker of all, traditional party "outsiders" Washington and Byrne were running in the Democratic party primary, while long-time party "insiders" Hynes and Vrdolyak were running as third-party candidates. If all of this was still not enough to convince observers that the Mayor Daley Democratic machine era was over, there was the fact that the Republican central committee and not the Democratic central committee held a slating session to endorse a mayoral candidate. As one Democratic committeeman suggested, "If we held a slating meeting, we wouldn't be sure if anyone would attend."[16] Perhaps the Mad Hatter and the March Hare would show up.

CHAPTER FOUR

Primary '87

A FEW DAYS INTO the new year of 1987 a white mid-level Byrne campaign aide stopped off at his local convenience store to buy some milk. His political loyalities were expressed by the Byrne-for-Mayor button he wore proudly on his winter coat. The store clerk, a black woman, told the Byrne staffer that she would not wait on him and urged the startled customer to shop someplace else. Shocked by the clerk's announcement, the Byrne worker asked why. The response was simple: "You are against the mayor."

This incident, hardly earthshaking, nevertheless reflected the near total commitment of the black community to the cause of Harold Washington. As would be demonstrated in both upcoming elections (the primary and the general), no elected official in Chicago history, including Richard J. Daley, ever had a more solid supportive core constituency than did Washington with city blacks. Given this solid black vote foundation, plus the chaos among his foes, Washington started his primary campaign against Jane Byrne, in the words of *Sun-Times* columnist Basil Talbott, "sitting pretty."

January Politics

As he had done during most of his first term as mayor, candidate Washington continued to use Vrdolyak as a political whipping boy to deflect political criticism aimed at him. And as had been the case previously, the press, the public, and the pols were more interested in the personalities and power conflicts of the combatants than in any serious discussion of major policy issues.

Another deft Washington move was the selection of his endorsed running mates (city treasurer and city clerk) for the primary. After some discussion, the mayor and his advisors agreed to support incumbent Cecil Partee, a black, for city treasurer and Gloria Chevere, a Hispanic, for city clerk. Washington forces recognized that in 1987, as was true in 1983, the city swing vote would be located along the independent lakefront and in the Hispanic communities. Though there was some thought of dumping Partee in favor of a white lakefronter, the mayor realized that Partee would be a tough man to beat. The announcement of an all-minority ticket was greeted with howls by antiadministration aldermen and other Washington political foes. The mayor's spokesman, Alderman Timothy Evans, answered critics by claiming that the mayor's ticket was based on talent rather than race, though, as it turned out, "they just all happen to be minorities." The mayor and his people rode this argument all the way through primary day, never answering the question of how it reflected their stated goal of a multiracial city. Moreover, on primary day the controversial Chevere selection would turn into a major plus, because Washington's numbers would rise significantly in the Hispanic wards.

For most of January, Washington's campaign was a study in moderation and professionalism. He used substantial funds to push voter registration in black neighborhoods. The majority of these dollars were not given to favorable ward organizations or community groups but were spent for advertising on Chicago's five black radio stations. These paid ads were then supplemented by these same stations' own public service announcements (PSA's), which also called for blacks to register to vote. The Washington campaign broke new ground in recognizing the importance of black radio in the black community. Washington combined his own unparalleled popularity among blacks with the notion of good and responsible citizenship to electronically energize his electorate.

Wesley South, general manager of WVON, a leading black station in the city, summed up the political use of black radio this way: "[In 1983] we just had a tremendous impact . . . we are like the grapevine for the black community, and we developed in it a positive fervor we hadn't known before. I see no reason why the same won't occur in 1987 too. . . ."[1] One can hardly imagine a white general manager of a major city radio station stating views and station policy anywhere close to those of Wesley South.

Perhaps the only risky political move Washington made in his primary battle against Byrne was the signing of an executive order, "mandating that virtually all companies that sell to the city or obtain financial incentives from the city consider hiring employees referred to them by City Hall." [2] The mayor called this new program "Chicago First"–the same name candidate Tom Hynes had given his new party. Mayoral aides labeled the hiring plan an imaginative effort to have private companies receiving city revenues help alleviate unemployment in Chicago. But critics said the employment proposal was a "hiring hall in City Hall" and that it would bring back all past patronage abuses, except that this time the jobs would come from the private and not the public sector. Sam Mitchell, president of the Chicago Association of Commerce Industry, was skeptical of the plan, saying, "There is no support for it in the business community." [3] Thomas Nayder, president of the Chicago Building and Construction Trade Council (a former Mayor Daley stronghold), voiced labor's fears that "making the mayor's office of Employment and Training the 'first source' of workers . . . [might effect] union hiring hall arrangements written into contracts." [4]

In a few days, following a storm of criticism, Washington softened his hiring edict by making the plan voluntary rather than compulsory. Though he had received some negative press, Washington had also put two strong chips on the primary table: 1) he told his core black constituency, many of whom were unemployed, that he was out there pushing for them (Washington was mindful of a few potential soft spots in his black base– poor south- and westsiders who were voicing concerns about the lack of improved job opportunities in their communities); and 2) he informed potential contributors, businessmen, and other city pols that Washington in 1987 was willing and able to play old-fashioned political hardball and that they had better think twice before going all-out against his re-election bid.

The Byrne Campaign

Almost overlooked in the wheeling and dealing of third-party filings was a simple fact: Jane Byrne had made her early political prediction stand up, that is, she was facing Harold Washington in the 1987 Chicago Democratic primary one on one. To be sure, she was not sure of the level of support for her from Hynes or Vrdolyak in the primary, given their own general election candidacies. But overall the former mayor was pleased to finally get down to some serious and publicized mayoral politicking.

To ease the controversies and minefields of dueling campaigns (Vrdolyak had openly – and Hynes had tacitly – endorsed her against Washington), Byrne launched a major campaign effort to convince Chicagoans that the winner of the Democratic mayoral primary would be the next mayor of Chicago. She knew that even a slight decrease in voter turnout on the part of Hynes and Vrdolyak loyalists could be critical to her candidacy. In sum, she needed every white ethnic vote in the city.

In early January a refreshed and relaxed Byrne hit the streets of Chicago with a full-court press campaign against Washington. Byrne slugged the mayor from all sides, letting Chicagoans know that she was as tough and feisty as ever and that she wanted the mayor to come down into the streets and meet her face to face. On the issue of whether she or Washington had done more for city Hispanics, Byrne rattled off the names of several Hispanic officials she had appointed during her administration and then told the press and TV news crews: "He [Washington] doesn't scare me with anything that he prints or anything that he says."[5] For over a century Chicagoans have loved this hard-nosed style of politics, and Byrne gave the voters what they wanted.

Byrne attacked Washington on crime, vowing to add 200 more police officers to fight drugs. She even suggested that gang graffiti would also disappear from building walls in crime-infested communities once she was elected. In grand Byrne fashion, she chartered a CTA bus and, acting as her own guide, led the press on a selected tour of the city, reviewing locked-up, stalled, and undone projects. A buoyant Byrne told a city press corps still fascinated by her genuine charm and sheer toughness, "There's nothing to back up what he's got in his commercials." [6] Parading past a padlocked gate at Navy Pier (a valuable piece of the city's lakefront property for which Mayor Byrne had proposed a privately funded major development and which Mayor Washington, via a special task force, had rejected) and a closed rapid transit station, Byrne artfully portrayed what she said was the major difference between her and Washington: she was a "doer," and Washington was a "talker."

Using a constant stream of accusations and proposals, Byrne, aided by her shrewd press secretary, Joe Pecor, kept the mayor

As in her past political efforts, Jane Byrne takes her campaign to the streets of Chicago. A basically shy woman, Byrne was outspoken and aggressive on the stump. *(Sun-Times)*

Byrne, campaigning for the 1987 Democratic mayoral nomination, tries to recapture some of the feisty combativeness that had won her the mayoralty eight years earlier. Here she speaks at a northwest-side senior citizens' home with 45th Ward aldermanic candidate Patrick Levar. *(Sun-Times)*

Byrne campaigning door to door in a far southwest-side 23rd Ward neighborhood. To gain free publicity, Byrne gave the press excellent "photo opportunities"—such as the traditional baby shot. *(Sun-Times)*

A few days before the primary, Teamsters Local 705 endorsed Byrne's candidacy. *(Sun-Times)*

1987 Chicago politics at its ambivalent best. Byrne greets a Hispanic supporter who is holding one of her signs while wearing several Washington buttons.

(Sun-Times)

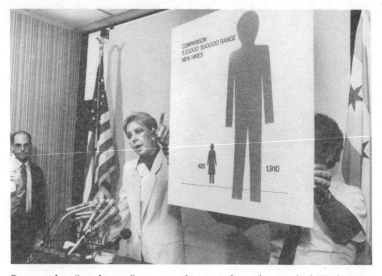

Byrne at her "gender gap" press conference, where she attacked Washington for not hiring more women for city jobs. *(Sun-Times)*

Byrne attending a service at the southside Life Center Church, in the heart of Washington country. As mayor, Byrne had been a big booster of the black church and was glad for the invitation to speak and be photographed.

(Sun-Times)

Harold Washington in political combat over the "gender gap" issue, refuting Byrne's claim in 1987 that the Washington administration discriminated against women. *(Sun-Times)*

A disappointed Byrne consoles supporters while conceding defeat in the February 1987 Democratic primary election. *(Sun-Times)*

Harold Washington claims victory in the 1987 mayoral primary, surrounded by three important supporters (left to right): the Rev. Jesse Jackson, the Rev. B. Herbert Martin, and the city treasurer, Cecil Partee. (*Sun-Times*)

Professor Donald Haider of Northwestern University left the groves of academe in 1987 to become the Republican mayoral candidate on the streets of Chicago. (*Sun-Times*)

Haider had debuted in 1979 as budget director for then mayor Byrne, who is here captured searching for meaning in his remarks. *(Sun-Times)*

Candidate Haider, always low on campaign funds, spent his remaining campaign budget on a case of red jackets to put his candidacy before the public. Here Illinois Governor James Thompson displays Haider's most visible campaign advertisement. *(Sun-Times)*

Undaunted by racial and political odds, Republican Haider takes his campaign to the black community, where, he said, he made half of his campaign visits. *(Sun-Times)*

Tom Hynes had difficulty energizing the Chicago electorate to his mayoral candidacy. Here he is seen in an ethnic restaurant speaking to a less than enthusiastic gathering. (*Sun-Times*)

Hynes (center), the Democratic Cook County assessor, files his mayoral petitions as a candidate of the Chicago First party. Hynes was one of three former Democrats running for Chicago mayor in 1987 under other party banners. (*Sun-Times*)

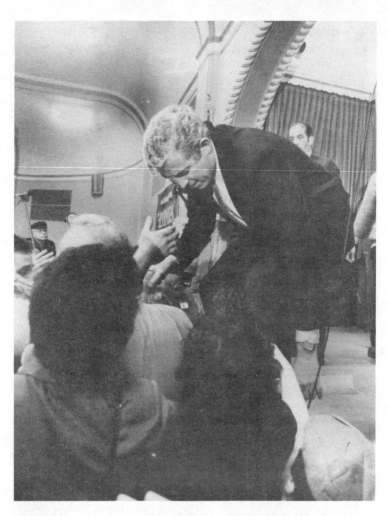

Tom Hynes stepping off the stage at Plumbers' Hall, where he withdrew from the mayoral race on a Sunday evening, only one and a half days before the election. His late withdrawal gave other candidates little time to capitalize on his faltering candidacy. *(Sun-Times)*

A crestfallen colleen depicts the gloom of Hynes's southwest-side Chicago ethnic supporters following his withdrawal from the mayoral race. *(Sun-Times)*

Mayor Washington liked to combine good campaigning and good eating. His campaign-stop snacks led to a grossly overweight condition and eventually to his death. *(Sun-Times)*

Candidate Edward R. Vrdolyak receives a warm welcome from members of the Chicago Mercantile Exchange. *(Sun-Times)*

Vrdolyak charms senior citizens at a southwest-side church bingo party. *(Sun-Times)*

A scene from Vrdolyak's incredible pre-election-day blitz of Chicago neighborhoods following the withdrawal of his rival for the white ethnic vote, Tom Hynes. Here the candidate is mobbed by well-wishers at the southwest-side Polonia Banquet Hall. (*Sun-Times*)

With his son Peter and his wife, Denise, Vrdolyak votes early at the family's polling place, St. Simeon Hall on the southeast side.

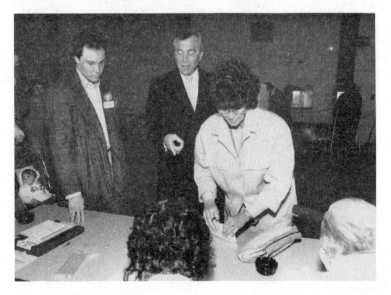

A snarling Vrdolyak denounces a Washington administration proposal to close a near westside police station because of budgetary constraints. Throughout his campaign, Vrdolyak portrayed the mayor as weak on law enforcement and public safety issues. *(Sun-Times)*

Between campaign stops, Mayor Washington strategizes with his press secretary, Alton Miller (left), and public works commissioner Paul Karras. *(Sun-Times)*

Candidate Vrdolyak acknowledges defeat in the April 1987 general election to the incumbent, Mayor Harold Washington. *(Sun-Times)*

on the defensive. She advocated a tax cut for owners of lakefront properties in order to help them repair their homes and the eroded beachfronts caused by the rising waters of Lake Michigan (on this point Byrne was prophetic, as will be seen later). She vowed to revive Chicago Fest, a city-sponsored summer entertainment and food festival that was held at Navy Pier during her administration, because "the people are hungry for it." She savaged Washington's record in hiring females; she lambasted his economic development program as mayor; and she so angered Washington with her ability to always be on the offensive by refusing to answer direct and difficult questions about her own record that he, in frustration, likened her to Hitler.

By the end of January, less than four weeks before primary day, Byrne was clearly on the move. Polls showed that she had narrowed the mayor's once substantial lead over her, and most experts agreed the primary race was now a tossup. Leading Chicago political columnists confirmed the Byrne surge. Raymond Coffey of the *Tribune* claimed that Washington was in trouble because he was unable to play defense against Byrne's repeated attacks: "Washington . . . seems to be trying to dismiss questions rather than answer them."[7] Columnist Basil Talbott argued that much of Byrne's momentum was due to the internal chaos of the incumbent's political operation. In Talbott's view, "His [Washington's] campaign of catch as catch can suffers from the lack of a strategic center, from erratic execution and an inefficient structure."[8] Even Washington's leading press defender, Vernon Jarrett of the *Sun-Times*, the city's most influential black reporter, revealed his surprise at Byrne's strong white support in the polls, especially in the so-called independent-minded lakefront wards. A somewhat shaken Washington campaign manager, Ken Glover, responded to negative press reports with positive bravado: "She [Byrne] is having a little fun at the moment but we're going to have fun in the next three weeks, and my idea of fun is winning."[9]

Glover's public optimism was not mere political rhetoric. Despite her excellent month of primary campaigning and new favorable polls, former mayor Byrne still faced enormous obstacles. At its roots, electoral politics always ends up being a contest of numbers. In order for Byrne to wrest the nomination away from Washington, she had to hit a political triple: 1) solidify her own white ethnic base in terms of loyalty and turnout; 2) do extremely well in the city's four main Hispanic wards (an achievement made more difficult due to an earlier verbal slip in the campaign in which she called Hispanics aliens); and 3) beat Washington in the six lakefront wards. If she could accomplish all of the above, Byrne could squeak out a victory even if Washington's black vote repeated its 1983 record percentage and turnout numbers.

To achieve her triple, Byrne went all-out to make peace with her former bitter intraparty foes, the Daley wing. Long-time Daleyites from the Southwest Side (most of whom were ardent Hynes backers) pledged fidelity to Byrne's *primary* candidacy. The big question looming was: how hard would they work for a candidate who, if successful, would be their major foe six weeks later? In the Hispanic community Byrne pushed her own mayoral record, her willingness to learn Spanish (she would never be mistaken for a linguist), and her gender and religion. On the lakefront Byrne was holding a series of coffees and attempting to contrast her administrative style to that of the incumbent. Of all the parts of the triad strategy, the lakefront effort seemed to be both the most delicate and the area where Byrne needed the most help. Thus, though bloodied by a few January battle losses, the Washington camp was still confident about the war; it would take a near miracle for Byrne to complete her political coup.

Haider and the GOP

On the Republican front, the Haider campaign received a tremendous mid-January jolt when publicity maker Bernard Epton, his main opponent, dropped out of the race. For reasons that will probably forever remain cloudy, Epton was unable to collect enough legitimate petition signatures to put his name on the GOP primary ballot. Epton's gracious acceptance of the Chicago Board of Election decision knocking him out was in marked contrast to his truculent behavior of 1983.

However, Epton's departure left Haider with minor-league primary opponents and little potential to improve his professorial name recognition. A victory over Epton would have given Haider a small bounce into the general election. Without his main challenger in the race, the Northwestern professor was reduced to shadowboxing in trying to capture headlines and recognition. Haider tried hard. He issued a series of position papers that called for, among other things: 1) creation of a mayor's office of labor relations to coordinate all union negotiations; 2) a phase-out of the monthly $5.00-per-employee head tax by trimming it $1.00 a year, beginning in 1988; 3) a 10 percent reduction in city spending (except for police and fire); and 4) increased use of private firms to perform tasks currently done by the city.

Though he often compared himself to another professorial mayoral candidate (Charles Merriam of the University of Chicago, the losing GOP mayoral nominee in 1911), Haider developed a very unacademic sense of humor about himself and his candidacy. For example, when asked where in the city his main strength lay, Haider replied, "Graceland Cemetery" (the burial ground for many prominent pro-Republican VIP's and Chicagoans from a bygone era). Or when a reporter asked him about his position on the abortion bill, the professor suggested, "If we owe it, pay it." Knowledgeable and witty, Haider might have been a force to be reckoned with in a different city and in a different era. But in racially divided Chicago the GOP hopeful was a political outcast who could not make any headway in the polls or in dollar donations against a crowded mayoral field of big-name, big-time players.

As for the "primary passers," Hynes and Vrdolyak, they paid lip service to the Washington-Byrne matchup and concentrated on trying to intimidate each other out of the April general election. Never in Chicago history had there been such a strange political situation as in early 1987. It was high stakes "power poker," and neither Hynes nor Vrdolyak was about to be bluffed or forced out. For Hynes, getting Vrdolyak to drop out was essential to any successful mayoral campaign strategy. No matter what issue positions Hynes took, they were meaningless if the April election turned into a four-way battle (Hynes, Vrdolyak, Haider, and presumably Washington). Hynes's filing under a new party gave him a political advantage over Vrdolyak, who was running as a Solidarity party candidate: Hynes Democrats allegedly could vote for Byrne in the primary, since their man and his Chicago First party were running only in the general; but Vrdolyak had to win the Solidarity party primary held on the same day as the Washington-Byrne battle.

Hynes charged that Vrdolyak would siphon off Byrne voters to guarantee his own primary victory. Vrdolyak countered that he had registered over 30,000 new voters to more than make up for any minor diversion away from Byrne on primary day. Confused Chicago voters had to be reminded that both of these men could be facing Jane Byrne in a general election six weeks after they supposedly went all-out for her in her campaign against Washington. It was sheer madness!

The bizarre nature of the campaign played directly into Vrdolyak's hands. Of all the candidates, he was the most relaxed and the one having the most fun; he was truly living up to his nickname, "Fast Eddie." One afternoon he could be a substitute disc jockey on a popular radio program (Steve Dahl and Garry Meier) demonstrating his quick wit by verbally dueling with a string of famous personalities, including the Reverend Pat Robertson. Later Vrdolyak would hold a press conference in which he would dub Hynes "a spoiler and a nonfactor" while deriding him as a "second-team player" (referring to the Daley connection). Finally, he would end the evening by attacking the Chicago *Tribune* for its fifty-six straight editorials critical of him personally and his candidacy (the *Tribune* did not take exception to Vrdolyak's count).

In the terms of Greek mythology his campaign would be subtitled "Vrdolyak Unbound." Free to speak for himself, the 10th Ward alderman even made light of poll data showing him with incredibly high negative ratings. "My negatives," Vrdolyak would argue, "all came from having very strong positions . . . but those ultimately will be my strengths in this campaign. People aren't looking for someone to be mayor who's going to sit back and pontificate and contemplate when things need to be done."[10]

February Politics

With Haider relatively unopposed in the Republican primary and Hynes and Vrdolyak privately blindsiding each other in a game of "political chicken," the public eye centered squarely on the Washington-Byrne race. Byrne increased her attacks on a whole series of issues.

First, on revenue and taxes, Byrne accused the Washington administration of lax collection procedures for moneys owed to the city. Supported by a Chicago *Tribune* study, she pointed out that even parking meter collections had dropped more than 40 percent since Washington took power. As for taxes, Byrne produced documents claiming that Washington and not she was the champion tax raiser. The mayor had an easier time defending himself against this charge since the Byrne administration also had imposed several huge tax increases.

The second subject was the Chicago Housing Authority. In early January the CHA announced a loss of $7 million in federal funds because of a missed application deadline. Moreover, the CHA's two top officials, Chairman Renault Robinson and Executive Director Zirl Smith, were openly feuding about who should take the blame for the blunder. Robinson, Washington's first campaign manager in the 1983 election, received the most heat. Through Robinson Byrne attacked Washington for mismanaging one of the nation's largest public housing programs. The issue exploded when Smith and Robinson both resigned, leaving the Washington administration clearly on the defensive. (Replacing Smith was former mayoral aide Brenda Gaines, while CHA board member and Washington's pastor, Rev. B. Herbert Martin, took Robinson's seat.)

The third subject was crime. Byrne was not as bold as Vrdolyak in condemning Washington's record on law enforcement because in her administration a major scandal had developed concerning the police department's "killing crime"—that is, reporting false crime statistics. Still, she was making some headway asking predominantly white and Hispanic audiences which mayoral administration, Byrne or Washington, made them feel safer on the streets.

Going into the primary home stretch, Byrne's campaign was charging on all cylinders; yet private polls revealed that Washington's impenetrable black support was holding solid. Given city election demographics, Byrne's only hope of victory lay in her trouncing the mayor in the six north lakefront wards. Simply doing well would not be enough. Though often labeled liberal, the residents of these lakefront wards (42, 43, 44, 46, 48, and 49), with gentrification and yuppification, had grown economically conservative. In a major gamble to appeal to the lakefront voters, Byrne escalated the charges that, between the two of them, Washington was the bigger taxer and spender. But she needed more than that. In her 1979 primary against incumbent Michael Bilandic, Mother Nature had become Byrne's best precinct captain. When snow and cold shut down the "city that works," Bilandic's pathetic responses to the weather crisis gave Byrne the boost she needed to nip him on primary day. In the first week of February 1987, man and God sent Byrne two spectacular surprise issues that gave her the opening she needed to consolidate the lakefront behind her candidacy.

At a Saturday Operation PUSH meeting, R. Eugene Pincham, a black Illinois appellate court judge speaking on behalf of Mayor Washington, said, "Any man south of Madison Street who casts

75

a vote in the February 24 [primary] election and who doesn't cast a vote for Harold Washington, ought to be hung."[11] The remark was injudicious at best and racial intimidation at worst, and Pincham's feeble efforts to back away from his remarks only escalated the issue throughout the city. Byrne's initial response to Pincham was careful: "There is no room in this election for racism, religious bigotry or any kind of discrimination. . . . I think more prudence could have been shown."[12] While other candidates and the media dealt with the crass belligerence and national embarrassment of the judge's comments, Byrne wanted to use them to further her appeal on the lakefront. She knew the mayor's support in the black community would not be affected by Pincham's statements; but she also knew that, played carefully, they could have a major impact in her six critical lakefront wards.

But for some unknown reason Byrne overplayed her hand on the Pincham affair. On the weekend following the judge's comments, Byrne produced a television commercial showing a lightning bolt and a scowling face of Mayor Washington splitting a picture of a peaceful Chicago. It accused Washington of racially dividing the city and ended with the tag line: "Jane Byrne – A Mayor for all Chicago." Immediate howls went up throughout the city attacking Byrne for exacerbating a racially tense situation. Sensing a backfire on Byrne, Washington cautioned his supporters to remain cool and not respond to this "outrageous commercial." The commercial was condemned by virtually everyone in the media, and Byrne pulled the spot a week later. She went back to a commercial showing her smiling and preaching love and unity, but the damage had been done. Instead of using Pincham's preposterous statement as a political weapon to win over critical lakefront voters, Byrne now had to backtrack on the issue, thus giving Washington a chance to regroup his forces and refocus the issue on Byrne's record and away from Pincham.

If Judge Pincham's comments represented a potential manmade gift to Byrne, Chicago's violent weather on Sunday, February 8, 1987, was potential divine intervention on behalf of her candidacy – especially along the lakefront. On that day sixty-mile-an-hour winds directly off Lake Michigan flooded and froze Chicago's Lake Shore Drive. The winds whipped water across the city's critical north-south thoroughfare, and the cold caused ice to form to a thickness of two feet in some spots on the road. It also flooded basements and buildings the entire length of the drive, knocked out electricity, downed trees, and generally made lakefront residents' lives simply miserable. The key question was: would the Drive reopen for rush-hour traffic on Monday morning?

As the story was unfolding, Byrne leaped into action. Even though city crews were working furiously to deal with the disaster, she held a Sunday lakefront press conference and denounced Washington for reacting too slowly to the winter storm and the flooding. Trying to re-create the 1979 blizzard imagery, Byrne stood up against the whipping winds and tried to make the race against time to open the Drive a referendum on Washington's ability to govern.

Like a plot from a Ken Follett novel, the entire direction of a major historical event – the 1987 Chicago mayoral election in this scenario – would rest mainly in the hands of one man, John J. Halpin, the commissioner of streets and sanitation. How ironic that the re-election hopes of the city's first black mayor would depend so heavily on the abilities of a short spunky Irishman! Halpin, a man with a brogue as wide as the Shannon River, was a career city employee who reflected the proudest traditions of Mayor Richard J. Daley's Chicago. Dedicated to public service and with a love for his job, Halpin was like many other Daley appointees – the professional government bureaucrats whose dedication gave Daley the political freedom to claim that Chicago was the city that works. Now Halpin, a native of county Clare, Ireland, would be the vital player in the drama of a frozen Lake Shore Drive.

According the Halpin, it was about 9:30 A.M. on Sunday when his assistant, Kirsten Svare, called him about the flooding problems on Lake Shore Drive. A brick wall (not a sea wall) used by residents for safety reasons at 1037 W. Northshore Ave. was crumbling, and large-scale flooding was taking place. Halpin raced to the scene, to be joined by other department heads from Public Works and Water, and began sandbagging efforts the length of the Drive. But the situation was deteriorating by the hour as the winds increased and the temperature dropped well below freezing. By early afternoon, segments of Lake Shore Drive had been closed, and television camera teams were filming the desolate-looking tundra conditions.

Calling out all his manpower and machine resources, Halpin decided that salt spreading was not enough. The key to the prevention of icing was to keep the water that was already on the drive moving; so Halpin ordered his salt spreaders and lift trucks to simply drive up and back under every viaduct along the Drive to prevent ice formation. This vital decision bought Halpin time; but he knew that, unless the wind that was splashing water over the length of the roadway ebbed, the battle was over. In Halpin's own words, "I couldn't fight Lake Michigan."[13]

By late afternoon, with Jane Byrne and television reporters clamoring to know whether the Drive would be open the next morning, Halpin boldly told one and all not to worry. "I would have had my people out there," Halpin said later "to suck the water up with straws if I had too."[14] Even so, late that night Halpin's confidence was waning as he and an assistant went for a corned beef sandwich at a Lincoln Park deli. Leaving the restaurant, Halpin suddenly noticed that the wind had died down; despite having been on the street for fourteen hours, he and his crew chiefs decided to go all-out, to work through the night and try to "clear the Drive–completely."

For the next several hours Halpin's street and sanitation crews and people from other city departments worked feverishly against the sunrise deadline. Stopping only to take phone calls from worried mayoral aides, city employees spread sand and salt up and down the Drive. By 3:30 A.M. only the infamous 31st Street viaduct and its impassable ramps remained closed. Still, nearly nine feet of water and clogged sewers stood between victory and defeat. Along with Myles McDerragh from the Department of Sewers, Halpin studied the viaduct problem. While trucks continued to keep the water moving, an unnamed city employee working in the area found the main clogged sewer, and the problem suddenly became manageable. By 5:45 A.M. the entire drive was open, except that drivers around 31st Street had to use the on-and-off ramps to bypass some frozen debris that was still blocking some of the lanes under the viaduct. By 8:35 A.M. everything was cleared.

For nearly twenty-four hours Halpin had led city workers on a race against nature and, as it turned out, a race against Byrne's candidacy. Who knows what the political ramifications might have been if lakefront residents had awakened Monday morning to find Lake Shore Drive closed like a rubble-strewn ice rink? It is probably not too much of an exaggeration to suggest that February 8th was the ballgame for Harold Washington. Once over the weather hurdle, his renomination and re-election became almost predictable. And like past successful mayors before him, Washington's political fortunes had rested with the loyality and tenacity of his city employees. Indeed, John Halpin had prevented the high-water mark of the Byrne campaign from drowning his boss and pal, Harold Washington. The orator from the Shannon had tamed the destructive power of Lake Michigan and deprived Byrne of an issue. Chicago's 1979 snow queen's efforts to exploit ice and flooding had turned into the ice follies.

In the last two weeks of the primary campaign, Byrne's hopes for victory began to fade. Unable to take full advantage of the Pincham affair or gain political mileage from the February 8th flooding, Byrne worked hard to consolidate her support in the ethnic wards. With thoughts of massive voter turnarounds in lakefront or Hispanic neighborhoods no longer possible, upbeat Byrne insiders now looked to voter turnout as the only hope for victory. As in the 1983 Washington-Epton contest, the Byrne-Washington primary turned into a census tract election: which candidate's hardcore voters would turn out in larger numbers — white or black?

To rouse and energize ethnic supporters, Byrne attempted to speak before predominantly black audiences. She was heckled and booed at a speech before a racially mixed group of North-eastern Illinois University students, who drowned her words with chants of "Harold, Harold, Harold." And she received considerable press mileage when a group of black Washington supporters physically prevented a small westside Byrne rally from taking place. According to newspaper reports, a pro-Washington precinct captain in Alderman Percy Giles's 37th Ward organization, Rev. Wesley Jackson, and his friends took over the Brothers Palace bar at 939 N. Pulaski, the rally location. When Byrne's people arrived for the meeting, they found that the owner, allegedly Byrne's host, had put a "Closed Today" sign on the front door, and a group of forty Washington loyalists were milling around on the sidewalk. The rally never took place. But the lockout of a white candidate from the black West Side failed to evoke the public sympathy the Byrne people might have expected.

Byrne also continued to work hard to reach total conciliation with the Daleys and their allies. A February Byrne fundraiser at the Hilton Towers Hotel saw the former mayor warmly introduce State Rep. John Daley (11th Ward committeeman and Rich Daley's brother). Back in 1955 — or even 1965 — this coming together of rival Irish-led factions would have been a major political event; in 1987 Chicago it was significant but hardly earthshaking. Times had indeed changed. Byrne also reintroduced her 1979 "poor Jane" image in the last few days of the primary campaign. She was the outsider struggling against a better-financed incumbent, who, unlike her, had the money for mailings, brochures, and commercials. She told her audiences that "it was better to run with the people than with the dollars, and she should know since she had done it both ways."[15] (The latter was a reference to her unsuccessful $10-million-dollar 1983 re-election campaign.)

Throughout most of January and February the Byrne and Washington camps had been negotiating the possibilities of a debate. Several side issues arose: for example, Washington wanted a live studio audience, while Byrne wanted a studio format. But the bottom line was usually the same: the current mayor was not eager to go one on one verbally against the former mayor. Incumbents always have less to gain than do challengers in debates. Desperate to rejuvenate her campaign, Byrne bought a half hour of debate time on WGN-TV. Knowing that Washington would not appear, Byrne put together a slick thirty-minute commercial highlighting her commitment to racial unity, safe streets, and old-fashioned fun. In Jane Byrne's Chicago, she concluded, "People loved their city."[16]

In the final days of the campaign Byrne pulled out all the stops, demonstrating once again a unique Chicago combination of energy, ambition, and intelligence. Unfortunately for her, all her efforts could not overcome some sticky points in her own mayoral record and, more importantly, new city demographics. Still, her final campaign whirlwind was remarkable. Byrne claimed that polls were showing that Washington's popularity had peaked (actually, the opposite was true). She derided the mayor for his "Atlanta Connection," citing evidence that huge city contracts had gone to the Georgia city in return for huge contributions to Washington's war chest. Byrne seemed to be working the supermarket circuit in lakefront neighborhoods every day, shaking hands with the coveted independents. She zigzagged through the city as if it were a single ward—dancing at Polish polka parties, lunching at Jewish delicatessens, and occassionally stopping off at a black church. Jane Byrne was indefatigable. David Axelrod, Washington's shrewd political consultant, who was both worried about possible overconfidence overtaking the mayor's supporters and truly dazzled by Byrne's closing efforts, told *Sun-Times* columnist Steve Neal: "Nobody should underestimate Jane Byrne. She's a fierce competitor, and if she gets a few breaks she's certainly in the ballgame."[17]

In the end Byrne, as always, gave it everything she had, going for broke against the odds. Fighting Washington upfront and fearing Hynes and Vrdolyak from the rear, the former mayor never took a backward step. She would lose not because she was outfought, but because she was outcounted.

In contrast to his primary election opponent, Harold Washington calmly and coolly eased his way through the hectic campaign's final weeks. Only the February 8th flooding and the injudicious Pincham comments momentarily clogged his well-oiled campaign machine effort. In a word, the mayor was in control. Crucial to his confidence was not only his splintered opposition but the fact that to a large segment of the city's population – almost all blacks and some Hispanics and whites – registering and voting for Harold was an act of faith in a historic crusade. Unlike four years earlier, Washington had few problems raising money: his fundraising efforts in Chicago and around the country gave him a two-to-one dollar edge over Byrne. Even sharp criticisms concerning contributions from individuals doing city business went unanswered or unexplained. Washington emphasized the limitations he placed on these contributions and that he was still the same man he was when he ran a "shoestring campaign."

By and large, Washington restricted his personal campaigning to familiar themes in familiar neighborhoods. He accused Byrne once again of leaving him with a $168 million budget deficit (a figure she rejected). He reiterated his belief that Byrne's famous Chicago Fests (the annual Navy Pier summer festival that Washington had abandoned) had cost the city millions of dollars. However, unlike Byrne, Washington did not dwell on his opponent. Washington knew that he did not have to convert too many people to his cause to win the primary. He had the voters; his only fear was low black voter turnout.

As he had done often during Council Wars, Washington resurrected the Democratic machine as a menacing monster to suit his political purpose. He told a black audience on the South Side: "Don't be complacent. Don't assume anything. You know and I know of one reason why the Democratic machine has been so powerful all these years – stealing. They can steal an election from you in a minute. One way to make certain that they won't is to bring in so many votes that they won't have time to steal any of them."[18] In classic Washington style, he never personally asked his audience to vote for him; the only question was not who would they support but simply how many would go to the polls.

On the major endorsement front, it was all Washington. The Chicago *Sun-Times* made him their choice over Byrne with a moderate to lukewarm editorial. Saying that the selection was not automatic, the *Sun-Times* recommended Washington to its readers because "his steady stewardship. . . holds greater promise" and because his four years in office "instilled among black voters a sense of racial pride and an empowerment long denied."[19] The Chicago *Tribune*, comparing the multicandidate/multiparty mayoral contest to the America's Cup yacht race elimination tournament, endorsed Washington because Byrne as mayor "was terrible." More than the *Sun-Times*, the *Tribune* praised Washington's administrative record, saying that his biggest achievement was having "a budget that is balanced without hidden deficits and other traditional City Hall voodoo."[20] Perhaps Washington's most gratifying endorsement came from the Chicago Federation of Labor, an organization long associated with former mayor Daley and the city's ethnic Democratic leadership.

As in 1983, the highlight of Washington's 1987 campaign stretch drive was a massive rally at the University of Illinois at Chicago Pavilion one week before primary day. Over 10,000 people, mainly black, rocked the rafters on behalf of their mayor. Speaker after speaker, including Jesse Jackson, county board president George Dunne, the main white pol in attendance, and a smorgasbord of community activists heaped praise on the mayor. Though the magic of the historic rally four years earlier was not matched, the message was loud and clear: this crowd and Chicago's black community wanted "Nobody But Harold."

Unlike in his first successful run, the mayor and his competent advisors—such as Jacky Grimshaw, a seasoned Chicago political professional long involved in reform causes—were not letting this election hinge on emotion. It was announced at the rally that the Washington campaign had purchased $200,000 of air time to run its final batch of political commercials (great cheers). It was also announced that the Washington campaign would mail one million sample ballots to Chicago voters (more cheers). And with his message going to the lakefront voters, almost none of whom were in the audience but who would read about the rally in the papers, Washington, in his own unique style, told the crowd: "Chicago is not only ready for reform, Chicago is luxuriating in reform" (a thunderous cheer). It was, in short, one hell of a rally.

A final twist livened up the final week of the Byrne-Washington campaign: the arrival of the so-called Freedom Riders. These were mainly Southern blacks who rolled into Chicago on two buses to help energize Washington's black vote. Embarrassed by their demeanor and style – and certainly not in need of any help in the black community – Washington nevertheless welcomed the uninvited riders and then proceeded to stay as far away from them as possible. Byrne called the southern visitors "outsiders," while her more colorful ally Ed Burke labeled them "carpetbaggers. . . who are being led by fly-by-night two-bit reverends who want to tell us how to run the affairs of the city of Chicago."

In the long view, the Freedom Riders were irrelevant to the primary's outcome, but their "ho-hum" reception by Chicago media and voters reveals just how different the city's electorate had become in the decade following Mayor Daley's death. Wards that were formerly filled with Catholic white ethnics were now home to Protestant blacks, and the latter folk simply chuckled at the Southern-style Freedom Rider's activities.

As primary day dawned, the Washington strategists were satisfied with their efforts. One City Hall insider joked about how silly the press was for considering the possibility that "Harold" would not run as a Democrat. "Even though the mayor transcends the Democratic party in the black wards," said the mayoral advisor, "our data showed a possible 5 percent slippage in Washington's black vote if he did not run as a Democrat. An independent candidacy was never a serious option."[21] Another Washington lieutenant philosophized that he was confident about the victory because the campaign accomplished its three basic goals: "First," he said, "we reignited the black movement; second, we exploited the confusion among our opponents; and third, we marginally improved our alliances with non-black Chicago voters."[22] Finally, a long-time lakefront liberal expressed faith in a Washington triumph for no other reason than that "a certain number of influential whites realize a Byrne victory might make this city ungovernable. . . they won't let it happen."[23]

As for the Byrne people, they were worried, angry, and bitter. One northside alderman condemned the media for allowing the Washington administration to rewrite its record. "The press bought their propaganda," he lamented. "The mayor's media people make Joseph Goebbels look like a piker." However, the same alderman heaped his biggest scorn on the lakefront independents and liberals who were supporting Washington. "Those people," he argued "disregard his tax increases and ignore his mayoral mismanagement. . . . Those idiots just love to be screwed."[24]

The Primary Results

Even before the polls closed, a new and fascinating election-day controversy raged on Chicago's radio and television stations. The issue was the confusion among election judges in mainly black wards in giving voters the proper primary ballot. The combatants were the Washington camp and their perceived enemy Michael Lavelle, Chicago Election Board chairman.

What happened? Primary voters had the option of asking for one of four ballots, each a different color: Democrat—green; Republican—yellow; Solidarity—creamy brown; nonpartisan vote (for alderman only)—white. In the early morning hours about 2,000 voters who asked for a Democratic primary ballot were given a Solidarity ballot instead. Since almost all of these voters were black and pro-Washington, the mix-up deprived them of casting a vote for the mayor.

By noon howls of protest and charges of deceit rose from the Washington forces. Jesse Jackson called the contest a "sabotaged election," and Election Board member Nikki Zollar, Washington's only ally on the three-person board, called the foul-up a "travesty." Racing into circuit court, Washington lawyers received an emergency favorable ruling that erroneously cast Solidarity ballots in nearly 300 precincts would be hand-counted in the polling place after voting hours.

Perhaps it is fitting that even on election day racial mistrust would be used as a political weapon. To be blunt, the Washington people were right in demanding that a voter's preference be reflected in the ballot count; but Jackson, Zollar, and even Washington himself manipulated the foul-up to boost their election-day black turnout. In reality it was black pro-Washington election judges, appointed by black pro-Washington ward committeemen, who were the culprits in the mix-up. In almost every ballot mix-up it was a matter of the polling place judge handing the wrong ballot to a voter who, without checking the ballot, voted in the wrong party primary. And even though the Washington people knew better, they spoke on white, and especially black, radio charging election-day machine manipulation and urging all potential Washington voters to go to the polls and overwhelm their scheming political opponents.

In actual numbers, Harold Washington defeated Jane Byrne by 78,158 votes (598,594 to 509,436). The mayor received nearly 54 percent of the Democratic primary vote, as Chicago voters went to the polls in staggering numbers once again. Of the 1,173,596 Chicagoans who voted on primary day, 1,146,245 (or 98 percent) voted in the Democratic primary; by contrast the Republican party primary had 18,501 participants.

A ward return breakdown reveals that Washington carried twenty-six of fifty wards; but the big news was the continuation of racial-based voting trends. This primary was a battle of ward landslides. In ten of his twenty-six ward victories Washington received at least *99 percent* of the votes. Not even Mikhail Gorbachev in his best Moscow precinct could match the loyalty and dedication of these hardcore Washington supporters. These nearly unanimous Washington "big ten" wards (Wards 28, 6, 24, 17, 21, 20, 3, 34, 16, and 8), located on the city's South and West sides, had one thing in common besides their devotion to Washington: none of them had more than a minute sprinkling of white residents.

In six other of his winning wards Washington received over 90 percent of the votes. Each of these wards had pockets of white residents who gave enough support to Byrne to limit Washington's victory percentage to merely astounding instead of unbelievable. Of the ten remaining Washington victory wards, only six were contested: that is, Washington's percentage was under 60 percent. As expected and predicted by pollsters, these wards were either heavily Hispanic or located along the lakefront.

As for Byrne, her twenty-four ward victories reflected the same racial voting patterns. Unfortunately for the former mayor, her pecentages were astounding rather than unbelievable. In six wards (23, 13, 38, 41, 45, and 36), the whitest wards in the city, Byrne received over 90 percent of the vote. Yet even in Byrne's two best wards. Wards 23 and 13, both located on the far Southwest Side of the city, Washington garnered approximately

TABLE I

Chicago 1987 Democratic Mayoral Primary Election
Results by votes, margins and percentages
Presented in ward rank order — for Washington — by percentage

Ward No.	Washington's Vote	Byrne's Vote	Washington's Margin	Washington's Percentage
28	18,517	152	18,365 W*	99%
6	31,302	294	31,008 W	99%
24	22,200	227	21,973 W	99%
17	24,493	254	24,239 W	99%
21	29,265	306	28,959 W	99%
20	20,964	226	20,738 W	99%
3	19,914	232	19,682 W	99%
34	26,537	328	26,209 W	99%
16	21,254	268	20,986 W	99%
8	28,714	388	28,326 W	99%
2	19,100	492	18,608 W	97%
37	19,808	817	18,991 W	96%
9	21,237	999	20,238 W	96%
4	19,720	981	18,739 W	95%
5	22,354	1,196	21,158 W	95%
29	18,883	1,117	17,766 W	94%
27	14,697	2,299	12,398 W	86%
7	15,447	2,825	12,622 W	85%
15	17,768	4,965	12,803 W	78%
26	8,927	5,658	3,269 W	61%
1	11,926	8,368	3,558 W	59%
31	7,894	6,177	1,717 W	56%
46	9,424	8,598	826 W	52%
48	8,808	8,159	649 W	52%
49	8,716	8,333	383 W	51%
22	3,831	3,801	30 W	50%
18	15,298	16,076	(788) B	49%
42	9,987	11,109	(1,122) B	47%
44	9,155	12,661	(3,506) B	42%
25	3,960	5,604	(1,644) B	41%
10	8,971	14,396	(5,425) B	38%
43	8,715	14,566	(5,851) B	37%
32	4,831	11,164	(6,333) B	30%
30	4,851	15,018	(10,167) B	24%
50	4,858	15,446	(10,588) B	24%
33	4,248	14,186	(9,938) B	23%
19	6,590	23,825	(17,235) B	22%
47	4,132	16,244	(12,112) B	20%
40	3,395	13,350	(9,955) B	20%
11	4,303	17,874	(13,571) B	19%
12	3,261	17,524	(14,263) B	16%
35	2,690	15,561	(12,871) B	15%
39	2,960	17,434	(14,474) B	15%
14	3,147	19,691	(16,544) B	14%
36	1,958	26,248	(24,290) B	7%
45	1,965	26,374	(24,409) B	7%
41	2,005	28,280	(26,275) B	7%
38	1,536	26,615	(25,079) B	5%
13	1,298	31,727	(30,429) B	4%
23	1,127	29,170	(28,043) B	4%
Wards Won	26	24		
TOTAL	587,594	509,436	78,158	54%

* "W" indicates wards carried by Washington and "B" indicates wards carried by Byrne.

4 percent of the vote. In most cities and in most elections this paltry support would have been catastrophic; but considering that Byrne received less than 1 percent of the vote in Washington's "big ten" wards, the mayor's 4 percent showing was significant.

Washington's black voters produced the greatest numbers in terms of the victory margin. In Alderman Eugene Sawyer's middle-class 6th Ward, Washington's victory margin was over 31,000 votes. Though not as spectacular as the 6th Ward, similar surrounding wards produced Washington vote margins of over 25,000 votes. By holding his own along the lakefront and in the Hispanic communities and by doing slightly better in Byrne's white wards than she did in his black wards, Washington pieced together his winning majority.

The sheer magnitude of Washington's black support can be seen best in a citywide precinct analysis (for the record, in this primary Chicago had 2,900 voting precincts). In 31 precincts Byrne was completely shut out (i.e., she received no votes), and in 110 other precincts she received only a single vote. Furthermore, in 912 precincts (31.5 percent of the citywide total) she received fewer than ten votes. Washington won 90 percent or more of the vote in 1,109 (38 percent) of the city's precincts.

To counter this black turnout and support for Washington, Byrne obviously had to do well in the white precincts, and she did. In 747 (26 percent) of the city's precincts the former mayor received 90 percent or more of the vote. (A look at their combined performances shows that Byrne or Washington received 90 percent or more of the vote in 64 percent of the city's precincts.) Almost two-thirds of the city's precincts went by landslide to one of the two candidates, and the overwhelming variable in determining which way the landslide would go was race.

In showing just how few politically contestable neighborhoods or precincts there were in this primary, the following facts are informative:

1) Washington won 1,368 precincts (47 percent); Byrne won 1,532 precincts (53 percent).
2) In only 92 (3 percent) of the city's 2,900 precincts did Washington win or lose a precinct by more or less than 6 percent.
3) Only 19 of the 50 city wards had precincts that were contestable.

4) The only wards with more than ten precincts in the 6 percent differential range were the 31st Ward (Hispanic), the 44th Ward (lakefront), and the 49th Ward (lakefront).

In sum, though Washington won a substantial and clear-cut victory, his black power base had expanded only marginally into other areas of the city.

The results of the other two party primaries were not surprising. Haider easily won the GOP primary, beating a bunch of no-names; Epton's withdrawal from the Republican race had limited the professor's triumph to a no-publicity sideshow status. In the Solidarity primary Vrdolyak was also an easy winner. He had countered any opposition write-in move by having over 3,800 of his 10th Ward loyalists take a Solidarity ballot and vote for him. After much early fussing and feuding over the possibility of Vrdolyak's candidacy splitting the antiadministration vote, Solidarity party voters had little influence in the end on the outcome of the Washington-Byrne primary battle. The responses of individual candidates to the primary's events were more cordial than they had been four years earlier. Unlike in 1983, Washington and his allies took the expected victory in stride as they geared their sights for the April 7th general election showdown. An obviously tired Washington told his supporters that this victory had "driven the spike of reform deep into the turf of this great city." The mayor never took his eyes off those lakefront voters, whom he would need in six weeks; and, as in 1983, he called for all Democrats to unify behind his candidacy. An equally subdued Byrne conceded defeat by saying, "The people have spoken, and we didn't make it." Unlike in 1983, when she refused to admit defeat until the following morning, there was little belligerence in her tone.

As for the three other candidates—Haider, Hynes, and Vrdolyak—each made a brave comment about how Washington's victory was not convincing nor showed that he was unbeatable. Still, the political handwriting was clear to anyone with his eyes open. In a slightly modified one-on-one contest Washington had whipped Byrne decisively. A far better indication of the status of Washington's foes was the fact that, for the first time since Anton Cermak had organized the city Democratic machine in the late 1920s, a critical election night saw the party's downtown headquarters closed. The days when Mayor Daley would receive ward returns from a battery of phones or candidates and ward committeemen rushing to see him with hot political stories were now memories. The city had changed, the individual pols had changed, and for the old-timers the party was over. It was now Washington's city, and though white Democratic party regulars could still fight him, they could not beat him.

CHAPTER FIVE

Harold Washington's Last Election

WASHINGTON'S ONE-ON-ONE victory over Byrne in the February 1987 primary did not scare off any of his three remaining white rivals. Each candidate proclaimed that the six-week campaign period between the primary and the general election would give him plenty of time to: 1) become the recognized chief alternative to Washington; 2) force one or both of the other challengers to drop out of the race; and 3) defeat the mayor in a second one-on-one contest.

The four-way party campaign made the race look more like a mayoral battle in traditional multiparty Paris than in Chicago. Washington was the Democratic candidate, and though he knew he would receive little support from white ethnic Democratic leaders, he believed that his party label would give him a few percentage points in each of their wards from diehard party supporters. Haider's Republican primary victory guaranteed him a place in the final four; but the professor knew he would need party support and finances from Republicans outside of Chicago in order to be competitive. Vrdolyak's Solidarity candidacy and Hynes' Chicago First party were convenient vehicles for them to bypass the Byrne-Washington battle, but each man knew he was appealing to the same constituency—white ethnic Chicago.

Ideology or philosophy have seldom played a major role in Chicago politics, and 1987 would be no exception. All four men claimed to be reformers. Washington's stated administrative and political philosophy of economic fairness and his belief in redis-

91

tributive social programs made him easily the most liberal of the bunch. But in reality, campaign strategy or even positions on issues were irrelevant in determining the mayoral winner as long as the incumbent faced divided opposition. Unlike in the primary, even organized crime's number one bookmaker/handicapper, Donald "The Wizard of Odds" Angelini, was offering no odds on the general election outcome. The wizard had come very close in predicting Washington's final victory margin over Byrne but even he took a pass on the four-way. Washington was unbeatable.

The Vrdolyak Campaign

First off the mark was Vrdolyak, whose personality and energy exploded onto the campaign scene. Aided by a $250,000 postprimary contribution from his long-time friend, Ohio millionaire Edward DeBartolo, Sr., Vrdolyak had the money upfront for the six-week dash to election day. He hired New York media consultant Tony Schwartz to produce his paid commercials, and then he bought $400,000 worth of television and radio air time. As for his main white ethnic rival, Hynes, Vrdolyak simply said, "He's gone, forget him."[1]

Many pundits and most Hynes supporters believed that Vrdolyak would quickly drop out of the race. For some reason, they believed that he would make a big splash and then in the name of anti-Washington unity would simply fade away. Strengthening this view were several polls that showed Vrdolyak's negatives as unmatched in Chicago political history, at times rivaling those of the Ayatollah. The question no one asked was, who would force Vrdolyak out? Just as in the preprimary maneuvering, there was not a single person in the city or the Democratic party who had the "hammer" (a stronger Chicago word for clout) to make Vrdolyak back down.

The Chicago *Tribune's* Mike Royko was one of the few major city commentators who from the outset predicted Vrdolyak would not fold. In his own colorful language, Royko asked: "What does Vrdolyak have to lose? If he's going to go out, at least it will be while swinging."[2] Royko concluded that "beneath Vrdolyak's tough exterior there is a very tough interior," and thus Chicago political observers and politicians should not "watch for Vrdolyak to blink [for] while you're watching, he'll stick a thumb in your eye."[3]

Since Washington's black support was untouchable in 1987, the campaign for the other three candidates become geographically more manageable. Politically, 40 percent of the city was simply "no white man's land." Ethnics, Hispanics, and lakefront neighborhoods and the electronic and print media were the only campaign targets for the challengers. With his unbridled enthusiasm to campaign, to talk fast and often, and to work long hours, Vrdolyak covered nonblack Chicago like a political blanket. He was everywhere.

Using an "alley fight" style of campaigning that Chicagoans have historically loved, Vrdolyak took on all critics and audiences. He verbally outpointed a DePaul University political scientist who accused him of being a racist by telling the prof and his student audience, "You can bum rap me . . . but you can't get a free shot today because I'm here." He went lip to lip with local, controversial WBBM-TV (CBS) commentator Walter Jacobson over the latter's belief that Vrdolyak was not a serious candidate because he was loaded down with "political baggage." "How dare you talk to me about baggage?" snarled Vrdolyak. "I paid my taxes. I never went to jail." Unlike Byrne, Vrdolyak was not afraid to mention Washington's past legal problems.

Of all the candidates, Vrdolyak was clearly having the most fun. Equally clear was a sudden surge in his political support from nonblack Chicago that propelled him close to Hynes in many public opinion polls. Boosted by his simple but hard-hitting television blitz (single message ads on specific issues, such as his position on crime), confident of his own ability, and encouraged by the lackluster campaigns of Hynes and Haider, Vrdolyak told one and all that March 13th (the deadline to withdraw from the mayor's race) would not see him drop out.

Perhaps the most pressure on Vrdolyak to fold his mayoral tents did not come from the political or business community but from the Chicago *Sun-Times*. Three days after Washington's primary win, a *Sun-Times* editorial entitled "Vrdolyak can't have it both ways" called for the 10th Warder to give up one of his positions—Democratic party chairman or Solidarity party mayoral candidate. Though the newspaper also suggested that Hynes give up his 19th Ward Democratic committeeman post if he stayed in the mayoral race, the editorial's major thrust was at Vrdolyak. "There is something terribly unseemly," wrote the *Sun-Times*, "about a party's official chairman running against the nominee of his party."[4]

On March 12th, the day before the mayoral drop deadline, the *Sun-Times*, in a somewhat unprecedented move, editorially called for Vrdolyak to withdraw. It suggested that the alderman ask himself the question: "What purpose do I serve by remaining in the race?"[5] The logic used by the *Sun-Times* was both curious and contradictory. In almost fatherly tones the newspaper said that if Vrdolyak stayed in the race he might cripple his future political prospects, whereas if he withdrew he would demonstrate "selflessness and courage." At the same time, it reintroduced poll data showing high negative voter attitudes about Vrdolyak. Lastly, it claimed Vrdolyak's continued candidacy "would undercut Hynes's chance of rallying supporters into a formidable opposition."[6]

Vrdolyak responded to the mayoral withdrawal deadline and the *Sun-Times* editorial by doing what he does best: he attacked. The Solidarity party candidate charged that the *Sun-Times* wanted him out because they were pro-Washington and they knew Hynes would be an easier opponent for the mayor. It was twisted logic at best, but Vrdolyak's anger was real and obvious, and it was his emotion and not his words that voters saw on their television screens. He accused Washington of not paying income taxes for *forty-nine* years – a major time-frame escalation. He charged that there was collusion between the *Sun-Times*, Hynes, and the newspaper's outside attorney, Samuel Skinner. Vrdolyak asserted that the law firm that employed Hynes on a part-time basis received lucrative bond business from the Regional Transit Authority, which was headed by Skinner. This was another wild charge at best, since Hynes's recent involvement with the firm was limited. But the message was clear as the withdrawal date came and passed: Vrdolyak was snarling back at his foes and not backing out meekly in favor of Hynes.

The Hynes Campaign

March 1987 was the worst of times for the Cook County assessor, Tom Hynes: he was suffering through a politician's worst nightmare. First of all, he was in a campaign in which he had no control over the events. To be competitive against Washington, let alone have a strong enough campaign to beat the mayor, Hynes needed his newly won worst enemy, Ed Vrdolyak, to sacrifice his own mayoral candidacy. Unlike Sydney Carton in Dickens' *Tale of Two Cities*, Vrdolyak was not about to play the noble gentleman; instead, it would be Hynes who would eventually end up on the political guillotine.

On the night of Washington's Democratic mayoral primary victory over Byrne, Hynes told reporters that Vrdolyak was not a factor in the upcoming general election because he was unelectable. Like a beleaguered general forced to fight a two-front war, the assessor could never concentrate his firepower fully on either Vrdolyak or Washington for any length of time. For example, in early March, Hynes's aides leaked to *Sun-Times* political editor Steve Neal a thirty-seven-page memorandum detailing the assessor's strategy for defeating Washington. The purpose of the leak was not to give the incumbent a sneak preview of his rival's game plan; rather, it was an attempt by Hynes to convince anti-Washington and undecided voters that he and not Vrdolyak was the serious alternative to the mayor. Such a move was a risky political tactic, but Hynes and his people had run out of ways of convincing Vrdolyak to leave the race.

Against Washington's hectic and controversial mayoral record, Hynes attempted to promote himself as a thoughtful and quietly competent administrator. His best effort to transmit this view to the voters was a TV commercial telling Chicagoans that, if elected mayor, Hynes would have a City Hall so quiet and efficient that "you won't even know I'm there." Hynes capped his "boring is beautiful" TV spot with a shot of his son falling asleep as he listened to his dad's low-key and professional approach to government. Unfortunately for Hynes, the cleverness of this ad was not duplicated in other areas of the campaign.

Hynes did raise some issues challenging the governing competence of the Washington administration. He claimed that Washington's "First Source" hiring program (the plan that urged companies doing business with the city to give preference to job seekers referred to them by City Hall) was antibusiness. He accused the mayor of keeping secret an audit report that criticized the city for the way it handled federal funds. Hynes hoped to smoke Washington out and force the mayor to reply directly to his assault. And he succeeded.

Washington countered Hynes's charges in a March 9th speech at Chicago State University. He attacked Hynes's "Mr. Clean" credentials, accusing him of conflict of interest because of his part-time legal work. The mayor suggested that the press refer to Hynes as "Mr. Former Clean." Perhaps never in the history of Chicago politics was a candidate so thrilled at being singled out and personally attacked by his opponent as was Hynes with Washington's outburst against him. Hynes now had his chance to go one on one verbally with the mayor—without Vrdolyak. And Hynes let loose! He responded to Washington's accusations with uncharacteristic emotion and abandon: "Who does Mayor Harold Washington think he is?" Hynes asked a Rotary Club luncheon crowd. "He should be the last person in the city to question the integrity of anyone. His history and his record are one of sleaze."[7]

"No more Mr. Nice Guy for Hynes" headlined the Chicago *Tribune*. For a few days Hynes's supporters believed that the publicized exchange between their candidate and Washington would force Vrdolyak out of the race. But they were wrong. Hynes's "sleaze response" to the mayor turned out to be the high-water mark of his mayoral campaign. It turned out to matter little to Vrdolyak and proved to be only a momentary diversion for the voters.

Hynes's problem with Vrdolyak soon became a campaign obsession with him and his political high command. A late March visit to Hynes headquarters at 350 W. Kinzie revealed how frustrated his people were over their inability to get rid of Vrdolyak. Located in a gentrifying neighborhood on the northwest outskirts of the Loop, Hynes's campaign office was as strange as his campaign. In order to get into the main campaign office complex, one had to walk up a winding narrow staircase that was similar to a fire escape. Once having negotiated the steps, one found several top Chicago political honchos, such as William Colson, State Senator Jeremiah Joyce, and Phil Krone, huddled in offices trying to explain why they could not force Vrdolyak out of the race. "It's Vrdolyak," said one Chicago old-timer from the Daley era. "If it was only 1963, we'd win this one easily. His [Vrdolyak's] ass would have been kicked out into the lake."

A Hynes fundraiser in March also revealed the helplessness of the assessor's campaign. Though the downtown hotel ballroom was filled with cheering Hynes supporters, the crowd did not reflect the new demographics of 1987 Chicago. Most of the people were middle-class whites, and several were former city residents now living in the suburbs. The attacks on Washington centered on his administrative mistakes at the CHA, his faulty crime-fighting record, and his inability to spur economic development. Fortunately for the listeners—and unfortunately for

Hynes—few lives of people in the crowd were affected directly by anything said about the mayor. When one final Hynes speaker said that it was "time for change," he was right—but a little late. The change had taken place in 1983 with the election of Harold Washington.

The Washington Campaign

Unlike the mood of elation that followed his upset 1983 Democratic mayoral primary victory, Washington and his supporters reacted in a subdued manner following their expected 1987 primary win. For a man who loved political combat as much as he did and practiced it as well as he did, the mayor looked and sounded tired. Part of the problem was his age and the personal toll that hectic first term had taken on his overall health; part was the fact that upcoming general election was going to be a relative breeze. Unlike 1983, the 1987 mayoral race against three opponents was Washington's to lose. All he had to do was avoid a major mistake, turn out his vote, and let his divided opposition chop each other up.

As in any campaign where one is an overwhelming favorite, Washington still faced some political problems. The first was the Jesse Jackson factor. Washington and Jackson were never close; they both used each other to promote their own political agendas, but philosophically and personally they did not trust each other. Washington and his chief advisors had not forgotten how the media-loving Jackson had tried to steal the mayor's thunder on the night of the 1983 primary win by shouting, "It's our turn." Furthermore, the mayor's strongest white support in the city came from the liberal Jewish voters living along the lake and in Hyde Park. And for them Jackson's pro-Palestinian views and his 1984 connection with Rev. Louis Farrakhan (the Chicago-based minister famous for his anti-Semitic statements) were unacceptable. Thus, limiting Jackson's activity in the general election campaign was a major goal of the Washington campaign.

Second, the mayor wanted to assure a high turnout of his core voters. Washington's experienced campaign team, led by Jacky Grimshaw, established a first-rate political network within the black community to counter voter overconfidence that might lead to election-day apathy. From the far southside middle-class black wards to the near south- and westside poor blacks living in public housing, Washington's organizers worked the black community. In the latter CHA areas, Washington activists who called themselves "Boss Busters" went on a voter registration blitz. Using words like "reform" and "movement," these political operatives actually put together a well-oiled machine. Unlike Daley's machine, it was monoracial and not multiethnic, and its main loyalty was to a man and not a party; but the dedication of its foot soldiers was equal to that of any precinct workers in Chicago history.

Third, the mayor did not want to let his rivals (especially Hynes and Vrdolyak) totally dominate the media. And as he had so shrewdly done in the 1983 mayoral primary, Washington also wanted to use his own campaign to both prop up a major foe's faltering campaign or cut down one that might be making too much headway. Divided opposition was Washington's political insurance policy; he wanted to help keep everyone in the race. This strategy explains his Chicago State University speech against Hynes, where he zeroed in on the assessor's alleged conflict of interest problem. Washington insiders were picking up signals that Hynes's campaign was in trouble; directly attacking him would boost the morale of the assessor's supporters, force Hynes to reply, and give him a public boost to slow down any Vrdolyak momentum in anti-Washington neighborhoods.

Another example of this little-discussed strategy was Washington's statement to his opponents in early March that he would not agree to a debate unless all three pledged to remain in the race until the bitter end. Washington realized that it was an absurd demand (even reformers cannot dictate the campaign choices or decisions of their opponents); but given the intense rivalry between Hynes and Vrdolyak, it helped keep both of them in the race past the withdrawal deadline.

Beyond his specific political concerns, Washington spent most of the general election campaign quietly pushing his theme that under his leadership Chicago was now "working together." And he reiterated that his reform administration had decimated if not destroyed old-style machine politics. On the campaign trail Washington's schedule was a calculated mix of governmental and political activities. Money was no problem; his campaign coffers were filled. Eager to expand his political base, the mayor spent considerable time courting and coalition-building with the city's growing Hispanic communities. As one antiadministration Hispanic said of Washington's efforts, "The mayor's reform principles include the use of City Hall clout to get what he wanted in Latino neighborhoods."

Unlike his three rivals Washington skipped the southside Irish parade (held on the Sunday before St. Patrick's Day). Instead, the mayor spent the day campaigning on the city's North Side in a variety of ethnic neighborhoods. He courted the Asian-Indian vote by donning ceremonial Hindu garments; he sampled goodies at a Greek produce market; and "he wolfed down at least five Jewish pastries at a Kosher bakery while posing in a baker's hat."[8] (Tragically, Washington's zest for food and his willingness to try all cuisines would help bring about his untimely death less than eight months after his re-election victory). In a way, that Sunday was a microcosm of the entire campaign: there were Haider, Hynes, and Vrdolyak working against each other and cajoling their same base crowd for support, while Washington, by himself, leisurely sought add-on support to his huge and untouchable black voter base.

The Haider Campaign

Don Haider would have won the 1987 Chicago mayoral election had the contest been decided by a written test on local government. Unfortunately for the GOP nominee, American electoral politics (especially in Chicago) and Ph.D. qualifying exams have little in common. At the outset of his campaign Haider told city voters that his first objective was "to raise the real issues facing Chicago." But the spectacular political machinations inside the local Democratic party, the unwillingness of his fellow Republicans at any level (national, state, or local) to give him genuine financial and political help, and the historic lackluster performance of the Republican party in Chicago overwhelmed any Haider effort to run a successful issues-oriented campaign. Instead, for six weeks Haider found himself calling for a "double drop" (saying that *both* Hynes and Vrdolyak should withdraw, leaving Haider as the only alternative to Washington) and seeking ways to garner free publicity for a campaign whose low ratings in public-opinion polls matched the level of his campaign funds.

Two days after his primary victory, Haider's campaign treasury had a total of $800. Plans for neighborhood campaign offices, phone banks, and volunteer organizations were canceled. On the advice of David Schultz, his former student and his successor as Mayor Byrne's budget director, the candidate spent his remaining bankroll purchasing a batch of red jackets with the words "Don Haider For Mayor" on the back. Haider then announced that he was taking his campaign, jackets and all, to the only place he could afford, the streets, and issued a press release detailing his upcoming thirty-day schedule. According to Haider, "This was the city's first walking mayoral campaign. . .that also included on-the-street, neighborhood press conferences."[9]

For the first two weeks in March, Haider kept himself in the news by continuing to urge both third-party candidates to withdraw. He stayed on the issues, and the print and electronic press generally took him seriously. For example, Haider's plan for Chicago's financial stability was delivered in a LaSalle Street press conference outside City Hall. Based on a report of the Financial Planning Committee for the City of Chicago, a high-powered business group that employed Haider as one of its main resources, Haider presented ten ideas to improve the city's fiscal future. However, once the March 13th mayoral withdrawal deadline passed without Hynes or Vrdolyak withdrawing, Haider's dreams turned from victory to respectability (10 to 12 percent of the election- day vote).

Still, Haider had fun as he continued to generate publicity with a series of unorthodox stunts. His most noteworthy was the elephant caper. On the day after St. Patrick's Day (a traditional slow political day in Chicago) Haider rode the mighty two and a half ton elephant Dondi across State Street. With TV cameras and news photographers recording the event, the distinguished Northwestern professor and his elephant became big news. Haider said that his campaign rented Dondi from the Shrine Circus which was appearing in the city because it is the GOP symbol and it signified the clear choice in the election between three Democrats and one Republican. *Tribune* reporter John Camper captured the ultimate explanation of Haider's "minisafari" from the candidate's wife. According to Jean Haider, "The elephant's head is just like Don's, lumpy and brainy."[10]

Cuteness and cleverness aside, Haider never had a chance. Having no political base, no party base, and no funds is not the prescription to win elections anywhere–especially not in Chicago. Though respected for his intelligence and admired for his whimsical sense of humor, Haider's thoughtful ideas about improving Chicago government never penetrated the voters' minds. Black voters were not going to heed Haider's message to dump Washington because his administration mismanaged revenue collections or was "unable to plan beyond next Friday's payroll" in the area of economic development. Ethnic Democrats and many lakefronters were unwilling to support a Democrat-turned-Republican who suggested that budget-cutting needs might require the closing of some neighborhood police stations or major cuts in other services. Whether Haider was right or off base on these and other issues he raised during the campaign was not the point. Beyond his organizational weakness, Haider forgot that a majority of Chicagoans today as in the past enjoy politics and political warfare too much to let ideas on government administration interfere with their fun. Moreover, the politics of race, ethnicity, and power were far more understandable.

Endorsements and the Silver Medal

Of all the candidates running for mayor, Hynes was the one who placed the greatest emphasis on seeking political endorsements. His strategists believed that if an impressive list of big-time political players would publicly announce their support for his candidacy, it might provide the push to force Vrdolyak out. Hynes people also realized that a potential negative factor in this process was that they would be asking mainly Democratic leaders to go against their party's duly chosen mayoral nominee, Harold Washington; but given their position, they had no choice.

Led by his friends in the Daley wing of the Democratic party, Hynes captured most of the endorsement headlines. From Washington, D.C., Congressmen Daniel Rostenkowski, William Lipinski, and Marty Russo pledged their support to the assessor; from Springfield, Attorney General Neil Hartigan endorsed his long-time pal; and in Chicago, Rich Daley and a bunch of state legislators, aldermen, and Democratic ward committeemen added their names to the Hynes effort. Unfortunately for the assessor and his campaign staff, all their hard work had no impact on Vrdolyak—who either politically ignored or verbally sniped at the daily stream of endorsement announcements.

The Hynes effort did have an impact on Washington. The mayor, seeking personal and political acceptability rather than an electoral boost, attempted to match Hynes in the endorsement sweepstakes. He received the expected endorsements of four Chicago congressmen: Charles Hayes, Gus Savage, Cardiss Collins, and Sidney Yates; State Comptroller Roland Burris added his name to the Washington column; and the mayor also received personal visits and endorsements from some national

Democratic leaders, including Sen. Edward Kennedy, Missouri Rep. Richard Gephardt, and former Virginia governor Charles Robb. However, it was in the local arena where the mayor's endorsements made the biggest splash.

Two of Washington's former aldermanic foes, Bernard Hansen and Eugene Schulter, were the first of the old "Vrdolyak 29" to throw their support to the mayor. A few other antiadministration aldermen and legislators who supported Byrne in the primary also publicly came over to the Washington side. But the big endorsement catch for the mayor was his former opponent herself, Jane Byrne. At a late March Washington fundraiser, Byrne announced: "The battle is over.... I wholeheartedly endorse Mayor Washington." That very night the Washington camp unveiled a new TV spot that featured Byrne telling city voters: "Harold Washington will be the next mayor of Chicago. He has my vote and my support...it's time to unite behind Mayor Washington."[11]

Though the mayor would also pick up critical labor endorsements, such as the Chicago Teachers Union and United Auto Workers, and received endorsements from both major city newspapers, the Byrne endorsement meant the most to him. Beyond the reform rhetoric and movement politics, Washington remained a ward and precinct politician whose ideal mayoral model more closely resembled Richard J. Daley than it did John Lindsay. Byrne's words put him closer to his goal.

Amidst the flurry of endorsements and campaign rhetoric, one newspaper story captured clearly and coldly the political reality of the 1987 Chicago mayoral contest. On March 19th, Steve Neal, *Sun-Times* political editor, in a front-page column, quoted Vrdolyak's chief political advisor and well-known political trickster, Joseph Novak, that the mayor's race had turned into "a contest for the silver medal [second place]."[12] Rep. Al Ronan, Byrne's political director in the primary, added that the Hynes-Vrdolyak race for runner-up meant that "Washington can't lose." To support these observations, Neal's story included the results of an Information Associates voter preference survey. The numbers read Washington – 51 percent; Hynes – 17 percent; Vrdolyak – 8 percent; Haider – 2 percent; and Undecided – 22 percent.

In a follow-up story, *Sun-Times* political columnist Basil Talbott expanded on the silver medal metaphor. Talbott revealed that long-time Democratic organization foes like the Better Government Association were gleeful about the Hynes-Vrdolyak street fight. "Some of the things that Vrdolyak is insinuating," said a BGA executive Terry Brunner, "are wilder than anything we've charged over the years." The message in the Neal and Talbott stories was expected but still shocking to lifelong ethnic Chicago Democrats. The Hynes-Vrdolyak contest was more than a race for second place; it had the possibility of destroying what was left of the once mighty Chicago Democratic organization. William Daley, another of the former mayor's sons and a recognized political expert, summed up the potential consequences of the runner-up race by saying, "It's the dismantling of the so-called Democratic party and a replacement of it by solo operators."[13]

Vrdolyak and the Mob Connection

As mentioned above, Hynes was desperate for Vrdolyak to leave the race. He was in political quicksand and faced an embarrassing possibility of coming in third in the race (Hynes supporters then and now claim that their private polls showed their man would have finished ahead of Vrdolyak). What to do? Late in March, Hynes decided to go for broke and risk it all by making an accusation that, even for Chicago politics, was unprecedented. Two weeks before election day, Hynes accused Vrdolyak of meeting with Chicago organized crime kingpin Joseph Ferriola to seek help for his campaign.

Equally newsworthy was the method Hynes used to deliver the bombshell. At a Sunday press conference the assessor said the following: "I *have heard* that Ed Vrdolyak met with Joseph Ferriola. I believe that such a meeting took place and that his candidacy for mayor of Chicago has received encouragement as a result of it."[14] Hynes did not elaborate on his charge, produced no eyewitnesses, and answered no further questions. In fact, the only additional information Hynes gave was that he did not initiate the Vrdolyak-Ferriola story; rather, he said that he was merely responding affirmatively to a Chicago *Sun-Times* inquiry about the meeting. But whether the *Sun-Times* or Hynes was making the accusation, its effect was the same: the assessor was saying to his rival, "It's your move, Eddie."

Vrdolyak took the challenge. He lived up to his nickname by responding with incredible speed and deftness to the accusation, calling the charge insane and McCarthyist. "It's absolutely, positively false," an angered but controlled Vrdolyak told the press.

103

"He's [Hynes] a liar and a sleaze, and his campaign is going nowhere. This is trash."[15] With typical Vrdolyakian wit, the alderman claimed that Hynes had met with Al Capone, John Wayne Gacy (the mass murderer), and Napoleon.

At stake was everything for Hynes and Vrdolyak. Joseph Ferriola was the recognized CEO of the Chicago crime syndicate and second only in total power to the mob's elder statesman, Anthony Accardo. If a Vrdolyak-Ferriola connection could be proved, Vrdolyak was not only out of the mayor's race but out of politics altogether. Not content with merely defending himself, Vrdolyak counterattacked! A day after the public accusation, Vrdolyak told Hynes, the press, and all voters that he was going to sue the *Sun-Times* for libel. Vrdolyak instinctively saw an opportunity to dominate headlines, turn the tables on Hynes, and perhaps even force *him* out. For the first time in his political life Vrdolyak was receiving public sympathy for a perceived low political blow directed *at* him.

The mob-connection story dominated Chicago headlines, and by the end of the day Vrdolyak's political standing increased. On radio and television talk shows, the Solidarity party candidate appeared more confident denying the accusation, while Hynes appeared more unconfident supporting it. Feeling the momentum, Vrdolyak played his victim status to the hilt. An out-of-town visitor witnessing the closing weeks of the campaign might have easily believed that Vrdolyak was the constitutional freedom candidate and the darling of the American Civil Liberties Union. Even GOP challenger Haider joined the fray on Vrdolyak's behalf, calling Hynes's action "innuendo and gutter campaigning." The Hynes bombshell had turned into a boomerang.

On day four of the story Vrdolyak made good on his threat and filed a libel suit against the *Sun-Times*. Claiming that all he wanted from the *Sun-Times* was "fairness," Vrdolyak did not even include Hynes in the lawsuit. Still taking the high road, Vrdolyak said through his well-known attorney William Harte: "There is no basis to sue him [Hynes]. He said he had heard it [the meeting story], which is true. We all heard Jane Byrne said she heard it—a rumor."[16] In politics, showing disdain for your opponent is even more effective than demonstrating anger; and through this lawsuit Vrdolyak, in mock pity, showed his contempt for Hynes and the entire episode. The public loved the action and more and more believed Hynes was out of step. To resolve this issue one way or the other, people said, either the *Sun-Times* or Hynes had to put up or shut up.

On day five the *Sun-Times*, through its political editor, Steve Neal, responded to Vrdolyak's lawsuit with more sensational headlines. According to (again) unnamed sources, the *Sun-Times* confirmed that Vrdolyak met Ferriola at the near northside Ambassador West hotel on two occasions following the mayoral primary. Behind the story, some insiders said that Vrdolyak met Ferriola to seek his help in preventing several northwest-side Italian committeemen from endorsing Hynes. Other insiders wondered why, even if Ferriola could help, he would personally meet Vrdolyak in a well-known hotel.

Vrdolyak's snappy response to the last *Sun-Times* accusation was, "Prove it and I'll bow out." Moreover, Vrdolyak demanded that Hynes apologize and quit the race if he or the *Sun-Times* could not produce credible evidence of the meeting in the next twenty-four hours. Clearly relishing his persecuted underdog role, Vrdolyak issued a copy of his personal schedule for both of the days he allegedly had met with Ferriola.

No other issue made news, and no other candidate received much press while the mob story dominated the headlines. Vrdolyak began telling his audiences that he was now on the "O" (offensive) and that neither Hynes nor the *Sun-Times* would intimidate him. As for Hynes, he moved further into the background as the battle between his rival and the newspaper escalated. More and more, he looked like a man who wished he had never raised the issue or, for that matter, entered the race in the first place. As for the other two candidates, Haider, in a "what about me, guys?" speech, wanted the campaign to get back to the issues of jobs, education, and taxes; Washington said nothing about the controversy, but even his most closed-mouth political aides had difficulty hiding their smiles over the Hynes-Vrdolyak- *Sun-Times* shootout.

One week after the Vrdolyak-Ferriola story burst onto the scene, it finally began to fade away. The issue was now in the courts, and both sides, especially the *Sun-Times*, declined to make any further comments. The *Tribune*, which had enjoyed seeing its rival newspaper squirm under severe public scrutiny, supported Vrdolyak's position. Their leading columnist, Mike Royko, claimed that "the mob story had a nutty taste" because it was illogical for any mayoral contender, especially Vrdolyak, to meet a leading mobster in a public place, and because "well-

placed sources [the unnamed story revealers] are often professional rumor leakers in the employ of a rival candidate."[17]

The ultimate winner of the future legal action was unknown,
but for the moment Vrdolyak was far ahead on political points.
Commenting on the entire episode, one old 50th Ward precinct
captain said, "Hynes was like the old boxer Bob 'Kill or be Killed'
Satterfield. He let it all go on one punch; if he had connected
Vrdolyak was out—unfortunately, he missed and Vrdolyak put
him on the canvas."[18]

The Debate and the Drop

All three of Washington's mayoral challengers wanted to
debate him. Hynes, Vrdolyak, and Haider wanted as many debates as possible, not only to demonstrate their differences with
administration policies but also to gain an advantage over each
other. Following the mayoral primary (where both Washington
and Byrne had effectively avoided a face-to-face confrontation),
Washington's deputy campaign manager, Jacky Grimshaw, announced that the mayor had tentatively agreed to one ninety-
minute debate on March 31st. "We are not talking about
unknown people," said Grimshaw in an obvious effort to differ-
entiate this proposal from the unknown Washington's demand
for many debates prior to the 1983 Democractic mayoral primary. "One debate is adequate to present your program to the
voters. . . ."[19]

Though disappointed about Washington's single-debate demand, all three candidates accepted the tentative offer; but it
was Vrdolyak who tried to make the mayor's unwillingness to
meet his challengers man to man a major campaign issue. Like
a cocky gunfighter who was new in town, Vrdolyak challenged
the mayor to come out into the street (or studio) for a verbal
duel. Incredibly, Vrdolyak sought the aid of Jesse Jackson to call
the mayor out. In early March he sent a letter to Jackson asking
him to moderate a series of four mayoral debates at Operation
PUSH (Jackon's political base in Chicago). Vrdolyak requested
that 1) the reverend use his influence to ensure that these debates
would take place; 2) they would include all four nominees; and
3) they would deal with the major issues facing Chicago. Jackon's
response was a carefully worded statement that he would study
the request, because "I have never closed my door to anyone."
In the end, nothing came of the exchange; but Vrdolyak had
again demonstrated to all that he had no intention of dropping

out of the race and that he and not Hynes had the guts to take on Washington.

Washington tried to avoid the debate dialogue by saying that both Vrdolyak and Hynes (who had also joined the "more debates" chorus) had forfeited their political legitimacy by not challenging him in the Democratic primary. "Why should I debate them?" Washington asked. "These three men [including Haider] ran out on their party."[20]

After gaining as much political mileage as possible from condemning his rivals as party turncoats and traitors, Washington confirmed the tentative single-debate agreement. A Washington advisor suggested that the mayor's real motive in avoiding more debates was his fear that Vrdolyak might anger or bait him into another "Council War" confrontation, which would leave Hynes as the cool administrator–and the big winner. However, two points turned the mayor's thinking around: 1) politically and personally, he could not let Vrdolyak charge that he was afraid to defend his record; 2) recent private polls had shown a significant softening in Hynes support, and the mayor became more confident that nothing could happen in the debate to resurrect the assessor's campaign. Considering the events of the Ferriola-Vrdolyak fiasco (which took place in the period between the debate agreement and the actual debate), Washington's thinking was right on target.

The actual debate symbolized the campaign standing of each candidate. Washington, assured of victory, played it cautious as he rattled off facts and figures in defense of his mayoral record; Hynes looked uncomfortable as he tried to convince viewers he would be a calming influence on the city in view of the ongoing flap over Vrdolyak's alleged mob meeting; Haider appeared bright and knowledgeable, but he was not taken seriously by any of the other debaters; Vrdolyak was his usual scrappy, full-of-fight self as he demonstrated his sharp tongue in boldy discussing the city's racial climate, lashing out at both Hynes and Washington.

The night's most memorable line came from Vrdolyak, who asked rhetorically, "Wouldn't it be interesting to see how this campaign would be if all of us were black or all of us were white?" Because the debate was broadcast live only on the city's public television channel, it gave the station its highest Nielsen ratings ever for a public affairs program. Chicagoans love their city politics–even when the outcome is not exactly in doubt.

The debate analysis in the press rated Washington and Haider boring but with passing grades; Vrdolyak garnered mixed reviews (high on style and guts–low on content and fair play); but Hynes was slammed hard by almost everyone. *Sun-Times* columnist Basil Talbott, the assessor's harshest critic, claimed that the debate left Hynes "a beat-up loser." Like the month of March, the Hynes campaign had come in like a lion but was now going out like a lamb. A strong debate performance had been Hynes's last major hope of turning the campaign around. It was, in short, his last possible momentum builder to gain the upper hand over Vrdolyak and still perhaps challenge Washington. Unfortunately for Hynes, it was not meant to be; in fact, the postdebate fallout found him slipping further down in the polls.

One week before election day, Hynes and his formidable political staff faced a gloomy end to their once hopeful campaign. Hynes was now caught in the middle. Washington had the black vote, and Vrdolyak was winning over more and more of the white ethnic vote. The assessor's campaign had been reduced to contesting his challengers in the overworked and overrated six lakefront wards (42-43-44-46-48-49), reinforcing alliances with old political friends (many of whom could no longer deliver the votes); and pushing the notion that, unlike Vrdolyak, he was seeking "the non-bigoted white vote." His campaign manager, the tough-minded state senator Jeremiah Joyce, was having a difficult time convincing anybody that a late Vrdolyak withdrawal could still give Hynes a shot at victory. And in a moment of candor, Joyce admitted that if Vrdolyak did not fold, Hynes could not win–a statement the candidate himself immediately rejected.

Three days after that Joyce statement, Hynes suddenly dropped out of the race. It was the Sunday before the Tuesday election date when Hynes made his surprise announcement at a Plumbers Hall mayoral rally for him. He told the shocked crowd, "I love Chicago enough not to be mayor." His aides claimed that Hynes recognized that he could not finish first and was not interested in coming in second.

Though some critics, like Mike Royko, claimed that the candidate's departure demonstrated that when "the going gets tough, Hynes gets going," most observers felt that Hynes made the only move left to him. By dropping out and not suffering a possible third-place finish, Hynes preserved his dignity and perhaps rescued his future political career. One old-timer likened

Hynes's mayoral bid to America's involvement in Vietnam: "It was a race he should not have entered because he could not win, and the longer he stayed in the more costly was the price for him to get out."[21]

Thirty-six Hours

From late Sunday afternoon, April 5, until early Tuesday morning, April 7, Ed Vrdolyak had the best day and a half of his life. It was Hynes, not he, who had pulled out of the race, and now it would be he and Washington going virtually one on one (the Haider campaign had atrophied following the debate). Vrdolyak graciously saluted Hynes for "putting the best interests of the city of Chicago before any personal ambition." He then asked for the backing of Hynes's supporters since the assessor, in his withdrawal statement, had pointedly declared that he was not endorsing any of the remaining candidates.

With political niceties out of the way, Vrdolyak turned his attention to Washington at full throttle. The mayor had casually dismissed Hynes's withdrawal as irrelevant to his own campaign. In fact, he had dubbed his three opponents "Wynken, Blynken, and Nod," and when Hynes withdrew he told a campaign audience, "Guess what? Nod dropped out—no surprise." However, some Washington aides were slightly edgy as a reinvigorated Vrdolyak accelerated into the campaign's home stretch in overdrive.

Vrdolyak burned the phone lines contacting formerly pro-Hynes Democratic committeemen and asking them for support. He told a large press contingent that was now chronicling his every move that he was calling everybody for help and, in true Vrdolyak style, added that he might even put the *Sun-Times* on his list (quite unlikely because of his pending lawsuit). On the day before the election he campaigned probably harder and in a more unorthodox fashion than any Chicago mayoral candidate in history.

Starting early in the morning, Vrdolyak greeted commuters at their bus stops in the independent-minded lakefront 43rd Ward. Stopping only to have a well-publicized breakfast at a famous near-north eatery, Vrdolyak began to work his way south. For lunch he marched into the heart of Washington's middle-class black turf and stopped off at the popular Army & Lou's soul food restaurant on East 75th Street. The eatery's front door sported a big Washington poster, but that did not deter Vrdolyak, who worked the restaurant shaking hands and exchanging quips with startled diners. He ended his long day with a huge night-time rally in his home 10th Ward, where he told his listeners and neighbors, "It's our turn. It's our turn to get this city on track."

Most of Hynes's major supporters switched openly to Vrdolyak in the campaign's closing hours. Illinois Attorney General Neil Hartigan was the only powerful Hynes backer to endorse Washington. The mayor, anxious to get the campaign over with, nevertheless worked all of election day on the streets urging black voters, especially CHA residents, to turn out. His workers in the white and Hispanic areas passed out fliers containing the *Tribune* and *Sun-Times* editorial endorsements of his candidacy (though neither newspaper's support was glowing). Of special interest was the campaign reappearance of Jesse Jackson, who accompanied the mayor on part of his day-long trip through black wards.

Perhaps the most poignant and politically telling scene of Washington's final day of street campaigning took place in the southside 20th Ward. In front of the Democratic ward headquarters, an elderly black man came up to Washington. The mayor thrust out his hand to his constituent; but instead of shaking it, the man took the mayor's hand and kissed it. No prince of the church was ever held in greater awe or was worshiped with more adulation than was Harold Washington in the eyes of this man. And as the results that night would indicate, this black voter was representative of an entire community.

And so the 1987 Chicago mayoral campaign ended. Critical policy issues facing the city received some candidate attention but garnered almost no publicity. To be sure, some new plans were offered in the area of economic development; but there was only limited debate on Chicago's massive affordable housing crisis, and no candidate wanted to deal with the city's crumbling educational system. The most unusual aspect of the campaign was that none of the mayor's opponents nor the press nor the public seemed overly concerned about the ongoing "Operation Incubator," the federal corruption investigation. The so-called *Sullivan Report II*, which detailed the misconduct of several administration officials and Washington political allies, was not released by the mayor's office. Instead, as he had done in the past, the mayor turned a "political lemon into lemonade" by pushing through the city council a strong ethics ordinance. Like Mayor Daley before him, Washington took the offensive when scandal or misconduct brought potential political harm to him or his administration. Washington also knew that Chicagoans were much more interested in the political showdown between him and Vrdolyak than they were in any truly substantive issues.

Chicago Picks a Mayor

"Harold Again" screamed the Chicago *Sun-Times* headline on the morning after election day. Washington had won a convincing, if not massive, re-election victory. He beat Vrdolyak by almost 132,000 votes while winning close to 54 percent of the total three-way mayoral votes cast. Approximately 72 percent, or 1,157,803, of the city's eligible voters went to the polls, and only 41,368 (3.5 percent) of them either did not vote for one of the three remaining major candidates, for some unexplained reason voted for Hynes, or skipped the mayoral race entirely.

As was expected, Washington was elated about the results. Not only did he win, but, unlike his first mayoral triumph in 1983, the Chicago City Council this time would be firmly under his control. The mayor told a cheering election-night crowd of 2,000 supporters huddled together at Chicago's Navy Pier that they were celebrating "not the victory of one candidate but a mandate for a movement." However, the night's two most memorable events took place when Washington first sang the city's unofficial anthem "Chicago, that Toddlin' Town," off-key, and then regaled the crowd with a personalized world geography lesson. With perspiration streaming down his face, the mayor rattled off a list of countries and cities around the globe where, if any Chicagoan were now to visit, the first question the locals would ask would be "How's Harold."

Vrdolyak took his defeat with dignity and pride. He was generous in congratulating Washington on his victory and proud of his substantial vote. "I expected to do better than Byrne," Vrdolyak told the press, "but then thirty-six hours wasn't long enough to focus between myself and Washington." [22] The Democratic party chairman refused at the time to speculate on either his future in the Democratic party or the possibilities of running for another office. But within a few short months Vrdolyak would switch parties and become a Republican candidate for a county office.

Haider was upbeat in accepting his predicted overwhelming loss. Calling himself a winner despite receiving only slightly more than 4 percent of the vote, the Northwestern University professor told his supporters, "We have an open road ahead of us." Most telling of Haider's concession statements was his warning to Washington that he and others would be watching the mayor's performance closely during the second term, because, unlike 1983, "he [Washington] has it all, he can't push the blame for things on other people. He will be held accountable."[23]

An analysis of the Washington general election victory reveals that he won twenty-seven wards (by barely winning the heavily Hispanic southwest-side 25th Ward, the mayor increased his total of wards won by one over his primary election performance), and like his primary victory over Byrne, his black ward numbers were overwhelming. Once again, the same ten black wards gave Washington over 99 percent of their vote, while six others gave him over 90 percent. As in the primary, only in the lakefront and Hispanic wards were Washington's victory or loss percentages not of landslide proportions.

A ward-by-ward comparison of Washington's general and primary returns reveals that despite the inclusion of a third candidate (Haider), the mayor made significant vote percentage improvement in the four Hispanic wards. In two of them (25 and 31) his vote percentage increased by more than 10 percent, while in the other two (22 and 26) they increased by more than 6 percent. The mayor's greatest ward percentage drop occurred in the six lakefront wards and in Vrdolyak's home 10th Ward. Haider's candidacy contributed in part to Washington's poorer lakefront percentage performance (the professor was in double-digits in each of the six east 40s wards); but Vrdolyak also did much better than expected in these still independent but now less "liberal" voting areas.

Vrdolyak's best support, like Byrne's in the primary, came from white ethnic Chicago. In two far southwest-side wards, 13 and 23, Vrdolyak received over 90 percent of the vote. In several northwest-side wards his percentages were in the high 80 percent range—held below the 90 percent figure because of some Republican voter support for Haider.

The GOP candidate Haider's best ward performance was in the lakefront's 43rd Ward (19 percent); in only nine other wards (almost all lakefront) did he win more than 10 percent of the vote. Two points reveal the inability of Haider to break off any

TABLE II
Chicago 1987 Mayoral Election
Results by votes, margins and percentages
Presented in ward rank order—for Washington—by percentage

Ward No.	Washington's Vote	Haider's Vote	Vrdolyak's Vote	Winning Margin	Wash %	Haid %	Vrdl %
28	19,141	75	82	19,059 W*	99%	0%	0%
17	25,339	99	126	25,213 W	99%	0%	0%
6	32,676	117	182	32,494 W	99%	0%	1%
24	22,741	107	125	22,616 W	99%	0%	1%
3	20,769	100	113	20,656 W	99%	0%	1%
16	21,954	86	154	21,800 W	99%	0%	1%
21	30,370	138	206	30,164 W	99%	0%	1%
34	27,407	94	231	27,176 W	99%	0%	1%
20	21,748	115	146	21,602 W	99%	1%	1%
8	29,847	102	340	29,507 W	99%	0%	1%
2	20,018	194	296	19,722 W	98%	1%	1%
37	20,522	130	551	19,971 W	97%	1%	3%
9	22,012	113	1,036	20,976 W	95%	0%	4%
29	19,389	153	927	18,462 W	95%	1%	5%
4	19,766	540	946	18,820 W	93%	3%	4%
5	22,543	642	1,256	21,287 W	92%	3%	5%
27	15,282	168	1,775	13,507 W	89%	1%	10%
7	16,072	108	3,049	13,023 W	84%	1%	16%
15	18,426	278	4,602	13,824 W	79%	1%	20%
26	9,027	432	3,543	5,484 W	69%	3%	27%
31	9,332	479	4,123	5,209 W	67%	3%	30%
1	12,179	977	7,245	4,934 W	60%	5%	36%
22	4,006	183	2,963	1,043 W	56%	3%	41%
46	9,944	1,844	7,564	2,380 W	51%	10%	39%
25	4,940	249	4,528	412 W	51%	3%	47%
18	15,810	568	16,146	(336) V	49%	2%	50%
48	8,789	1,966	7,348	1,441 W	49%	11%	41%
49	8,269	1,809	7,496	773 W	47%	10%	43%
42	9,680	3,100	10,215	(535) V	42%	13%	44%
44	8,002	2,756	10,389	(2,387) V	38%	13%	49%
32	4,832	605	9,067	(4235) V	33%	4%	63%
10	9,052	241	19,906	(10,854) V	31%	1%	68%
33	4,737	1,003	9,837	(5,100) V	30%	6%	63%
43	7,723	4,897	13,707	(5,984) V	29%	19%	52%
30	5,160	1,011	13,319	(8,159) V	26%	5%	68%
47	4,161	1,896	13,008	(8,847) V	22%	10%	68%
50	4,385	2,155	14,673	(10,288) V	21%	10%	69%
11	4,460	432	16,894	(12,434) V	20%	2%	78%
19	6,248	1,992	23,634	(17,386) V	20%	6%	74%
40	3,050	1,724	11,518	(8,468) V	19%	11%	71%
12	3,337	657	16,186	(12,849) V	17%	3%	80%
14	3,342	585	17,766	(14,424) V	15%	3%	82%
35	2,628	1,454	13,871	(11,243) V	15%	8%	77%
39	2,731	1,632	16,308	(13,577) V	13%	8%	79%
36	1,886	1,372	25,096	(23,210) V	7%	5%	89%
45	1,562	2,064	24,812	(23,250) V	5%	7%	87%
41	1,582	2,461	26,530	(24,948) V	5%	8%	87%
38	1,292	1,659	25,024	(23,732) V	5%	6%	89%
13	1,123	1,092	31,018	(29,895) V	3%	3%	93%
23	961	994	28,567	(27,606) V	3%	3%	94%
Wards Won	27		23				
TOTAL	600,290	47,652	468,493	131,797	54%	4%	42%

* "W" indicates wards carried by Washington, and "V" indicates wards carried by Vrdolyak.

significant chunk of support from Vrdolyak or Washington: 1) in only four wards (45, 38, 41, 23) did Haider finish second in the balloting; 2) he was unable to win a single precinct in the entire city.

In terms of margin, it was a primary replay for Washington. His popularity in the heavily turned-out middle-class black wards was greater than Vrdolyak's strength in middle-class white ethnic wards; moreover, the mayor had more of them. For example, *five* wards (6, 21, 8, 34, 17) gave Washington margins of over 25,000 votes, while Vrdolyak had only *two* wards (13, 23) in the same category. In Washington's big five, Vrdolyak's combined total vote count was 1,085; in Vrdolyak's big two, the mayor received 2,084 votes. Washington's lowest vote count came in Congressman Lipinski's 23rd Ward (961 votes). Vrdolyak's lowest total was in Alderman Ed Smith's westside 28th Ward (82 votes). Moreover, in thirteen other black wards Vrdolyak's vote was less than Washington's worst ward performance of 961 votes.

A citywide precinct-by-precinct analysis reveals that Washington shut out his opposition in thirty-two precincts (one more than in the primary) and in 890 precincts (31 percent of the citywide total number) Washington garnered 99 percent of the vote. As in the primary, his opposition could not match Harold Washington's massive and near-unanimous black support.

The mayor's best precinct was the 32nd precinct in the far South Side, the nearly all-black and middle-class 8th Ward. The precinct captain, Donne E. Trotter, was not only dedicated to the mayor but was also a loyal member of Committeeman John Stroeger's 8th Ward regular Democratic organization. Most residents in Trotter's precinct live in a townhome complex located on 101st and Cottage Grove Avenues. According to Trotter, "His people are family people . . . many have lived in the community for three generations, and they are very proud of their neighborhood."[24]

The precinct is a big one—with approximately 1,000 registered voters. Trotter's goal was an 80 percent turnout. "I went door to door before the election," Trotter said, "reminding people to vote. I did not have to sell the mayor to the voters. . . . Harold Washington is his own best precinct captain." Final results from Trotter's precinct: Haider—1; Vrdolyak—2; Washington—795.

Though proud of these totals, Trotter clearly gives credit for these remarkable numbers to Washington and the people themselves living in his precinct. "We want to become part of the American dream," Trotter philosophized, "even the new people coming here from DuSable and Phillips want it [high schools in a very poor section of southside Chicago, where, unlike the old Irish, who divided the city into parishes for geographical purposes, many blacks divide it by high school district]. Harold is a major step in that direction.... Not voting for the mayor is like killing your own dream."

Given Chicago's changing demographics and the intensity of Washington's black support, it would have taken a miracle for anyone to deny him renomination and re-election. In effect, any opponent would have had to achieve the nearly impossible—that is, win over almost all the city's nonblack voters. Washington had an iron grip on his core constituency, and no one could take that vote away from him. Add incumbency and a growing personal attraction to city Hispanics and liberal whites, and you have a simplified blueprint of the Washington victory coalition.

II.

The Meaning

OF THE WASHINGTON YEARS

CHAPTER SIX

The "Hollow Prize"
Thesis Revisited:
The Chicago Case

WINNING BLACK POLITICAL control of central U.S. cities was written off at the end of the 1960s almost before it began by an enormously widespread idea called the "hollow prize" thesis, which was published in the influential *Journal of the Institute of American Planners*. Black control of the central cities, argued Paul Friesma, would result in winning only a "hollow prize."[1] Written at a time when visions of the apocalypse gripped some of America's leading liberals, the essay expressed the author's fears about whether the nation would survive as a unit, of the possible "destruction of its major political institutions," and "protracted racial turmoil and peril" extending perhaps into the twenty-first century. Burned-out cities, white flight, and a business exodus would leave but hollow shells for the political invaders. The anticipated black political capture of the central cities would be mostly "psychic" and "symbolic," for there would be very little left of substance. This gloomy prognosis was written in 1969, at a time when the expectations of other white liberals and black leaders were unrealistically high; and thus Friesma's prediction sounded even gloomier at the time it was issued than it would today. The "hollow prize" thesis struck a responsive chord among intellectuals and political activists. It was one of the most discussed ideas of the period.

Did the "hollow prize" thesis correctly divine the future? Were cities empty shells plucked bare of their largesse by ethnic and machine politicians and left as rotting stumps of an industrial civilization gone to seed, ragweed, and vacant lots with nothing to offer the black empowerment movement? This gloomy prediction seemed plausible and even possible at the time it was uttered. Yet already by the mid-1970s the "hollow prize" thesis seemed at least partly wrong. There was increasing evidence that black political capture of the central cities delivered more than "psychic" and "symbolic" rewards—though it clearly did that also. Black mayors during that decade took over city halls in Atlanta, Cleveland, Detroit, Gary, Washington, D.C., Los Angeles, Newark, and elsewhere.

The capture of central city governments by blacks could have important economic consequences, and the patronage system once practiced by traditional white political organizations of delivering jobs and favors to the faithful could also be practiced even under a reformed and rationalized bureaucracy in the 1970s and 1980s. Despite the classic municipal reform movement, which put into place (three-fourths of a century ago) civil service laws, merit employment, competitive bidding, and contracts to the lowest bidder, black mayors have been able to use the system for racial advancement. Through the use of aggressive affirmative action strategies; through the use of racial criteria in appointing policy makers to city government; through the promulgation of city residency requirements for city jobs, which tends to slant hiring in favor of the black inner-city majority over the white suburban periphery; and through contract set-asides and disregard for the principle of "to the lowest bidder goes the job"—black mayors have been able to tilt the scales heavily in favor of black job seekers and businesses.[2]

Stronger confirming evidence of black economic advance in employment in America's big cities came in a benchmark study of black employment in city government released in 1983. Prof. Peter Eisinger's *Black Employment in City Government* shows that blacks had gained in the number of public jobs even as cities were laying off workers. Between 1973 and 1980 some 25,000 city jobs were lost, but the number of blacks employed in big cities increased by 9,000. This study also devised something called a "fair share score," which was calculated by matching the black percentage in the public work force with the black percentage in the city's population, whereby an equal match would yield a score of 100. The forty-one big cities studied showed that blacks had more than their "fair share" at the beginning of the period (1973) with a score of 107, and even after massive city layoffs and labor force shrinkage, blacks finished the decade (1980) still exceeding their "fair share" with a score of 104. Actually, Eisinger's "fair share" formula is probably flawed in that it tends to understate the degree of overrepresentation in public employment by blacks: blacks with a much lower median age (26) than the white median age (32) statistically have fewer available persons in the adult work-age group than do whites. At the same time, it should be said that this black overrepresentation is partly accounted for by a high concentration of minority workers in the lower level of municipal jobs. Yet the larger truth remains: the most reliable body of data assembled under the federal Equal Employment Opportunity Act (1972) showed a black overrepresentation in public jobs in our largest cities.[3]

How did Chicago compare to the forty-one-city study with regard to hiring blacks and minorities? During his last four years as mayor (1973-76), Richard J. Daley was often pilloried as a bane to blacks, women, and other minorities and charged publicly in the most lurid terms with being a racist, a political antediluvian, and an urban primitive on affirmative action. The city's first black mayor, Harold Washington (1983-87), frequently criticized the departed boss as a benighted part of Chicago's past and an unmitigated racist. In the 1983 mayoral campaign candidate Washington condemned administrations preceding his as being unfair and discriminatory in hiring Chicago's city work force, and he promised to correct the wrongs of the past. By year three and four of his first administration, Mayor Washington was boasting that he had brought "fairness" to Chicago public employment. (By "fairness" Washington meant choosing the city's work force so that it closely paralleled in race and gender the city's population.) Washington and his administration's spokesmen repeatedly presented "fairness" as the centerpiece of his mayoralty, as compared to the discriminatory bad old Daley days.

What does the record show? What do the objective statistics and hard numbers show concerning Daley's alleged "racism" and "unfairness"? Let us turn to an examination of the Daley years. In broad terms and in viewing the entire city work force as a unit, Mayor Daley's Chicago in the 1970s (especially after 1973, when the federal Equal Employment Opportunity Act required the kind of statistical reporting used in this chapter) had been keeping abreast of population changes and hiring more blacks in what appears to be a remarkably statistically responsive fashion (Table III). For example, in comparison to Chicago's "external work force," which covers all those employed in either private or public employment within the city limits, one finds that in

TABLE III
Total City Workforce

		Black	White
External Workforce – 1970		17%*	78%
Richard Daley	City workforce, 1973	23%	75%
	City workforce, 1976	25%	71%
External Workforce ** **– 1976 est.**		26%	62%
External Workforce – 1980		32%	52%
Jane Byrne	City workforce, 1981	29%	65%
Harold Washington	City workforce, 1985	30%	64%

Source: Official Report of the Task Force on Affirmative Action, City of Chicago, December, 1985, pp. 1,2.

*All percentages report only the whole number and are not rounded.

**Note: the 1976 estimate of the "external workforce'" is derived from a common technique used by demographers by taking the 1970 and 1980 census data on the "external workforce" and estimating a uniform growth rate per year for the intervening decennial years.

1973 the "external work force" was about 17 percent black and 78 percent white; the "internal work force," which was that employed by Daley's City Hall, was 23 percent black and 75 percent white. That was the first year in which solid statistical EEO data was available. Thus blacks employed under Daley, despite popular perceptions to the contrary, clearly had more than their "fair share" (to use a popular affirmative action phrase) of the city's work force as measured by the "external work force." In fact, blacks were "overrepresented" by one-third, to express it in fractions, or 6 percentage points, whereas whites were about 1/25, or 3 percentage points, underrepresented or below their "fair share." Although it is likely that in 1973 blacks were heavily clustered in manual and semiskilled jobs, with a few in "soft-money" federal jobs, the fact remains that, as a percentage of the total city work force, they were overrepresented when measured by the "external work force yardstick."[6]

Even during Mayor Daley's last year in office (1976), the EEO figures (published by the Washington administration) show that the city's white work force had fallen several percentage points (to 71.6) and the black work force had grown to 25 percent. The 25 percent black employment figure in Daley's last year is probably very close to the size of the "external" black labor force, which can be estimated to have been about 26 percent at that time (Table III). The city's white work force had shrunk, but admittedly not as dramatically as the white external work force had. Yet one can conclude that blacks as a percentage of the total city work force had been close to mirroring their numbers in the "external workforce" and by that measure getting their "fair share" under Mayors Daley and Byrne.

Mayor Washington's Official Affirmative Action report, issued in 1985, also claimed that minorities and women "were even more seriously underrepresented" in the city work force from 1980 through 1985.[7] This charge contains both more and less than meets the eye, and the story is more complex than the aggregate figures by gender suggest. When compared to their numbers in the external work force in the past (which is a fair measure of the number of available workers), it turns out that women were 17 percentage points underrepresented under Mayor Daley, but 25 percentage points underrepresented under Mayor Washington in 1985 (Table IV). Another minority, Hispanics, also remained underrepresented on the city payroll under Mayors Daley, Byrne, and Washington, although their degree of underrepresentation under Washington was actually greater than it was under Daley.

TABLE IV
Total City Workforce *

	White	Black	Women	Hispanic	Asian
1970 Census External Labor Force	78.2%	17.2%	33.3%	3..2%	1.0%
Richard Daley – 1973	75.0%	23.0%	16.0%	1.7%	0.3%
Jane Byrne – 1981	65.4%	29.7%	21.3%	3.9%	0.9%
Jane Byrne – 1982	68.1%	27.2%	19.8%	3.7%	1.0%
Harold Washington – 1985	64.1%	30.3%	19.9%	4.5%	1.0%
1980 Census External Labor Force	52.8%	32.1%	44.2%	11.6%	3.3%

*Total City Workforce includes both full time and part time. Official Report of the Task Force for Affirmative Action, Chicago, Dec. 1985, 1,2.

Using the 1970 and 1980 benchmark census data on the "external labor force," we see (Table V) that Daley in 1975 employed 2.6 percent Hispanics on the city work force in comparison to 3.2 percent of the "external labor force," whereas Washington's administration was further from the mark, with only 4.5 percent Hispanics on the city payroll in 1985 compared

TABLE V
Comparison Internal, External Labor Force, Chicago

	Hispanic	Asian
External Workforce – 1970	3..2%	1.0%
Richard Daley – 1975	2.6%	0.4%
Harold Washington – 1985	4.5%	1.0%
External Workforce – 1980	11.6%	3.3%

Source: Official Report of the Task Force on Affirmative Action, City of Chicago, December, 1985, pp. 1,2.

to the Hispanic "external work force" of 11.6 percent (Tables IV, V). Thus both the degree and ratio of underrepresentation of women and Hispanics was greater in Mayor Washington's first term than it was a decade earlier under Mayor Daley. The "Boss" did not, as is often charged, turn a blind eye and a deaf ear to historical and demographic change. He was moving with the tide of ethnic and racial change.

Another historical look at the numbers on women – beginning with Daley's last full year in office (1976) through Byrne's last full year (1982) and the last full year for which comparable data exist in comparative form for Washington (1985) – reveals at first glance more continuity than change in the gender and race of city employees. During this period, extending for nearly a decade, from Daley in 1976 to Washington in 1985, the differences are minuscule; to make the case that either Byrne or Washington improved markedly on the Daley record in minority employment, one is reduced to cheese paring, quibbling about skimpy fractions of differences, and arguing that a change of 100 or so employees – seen against a base figure of 7,000 to 10,000 – can be called significant change. As the performance data show, Washington improved on the Daley record of hiring women employees by under two percentage points, and in the case of blacks, by only five percentage points (Table VI). As the actual job count shows, in 1976 Daley employed more women than

Washington did in 1985 and almost as many blacks, although Washington increased the *percentage* marginally in both cases. Again, it is likely that Daley's relatively good showing on minor-

TABLE VI
City Total Workforce
Full Time & Part Time

	Women		Blacks		Total Size City Workforce
	%	Number	%	Number	
Richard Daley — 1976	18.2	(7,936)	25.2	(11,030)	43,609
Jane Byrne — 1982	19.7	(8,342)	27.1	(11,471)	42,185
Harold Washington — 1985	19.9	(7,814)	30.3	(11,886)	39,197

Source: *Official Report of the Task Force on Affirmative Action*, City of Chicago, December, 1985. Appendix I labels its data "City Total, EEO – 4 Full Time/New Hires."

ities and women may have found them clustered in the lower rungs of the job ladder and some on federal "soft money" projects. Yet the gross employment figures suggest not a hard-hearted "racist" ogre but a mayor who was responding to change.[8]

New Hiring

The new direction of the Washington administration, when it took over in 1983, can be seen much more clearly in the new hiring data and also in the controversy that it was to provoke.

"She's gotta be nuts! Wow, that is one of the most damnable lies ever," roared the incumbent Mayor Washington at challenger Jane Byrne in 1987. As the Democratic primary campaign ground down in late January, both candidates claimed to have done more for women; Washington reportedly made the claim on several occasions that he had done more for women in government than any mayor in the city's history. Jane Byrne asserted the contrary and argued, furthermore, that there was a "gender gap" in the Washington administration because it hired women at much lower salaries than men. Washington railed at Byrne with his typical rhetorical overkill, assigning her again to the nether regions in company with Lucifer and the forces of prevarication and darkness. Washington backers, led by the mayor's

125

deputy chief of staff, Brenda Gaines, rallied 200 female city employees at City Hall to repudiate Byrne's charges and condemn her. Both major daily newspapers gave Byrne poor coverage on the issue: the *Tribune* said, "Byrne's Equality Attack Backfires"; the *Sun-Times* dismissed it as another quirky and ill-founded attack by a sometimes "batty" candidate.

The following day, however, the *Tribune's* research into the city records revealed that there was some substance to Byrne's charge and that indeed there was a pay gap: men hired by Washington had average salaries of $21,000, whereas women lagged behind at about $15,000. Additional digging into city records by the present authors shows that during the first three full years of the Byrne administration (1980-1982), the city's first female mayor hired twice as many women – 4,309 – as Washington did

TABLE VII
Total City New Hires All Categories
FEMALE

		White	Black	Hispanic & Other	Total Females Hired
Jane Byrne	1980	385	830	96	1,311
	1981	768	1,433	163	2,364
	1982	330	254	50	634
				Total Women Hired by Byrne	**4,309**
Harold Washington	1984	117	216	43	376
	1985	163	601	84	848
	1986	270	551	93	914
				Total Women Hired by Washington	**2,138**

Official Report of the Task Force on Affirmative Action, City of Chicago, December, 1985, Appendix IV, New Hire Data; supplemental New Hire data, 1986.

in a comparable period (1984-1986) – 2,138 (Table VII). Although this might have provided good grist for the Byrne campaign mill, she fumbled the ball and failed to focus sharply on the issues. Apparently not certain enough about the validity of her own statistics, Byrne retreated.

That was a serious mistake to make with Harold Washington, who possessed the never-let-go oratorical talents of a bull terrier and moved in for the kill. He unloaded a barrage of *ad hominem* rhetoric designed to bowl over Byrne on the issues: "You know her style. Tell the big lie. L. I. E. She's always had trouble with numbers, and now it's gotten chronic."[10] Mayor Washington publicly bulldozed over the gender-gap issue and bullied Byrne into silence on the question. The old Jane Byrne of fire-in-the-belly and feisty combativeness was gone, and Washington won the public showdown on the "gender gap."

What do the Washington administration's numbers on new hiring show with regard to the alleged "gender gap"? The larger picture is complex and shows some contradictory directions. The biggest losers during the Washington years among females

TABLE VIII

City Total of New Hires in All Categories

	MALE				FEMALE				Total No. of New Hires
	Black		White		Black		White		
	%	no.	%	no.	%	no.	%	no.	
Jane Byrne – 1981	23.8	(1,489)	31.4	(1,963)	22.9	(1,433)	12.2	(768)	6,252
Jane Byrne – 1982	18.2	(452)	50.2	(1,249)	10.2	(254)	13.2	(330)	2,484
Harold Washington – 1985	43.0	(1,230)	18.7	(537)	21.0	(601)	5.7	(163)	2,858
Harold Washington – 1986	31.7	(746)	18.8	(442)	23.4	(551)	11.5	(270)	2,348

Official Report Task Force on Affirmative Action, City of Chicago, Dec. 1985, Appendix IV, New Hire Data; supplemental New Hire Data, 1986.

were white females, whose rate of all new hires dropped from 13 percent under Jane Byrne in 1982 (her last full year) to 5 percent in 1985 under Washington and about 11 percent in 1986 (Table VIII). Mayor Washington's first two full years in office (1984 and 1985) were the worst for white women hires up to that time in the decade of the 1980s: the absolute number of white women hired was cut to less than one-half of Jane Byrne's average. As the re-election campaign got nearer, Washington, either for that reason or others, jacked up the number of white women hires in 1986. Whereas Jane Byrne hired 768 new white women as city employees in 1981, Harold Washington hired but 163 in a comparable period, 1985, and increased the number by only 270 white women hires in 1986 (Table VIII).

Black women benefited most during the first three full years of the Washington administration: they averaged 21 to 23 percent of all new persons hired, whereas white women averaged under 9 percent of all new employees in Chicago during the same period. In Jane Byrne's record year for females hired (1981), about 23 percent of all new hires were black females (numbering 1,433). Washington's comparable high-water mark was achieved in 1986 with 23 percent, or 551 new black women hired (Table VIII). If one combines black with white women and all minority women, it becomes clear that Jane Byrne's hiring binge of 1981, which placed more than 2,200 new women into city employment, was unmatched by Washington in his first term and, given the budgetary constraints of the 1980s, may not be matched in this decade. In defense of Washington's lower female hiring figures, it should be pointed out that 1981 was an extraordinary year for the large number of new employees hired by the city.

The deVise Affair

A second public relations brush-fire war over personnel data broke out after the election, in late May 1987, when Roosevelt University urbanologist Pierre deVise took the Washington administration to task for ignoring merit hiring – and possibly violating federal civil rights laws – with its "it's our turn now" policies. By slanting hiring heavily in favor of blacks, who were given two-thirds of all new jobs by City Hall in 1985 and most of the top administrative posts, Washington "denies qualified whites and Asians public employment opportunities," deVise asserted.

DeVise's criticism provoked Mayor Washington into one of his rolling-thunder, days-of-wrath verbal bombing raids against the Roosevelt professor and his modest eight-page paper. "Pierre deVise should be ashamed of himself," roared the mayor at a southside speaking engagement. "I have never seen a more mixed-up, botched-up, unprofessional report in my life. It's five pages of just plain junk." Warming to the subject, Washington, a 1949 Roosevelt graduate, blustered, "I am astounded that a man who would put out such a horrible piece of work would be teaching at my own college, my own university. It is amazingly inaccurate, so patently false that you wonder at the motivation of a person who would write such a thing." Not only did the mayor question deVise's study and its motivation but also his mental condition, possible sanity, and his right to hold a job at Harold Washington's alma mater. "I don't know what's gone wrong with the man. He has lost his moorings."[11]

While Washington was assailing deVise on the South Side, his press secretary, Alton Miller, was tearing into deVise on downtown public radio, calling his eight-page study "unscientific, intemperate, inflammatory" and "neo-racist." Finally, at the end of the week, in a musty whiff of something reminiscent of 1960s radical chic patronizing, the Chicago *Tribune* upbraided deVise for his naiveté: "A professor discovers human nature." The editorial offered a feeble defense of black patronage hiring, an interesting reversal of the paper's decades of condemnation of white patronage.[12] The editor's confused moralizing about the facts of human nature and the inevitability of black patronage was the *coup de grace* for deVise.

Although deVise's figures for 1985 were correct, he fared no better on the "reverse discrimination" issue than had Byrne on the "gender gap." The press first printed his study as a titillating piece with great fanfare and then, having built him up, went into a shark frenzy to cut him down. The big dailies and other media unleashed a counterattack as if Attila the Hun had just breached the wall. Poor deVise and his mimeograph machine were no match for the media establishment. It was a David-and-Goliath contest; only this time the Goliaths would win. The mayor, who had learned the political utility of name-calling in the "gendergap" fight, moved in and decked deVise.

What were the facts of the case? Drawing upon data from the mayor's own personnel office, deVise focused on the most lopsided hiring year (1985) and correctly reported that black preferential hiring had reached 64 percent. DeVise did not cite data for 1984 and 1986, when black hiring was not quite as high (about 55 percent). His provocative interpretation was that black patronage had squeezed out merit employment, which cut to the quick a mayor who claimed to be a "reformer." DeVise suggested that what we call "affirmative action patronage" in this book had replaced civil service, and that qualified Asians and whites had suffered. When pressed on this point, the mayor argued that his hiring policies "were driven" by the relative numbers of the races in the job pool, which is fairly close to an admission that pure merit was not the governing first principle in City Hall.

Officials and Administrators

In examining the top of the municipal job ladder, officials and administrators, it becomes apparent from Table IX that under Mayor Washington white males and females lost most of the new executive opportunities, and black males and females gained most. Hispanics made some modest movement, but Asian-Americans and American Indians moved hardly at all from 1981 to 1986. The only female category that experienced an actual loss in numbers and percentages were white females, who comprised 22 percent in 1981 and 45 percent in 1982 of all newly signed on "officials" under Jane Byrne, a figure that fell dramatically to an average of about 9 percent during the first three full years of the Washington administration. Jane Byrne's 1982 hiring binge was a banner year in the "officials" category, when an astonishing 45 percent of all new hires were white women. If one adds black women to Byrne's 1982 hiring crest, then exactly one-half (50 percent) of all of the city's new "administrators" and "officials" came from the female executive labor pool. Never before or since have women comprised so large a percentage of the new "officials" and "administrators" hired. Mayor Washington's best year for women was 1986, when 41 percent of "officials" and "administrators" hired were women. Washington's three-year average was about 36 percent.

As in the case of general hiring, black men emerge as the largest single beneficiaries in the new upper echelon hired, averaging 32 percent, or about one-third, of new officials and administrators in Washington's first administration. Black women, by comparison, averaged about one-fourth of new officials, and white women lagged behind at fewer than one-tenth (9 percent) of the new officials hired by the city. White men comprised slightly less than one-fifth of the new officials hired.

It is possible to impose several different interpretations on this gross aggregate employment data when it is seen in its historical and comparative context. The questions raised by Jane Byrne and Pierre deVise immediately come to mind. A careful examination of the data indicates that Jane Byrne's record on the gender issue was not as bad as Washington claimed during the campaign, but not quite good as she claimed. Yet in total number of females hired by City Hall and the total number hired into

TABLE IX
Officials and Administrators
NEW HIRES

	MALE						FEMALE						Male & Female American Asian	Male & Female American Indian	Total New Hires
	Black		White		Hispanic		Black		White		Hispanic				
	%	No.	%	No.	%	No.	%	No.	%	No.	%	No.			
Jane Byrne—1981	15.9	(7)	45.5	(20)	4.5	(2)	11.3	(5)	22.7	(10)	0	0	0	0	44
Jane Byrne—1982	8.3	(2)	33.3	(8)	8.3	(2)	4.7	(1)	45.8	(11)	0	0	0	0	24
Harold Washington—1985	37.2	(22)	20.3	(12)	8.5	(5)	22.3	(13)	8.4	(5)	3.3	2	0	0	59
Harold Washington—1986	31.9	(23)	20.8	(15)	5.5	(4)	25.0	(18)	9.7	(7)	5.5	4	1	0	72

Source: Dept. of Personnel, City of Chicago, 1986.

131

higher office, Byrne's record is slightly better than Washington's first term. DeVise's charge that Washington had shelved the traditional merit system and given two-thirds of all new jobs to blacks and 60 percent of the administrative jobs to his own race is also correct, as far as the figures for the single year 1985 are concerned. DeVise surmised that using the merit system would not produce this high an overrepresentation of newly hired blacks. Another affirmative-action group, Hispanics in Chicago, did not fare half as well as blacks did under the Washington administration. Their underrepresentation seemed to be part of a larger national trend: a study by deVise of thirteen big cities under both black and white mayors discovered that Hispanics got a larger share of jobs in white-mayor cities than in black-mayor cities.[13]

In Chicago, underrepresentation of some minority groups should not come as a surprise, because hiring policies that disproportionately favor blacks were implicit in Washington's campaign promise, "It's our turn now." Washington's pledge to make the public work force a mirror reflection of the city's racial make-up also suggested that merit would not be the leading criterion used in city hiring. Whether the Washington administration, as deVise claimed, violated the civil rights of white males and females, Hispanics, and Asian-Americans, and disregarded merit by favoring blacks, is a question the courts will probably have to decide. Whether this is affirmative action or reverse discrimination is a matter of interpretation.

Another plausible interpretation lies in the hypothetical world of what did *not* happen. Washington did not bring about what whites feared he would: "Papa Doc" policies, a wholesale sacking of whites, and purges that might have changed the complexion of the City Hall labor force overnight. Such fears were probably unrealistic simply because of the Shakman rulings and some civil-service job protection. Yet there is little doubt that Washington dramatically and drastically altered hiring for new jobs in Chicago's public work force and massively changed hiring priorities. Blacks have benefited enormously; Hispanics have benefited more modestly and are in a distant second; Asian-Americans and American Indians have benefited hardly at all; and white males and white females have borne the brunt of the loss of job opportunities in this racial and gender shift in hiring.

Other Gains

Other benefits have also accrued to black Chicagoans. One of the unanticipated gains reaped in many black-mayor cities, including Chicago, was first noticed by Detroit mayor Coleman Young: the white exodus was creating "housing bargains" for blacks who displaced whites. A more detailed study by deVise suggested that blacks pay far less for more housing than do whites. White movement to the suburbs, he argued, created a huge surplus in housing and fewer buyers; thus housing prices have dropped dramatically in many city areas. This surplus has created bargains for blacks. The 1980 census data show that the average white-owned home costs 45 percent more than the average black-owned home of the same size in Chicago.[14]

Chicago was not a "hollow prize" after black mayor Harold Washington took over in 1983. There were jobs and contracts to be had going into the millions of dollars. Placed in the historical perspective of the forty-one big-city study, Chicago's black public work force followed a parallel course with a steady and incremental increase in black employees both in percentages and actual numbers, accompanied by an even more dramatic decline in the number of white city employees. Although the city work force between 1973 and 1985 lost some 4,500 jobs, black workers actually increased their numbers in city employment. The total number of new blacks hired by the Washington administration between 1983 and 1986 was 5,897, or more than half of all new hires—compared to only 3,661, or 32 percent, newly hired whites.[15] For twelve years and under four different mayors, Chicago moved in the direction of more black public employment and participated in a larger national trend that was operating in other big cities, whether they had black or white mayors. Much of the campaign charging and countercharging of who employed more blacks and women and at what salaries is best viewed, in the larger historical perspective, as campaign rhetoric intended not to describe reality but to meet the exigencies of winning election or re-election.

Contracts

Neither was Chicago a "hollow prize" when it came to parceling out contracts for the city's purchase of goods and services. "There's millions and billions out there for blacks," said Clarence McClain, former mayoral aide and political confidante to Harold

Washington, in viewing the mayor's program to steer 30 percent of a $100 million airport "People Mover" contract to blacks and minorities.

The first of the "millions" under a formal program for minority preference began in 1979 in the Jane Byrne administration, which set aside 10 percent of federal contracts. Following up in 1984, during his first year in office, Mayor Washington raised to 25 percent the city's purchasing of goods and services from minorities. Washington then commissioned a black Atlanta-based consultant to conduct a $600,000 study on how to increase the black and minority share of city-funded business. The result was the James H. Lowry Report, which became the basic blueprint for Chicago's program of set-asides and preferences for blacks and minorities.[16]

The Lowry report suggested increasing the size of the minority-preference quota from the city; it argued that in the existing no-holds-barred, free-and-open bidding competition, blacks and minorities could not compete successfully against "majority" contractors. Accordingly, on April 3, 1985, Mayor Washington issued a formal executive order raising contract set-asides to 25 percent for blacks and minorities and 5 percent for women on all purchases of goods and services by Chicago. To meet the "25 and 5" goals, the city set in motion an elaborate process, including a widespread solicitation of minority businesses and potential minority vendors, along with seminars and how-to help sessions; cookbook plans on how minority subcontractors might get into "majority" prime contracts; a 2 percent preference for Chicago-based businesses and a target of awarding 60 percent of all business to local companies; the drawing up of a list of "certified" minority contractors who would have exclusive rights to the 30 percent set-asides; and the reserving of no-bid purchases of $10,000 or less for minorities and local businesses. The program also provided for low-interest loans for blacks and minorities; a "Chicago First" hiring program (which Washington announced in 1987) asking recipients of city contracts to turn first to City Hall as a hiring hall and hire from a list of "prepared" workers approved by the mayor's office; and finally, a provision for severe penalties to "majority" contractors who did not meet minority quotas, assessing "dollar-for-dollar" damages against those who even in good faith fell short of the city's "goals."[17]

A zealous application of the "25 and 5" diversion (order for set-asides) in purchasing saw that minimum figure exceeded in

1985; the quota of 30 percent was also exceeded in 1986, with about 35 percent of all purchases going to blacks, minorities, and women: that is, about 35 percent of approximately $400 million was divided up, with 27 percent, or $116 million, going to blacks and minorities and 8 percent, or $34 million, going to women.[18]

The 1969 "hollow prize" thesis that predicted a bleak and gloomy future for black-mayor cities did not correctly divine the future. The cities did not turn out to be hollow shells plucked bare of their largesse by white machine politicians. The rewards to blacks of coming into power in many city administrations were more than "psychic" and "symbolic," although they were that too. They were also substantive rewards, as the Chicago case shows: thousands of jobs; contracts for city work that numbered in the multimillions for black businesses; entry into political positions seldom held by blacks before; and the cultivation of a new minority business class of suppliers, food vendors, insurance brokers, contractors, bond salesmen, and every other line of business that municipal corporations deal with.

Efficiency vs. Equality: The Big Tradeoff

Were the shifts ordered by Mayor Washington toward racial and gender preferences in hiring city personnel and awarding city contracts economically wise for the city? Were they morally healthy and ethically correct substitutes for the concept of merit and excellence? Few Americans, either black or white, would be happy in a society that discarded wholesale both the principle and the practice of merit hiring. Using some principle other than merit to select people for jobs and contracts presents hazards that should be carefully examined. At the lower end of the skills and occupational scale, many blacks and whites would not object to abolishing classic merit exams and substituting racial preferences or patronage – or even a lottery, which is, in fact, what Chicago currently does with laborer's jobs. On the other hand, a far greater number of whites and also many blacks would object if the principle of racial preferences and quotas began to replace skills and abilities altogether, and if race rather than qualifying merit became the dominant factor in determining, say, who practices medicine or pilots commercial aircraft. (Though even here there is room for disagreement: Chicago's black congresswoman, Cardiss Collins, who sits on the airline safety committee, has indicated to the press that she thinks quotas might be all right in selecting airline pilots as well as laborers.)[19]

There is also a political price to be paid for using criteria other than merit principles. Quotas and preferences for favored groups rub raw the psyches of yesterday's ethnic minorities. Jews and Japanese-Americans, for example, have been quota-ed out or cut out of society's reward system in the past, partly at first because they were underachievers but more recently because they were overachievers. As yesterday's dispossessed have learned, even the most benign quotas, which are intended to help someone else, generally end up hurting someone – offering one group gains at another group's expense, often the more qualified group. As one observer of quotas in Chicago's black newspaper, the *Defender*, saw it: "Blacks are continuing to use 1960s legal tactics in hopes of circumventing mainstream standards versus demonstrating high caliber performance."[20]

At the heart of the conflict between blacks and whites is the effort to use racial quotas to achieve some measure of equality. The old doctrine was equality of *opportunity*, which was simply concerned about getting all of the runners up even at the starting line. The new doctrine of equality of *result* aims at having everyone finish the race by predetermined racial, ethnic, and gender quotas, a form of egalitarian pluralism.

Quotas also have cost implications. The most elegant and pithy theoretical formulation of the problem and its cost implications was stated by the distinguished economist Arthur Okun in his book *Equality and Efficiency: The Big Tradeoff*. Okun says that some economic policies designed to reduce the scope and magnitude of inequality weaken incentives to produce and thus they unintentionally impair efficiency. At some point along the way society is then faced with a choice that offers more equality at the expense of efficiency or more efficiency at the expense of equality. In the idiom of the economist, "a tradeoff emerges between equality and efficiency." When put into operation, this question is generally not so polarized that the choices are a straightforward alternative between equality at all costs or efficiency with no reservations, but generally one of degree: how much efficiency are you willing to lose for equality? As Okun argues, there is an easy answer to that question: "Promote equality up to the point where the added benefits of more equality are just matched by the added costs of inefficiency."[21] That insight is difficult to apply in the real world because of the imperfection of the measuring sticks; furthermore, each person has his own measuring stick. Blue-collar workers see it differently than do middle-income and high-income professionals or the independently wealthy. Chicago's lakeshore and "limousine liberals" can tolerate inefficiency and the sacrifice of merit at the lower ends of the job ladder, where the impact is most heavy on ethnic, blue-collar, bungalow-belt workers. Those furthest from the threat of race and gender preferences are often the most tolerant of it, that is, unless preferences adversely influence the selection of psychiatrists, neurosurgeons, airline pilots, and stock brokers—occupations that the "chablis and brie" set want chosen purely by merit principles.

We posed the question of the "big tradeoff" to Chicago's deputy commissioner of personnel. Samuel Ackerman argued that racial preferences in hiring had not negatively affected the work force or the city's efficiency. His reasonable-sounding argument was that some city departments were so overstaffed by past administrations with patronage workers and no-show inefficiency that an actual reduction in the work force in the Department of Streets and Sanitation and racially preferential hiring had improved efficiency.[22] The reduction in the size of garbage crews offered some evidence to support his point; and during Washington's first administration the city appeared to be looked after about as well or possibly slightly better than before—and with a smaller work force.

It is possible and even plausible that the hiring policies of previous administrations had kept out of the city work force a highly skilled segment of mostly black workers, and that the new administration's use of racial preferences had produced a surge of qualified and meritorious black employees who would outperform their white predecessors. One might further argue that the end of no-show jobs and patronage would also contribute to efficiency. And it is possible that Streets and Sanitation was more efficient with fewer workers, returning to the taxpayers their money's worth.

Even assuming that all of the above were true, one could also argue—as did a former city commissioner of personnel—that this new surge of efficiency may be a temporary phenomenon that may run its course within a short time. As the pool of qualified blacks is exhausted and the external labor market continues to compete even more vigorously for the best black employees, within a few years Okun's iron law may return to haunt the city.

137

As Okun puts it, ultimately "the conflict between equality and economic efficiency is inescapable."[23] The teeter-totter analogue applies: when you raise the equality end, you depress the efficiency side. We do not offer an easy answer to the problem, but we do believe it is important for Chicagoans to be aware of some of the consequences of the choices they are making or are having made for them. The "equality and efficiency tradeoff" is not going to go away or stop operating just because an articulate mayor tells it to cease and desist. Just as the ancient Scandinavian King Knute could not command the tides to stop, no mayor is likely to have the rhetorical powers to repeal the big tradeoff and the attendant economic inefficiency and higher taxes that the drive for equality at any cost is likely to bring to Chicago.

Clearly, the "hollow prize" thesis did not accurately predict Chicago's black political takeover. When it came time to fulfill the "it's our turn now" campaign pledges, there was much to be passed out to Chicago's former have-nots. Although certainly no "boss" in the William M. Tweed or Richard J. Daley manner, Mayor Washington found ways in his first administration, mostly through executive orders and affirmative action programs, to reward his core constituency. Fragmentary and incomplete evidence indicates that "affirmative action patronage" may not be any more inefficient (at this writing) than machine patronage was in the past; in fact, gross figures suggest that it represents at least a modest step upward in the efficiency-reform equation. Whether affirmative action patronage will ossify over time and become a sluggish drag on the city and the business community, as the old-style patronage was, is something only time will tell.

Finally, there is another "tradeoff" that has been almost forgotten by our generation: it is the fact that contract set-asides and quota hiring began at the federal level in 1969 to buy racial peace and extinguish the fires that were burning down America's cities. The fires have long ago gone out, but we still have racial quotas and preferences. We will know in another decade or so whether it was a good bargain or the price was too high.

CHAPTER SEVEN
The Chicago Political Tradition

W E WILL EXPLORE briefly in this chapter some of the Chicago political traditions that were confirmed by Harold Washington's mayoralty, as well as some that were denied. Traditions and political behavior accumulate and pile up in the history of cities, and often by their very dead weight they develop a remarkable grip on the polity and capacity to guide the future – or at least determine the parameters in which the future will operate. Some of these political traditions accrete and encrust like barnacles, and others age like fine wines. Some rise from the logic inherent in historical situations; others from the whim or choice of an individual political leader; and yet others from a mix and match of the individual and the historical situation. In examining some of the mainline Chicago political traditions and their relationship to Harold Washington's mayoralty (1983-1987), we will also discuss the city's passage through a great political and historical watershed, which is one of those rare epochs of wholesale change that come but infrequently in the history of a city.

Builder Mayors

During his first term Washington defied what has been a long-standing political tradition in Chicago of "builder mayors." Mayor William B. Thompson was known as "Big Bill the Builder" in the 1920s. Mayor Edward Kelly was a bricks-and-mortar man to the extent that the threadbare thirties and federal works projects money permitted. Reformer Martin F. Kennelly helped set off the Loop building boom of the mid-fifties with the construction of the landmark Prudential Building, the first new skyscraper in Chicago in many a year. Richard J. Daley rewrote the builder tradition by presiding over the biggest public and private building boom the city had seen since the Great Fire, ranging from a new city campus for the University of Illinois to a new airport called O'Hare on the outskirts of town. In the Loop, Mayor Daley helped turn around creeping blight with policies that encouraged the rebuilding of the Central Business District; from that encouragement came the execution of many architectural triumphs, including the John Hancock building and the Sears Tower, the world's tallest. Jane Byrne gave every evidence of continuing the "builder" tradition with her projected North Loop construction, Navy Pier revitalization, new public library, O'Hare expansion, and rapid transit lines to O'Hare and Midway airports–all massive, multimillion-dollar projects.

The political game plan in the public "builder" tradition suggested that a mayor, in the first year of his term, should announce with great fanfare and publicity the big plan or plans; in the second year he firms up the financing, developers, and contractors; the third year sees dirt flying and bricks and mortar rising; and, with luck, the fourth year is ribbon-cutting time (at least for Phase I), with the mayor proudly beaming and posing for television cameras while he surveys a new glittering glass edifice or a public building just in time for re-election. That, in essence, is the model of the "builder" mayor of Chicago.

Mayor Washington rejected the "builder" tradition out of hand, because of a shortage of money for public projects, because it was associated with his old enemies Daley, Byrne, et al., and because he favored small-scale "people projects" instead of public monuments in the Loop. Washington and his advisers took a kind of perverse pride in smallness, reversing the old Daniel Burnham motto of "make no little plans." The city's commissioner of economic development, Dr. Robert Mier, pointed out that the new administration would eschew the "monumental and grandiose" and emphasize instead small and minority business and neighborhood development. According to Mier, the just-preceding Byrne administration had worked out a bad deal on Navy Pier revitalization, which the Washington administration had to junk.

None of the "big-bang-for-the-buck" Daley megaprojects were initiated in Washington's first term. In fact, the administration experimented with what many investors considered to be the antigrowth idea of "linked" development, which required private downtown developers to divert some of their investor capital into nonprofitable charitable and public purposes in the neighborhoods. Other public-private projects either atrophied or were barely kept alive on life-support systems. Navy Pier continued to deteriorate because it was in need of expensive infrastructure repairs; North Loop moved jerkily ahead, almost stalling out from the confusing stop-and-go signals; the proposed new library continued to flounder, as it had for a decade, mired in site fights; and the new sports stadium stayed in limbo. "Show me a project he's started and finished," blurted out mayoral challenger Jane Byrne before the Democratic primary in February 1987.

Two projects that the administration could point to by election day 1987 were the preservation of the Chicago Theater, a darling of the preservationist lobby that got more press than its economic significance warranted (and which would be bankrupt by September 1988), and a new public parking garage. These were small potatoes in the "builder" tradition. Other projects begun by previous mayors, such as the airport transit systems and the O'Hare expansion, were continued in a reasonably competent manner by the Washington administration; and the mayor permitted private developers to continue to do their thing in the Central Business District. Finally, the mayor, fearing a fiscal disaster, prudently killed the project that would have been a "builder" mayor's dream – the 1992 Chicago World's Fair.

When Washington opened his 1987 mayoral re-election campaign, the "builder" cupboard was pretty bare. He had broken the mold and defied a Chicago political tradition. No monuments along the Chicago river or, as Commissioner Mier put it, "edifice complexes." This uncharacteristic turn in the Chicago mayoralty was not necessarily good or bad, but it was different. Washington's rejection of showplace public projects was partly out of economic necessity and partly a new model of political leadership that rejected the "builder" tradition of Chicago mayors.

Bons Mots by the Mayor

When it came to the language of politics, Harold Washington, among Chicago's contemporary mayors, was *sui generis* – in a category by himself. Mayors Bilandic, Daley, and Kennelly were generally conflict minimizers, fuzzying up the issues in their public statements, if need be with fractured syntax. When the questions got tough, they would duck and run away and "live to run another day." Washington's immediate predecessor, Jane Byrne, was more feisty and combative and seemed to delight in what reporters called her "gang bang" press conferences. She played "fire-away-Flanagan" and hurled half-thought-out verbal bombshells before disappearing behind an elevator door or exiting in a chauffered car. Yet Byrne never developed the knack of invective and verbal assault that Washington visited upon his opponents. A politician with Washington's demagogic gifts had not been seen in Chicago since William "Big Bill" Thompson, the city's last Republican mayor, left the scene in 1931. Big Bill once threatened to "punch King George in the snoot," roared during the middle of prohibition that his honor "was wetter than the Atlantic Ocean," and debated two of his political enemies in a public theater in absentia, providing for their symbolic presence with two caged rats.[2]

No matter how Washington would perform as mayor, observed one keen student of the mayoralty, "the city's vocabulary is bound to expand." Robert McClory foresaw that Washington's command of words would become legendary as he routinely spun off multisyllable attention-getters such as "eschewed," "contretemps," "surcease," and "anathema," offered biblical allusions like "plagues of locusts," quoted Shakespeare, or paraphrased one-liners from what sounded like Bartlett's book of quotations. Famous for his colorful alliteration, such as "ministerial minions," he used such lofty metaphors that ghetto kids took to calling him "Harold Skytalkin'." Washington was a voracious reader who often dipped into the social sciences and tucked away words, phrases, and information that would serve him well. "You don't have to feed Washington any lines," said his media adviser. Washington's conversational range was phenomenal. He could address bankers in the staid language appropriate to that group in the late morning and in the afternoon engage in downhome banter with welfare recipients and street people. "Not only could he speak the king's English," said the mayor's pastor, Rev. B. Herbert Martin, but "Harold could fuss and cuss black folks' style. He knew every idiomatic expression." Rugged, macho-looking, and imposing, Washington could paint sharp word pictures that evoked both sympathy and defiance at the same time.[3]

Washington's use of the language was expansive and entertaining, sometimes funky, and almost always effective. On the campaign trail or in a fight with his real or imagined political enemies, his language took on the tone of an irate Southern preacher or an Old Testament prophet as he levied a writ of rhetorical fire and sword upon the blasphemers who crossed his path or were otherwise vexatious by disagreeing with him. No pussyfooter or pettifogger, the mayor spewed out barrels of wrath upon gainsayers and other rabble who carped at him and his administration. His style was not that of a deft fencer, who parries and thrusts his way forward, but of a broadswordsman, who wades in smiting the enemy hip and thigh. Like the angered preacher or prophet, Washington often seemed persuaded of his own righteousness in all things and of the perfidy, malice, and black-hearted skulduggery of the benighted few who opposed him. The mayor's expressions lived in a Manichean world of good and bad, black and white. His principal council opponent, Edward Vrdolyak, for example, was known in the inner circle as "the Prince of Darkness," "Darth Vader," or "Mr. V.D." Subtlety and the polite and measured debate of the drawing room or the academy were not part of the mayor's rough-and-tough political style.

It was in the tradition of "Big Bill" Thompson and of that talented backwoods demagogue Huey Long that Washington lashed out at those in his way. When vexed, Washington often burned with visible anger as he publicly excoriated and lambasted his political enemies with an ever-expanding lexicon of insults. He called former Mayor Richard J. Daley "a dictator," and argued that his son, State's Attorney Richard M. Daley, should be "hauled off to jail" for petitioning for a nonpartisan mayoralty election. When Congressman William Lipinski sided with the Daley petitioners, he earned the sobriquets "lunkhead," "noodlehead," and "slug." City elections commissioner Michael Lavelle, who stood in the way of Washington's takeover of the elections process, was branded by the mayor as "stupid," a "flunky," a "saboteur," and "a thief in the night." Opposing one of the largest property tax hikes in the city's history earned Alderman Bernard Stone the title of "stonehead." Archenemy Ed Vrdolyak was further labeled a "dodohead," "an unmitigated four-flushing hustler," "a treacherous rat," and his aide, Joseph

Novak, "a scurrilous geek." Vrdolyak's twin commander of the council opposition, Edward Burke, Harold socked with "draft dodger," "a twerp," "the pits," and "a pimple on an elephant's butt." Council newcomer Edwin Eisendrath came off in the Washington argot as a "little fart."[4]

The mayoral tongue-lashing even reached downstate and sometimes even out of state. President Ronald Reagan was a "slumlord," and, according to Mayor Washington, when Illinois Governor James R. Thompson was not playing "hocus, pocus, dominocus" with the voters, he was "a South Africanite . . . an aparthedite," a "no good," and "a disaster." In a somewhat sprightlier name-calling mood, Washington issued a mock apology on Chicago radio for calling Governor Thompson a "nincompoop," adding, "It's all right to call someone an S.O.B., but nincompoop is going too far." "When you were denounced by Harold," observed the governor in his funeral eulogy for the fallen mayor, "you were denounced."[5]

Sometimes the mayor even bit the hand that fed him, such as when he took after a group that had helped put him in office, the Black Independent Precinct Organization (BIPO), because it opposed his choice of a Hispanic female for city clerk. Tearing into BIPO on evening television, Washington ridiculed the group as "Flippo, Bippo, Dippo," implying that the last part characterized its state of mind. Council ally Dorothy Tillman, often an unguided black missile, was, by the mayor's lights, "abrasive," "crude," "too loud," and "a loser." When U.S. Congressman Daniel Rostenkowski endorsed Washington's mayoral opponent Thomas Hynes, Washington spat out, "Was he driving when he said that?" It was a snide reference to the solon's recent arrest on drunken driving charges. At the time he issued the public insult, the mayor was still dependent on the good will of Rostenkowski, chairman of the powerful U.S. House Ways and Means Committee, to exempt from new tax bonds two of Washington's proposed stadium projects. City Treasurer Cecil Partee, who had saved Washington from a political defeat early in his career, the mayor called "the biggest Uncle Tom on God's green earth."[6]

Press

Mayor Washington also lobbed a high-explosive vocabulary of invective on the press and media when he was unhappy with unflattering stories about his administration. He castigated them as "rats," "liars," and "a bunch of slugs," who were "arrogant," "abominable," "crazy," and "frenzied," and who wrote "slimy," "hysterical," and "scurrilous" copy and "single-handedly polarized the city" racially. Gossip columnists who reported on his honor were "slinky, funky rats who tell base lies." A trio of Chicago *Tribune* reporters who had written an incisive and probing profile of the mayor were caricatured as a bunch of "cottonheads" who should be taken out and "bull-whipped." Other local journalists drew such endearing appellations as the "culprit," the "fool," and the "ambushers." He labeled a Chicago television commentator the "lowest of the low" and the "bottom of the barrel." When CBS television's Ed Bradley tried to bring together Washington and his council nemesis Vrdolyak for a joint interview at the 1984 National Democratic Convention, the mayor lashed out at the black reporter: "You're one of the lowest possible individuals I've ever seen. You're an insult to common sense." It is clear from his many encounters that Washington expected more favorable treatment from the black press. Unfortunately, "if you challenge him," said black *Newsweek* writer Monroe Anderson, "he verbally beats up on you. Washington loves to beat up on the media. He's a master manipulator." In his first term in office Washington "had started more confrontations with the press than Richard J. Daley did in sixteen years," according to *Sun-Times* reporter and mayor watcher Tom Fitzpatrick.[7]

Mayoral Challengers

In 1987, Washington's contempt for his principal challenger, Jane Byrne, seemed not to have abated one whit since the 1983 inaugural. At that event the newly elected Washington, against the advice of saner heads, decided to verbally "kick the lady in the ass in public," in the words of one of his cabinet members, in front of the press, the clergy, and a television audience of millions of Chicagoans. Washington's inaugural was no love fest or healing ceremony, but a bitter denunciation of the vanquished in which he rubbed in their defeat and vowed to purge the earth of his political enemies. During his 1987 campaign exchanges with Jane Byrne, the mayor exuded a kind of political nastiness and resorted to regular *ad hominem*, calling his female opponent at various times "big mouth," "fuzzy," and "a prolific mother," even though Byrne had only one child. In an encounter over spending and taxes, Washington dismissed Byrne's criticism with "she's always had trouble with numbers." Or when Jane Byrne offered to debate Washington on a Spanish-language television station, the mayor balked and ridiculed her: "She can't use English; how does she expect to try Spanish?" The mayor had also tried to associate Byrne with Adolph Hitler, and when chided by the press for his demagoguery, Washington responded: "I said she reminds me of Hitler in reference to her use of the 'big lie.' I should have said Goebbels; she probably wouldn't know who Goebbels was. We wouldn't have an argument."[8] Washington also knew how to smear the enemy with guilt by association. He unloaded emotional blockbusters that flustered his opponents and then mockingly backed off when chided by the press.

So excessive and ferocious had Washington's rhetoric before black and special-interest ethnic audiences become by the end of the 1987 campaign that Operation CONDUCT, a group dedicated to keeping racial, ethnic, and religious slurs out of the campaign, censured him for his zealous effort to exploit anti-Semitism. Mayoral challenger Edward Vrdolyak had called upon Washington to repudiate Black Muslim leader Louis Farrakhan (who had said Jews had a "gutter religion" and Hitler was a "great" but wicked man), but the mayor refused. According to the mayor's press aide, Washington was "not in the business of denouncing people." Yet following that disclaimer, speaking before a Jewish audience, he let fly with a no-holds-barred denunciation of Vrdolyak as "sick and insane" and "an anti-Semite." For the unproved and reckless "anti-Semite" charge Washington earned another censure from Operation CONDUCT. (Vrdolyak would also earn a censure for a racial slur.)

The mayor's intemperate and heavy-handed assault on anyone who opposed him prompted even a dyed-in-the-wool partisan Washington newspaper called the *Reader* to cry out: "Lighten up, Harold. Anyone in his way he lets have it. Dan Rosty is a drunken driver. Mike Lavelle is 'dumb.' Ed Vrdolyak is an 'anti-Semite.' " During an earlier exchange, Mayor Washington had ridiculed Chicago Board of Election Commissioners spokesman Thomas Leach as "a man who lives up to his name." To which Leach riposted, "Unfortunately, the mayor is a man who doesn't live up to his."[9]

Did Washington's trenchant attacks on his political foes and the press serve any rational purpose, or were they, as many have suggested, merely letting off emotional steam and evening up past scores by honky bashing? According to onetime mayoral

Operation CONDUCT, a group brought into being by the Community Renewal Foundation and the American Jewish Committee, worked hard and successfully to curb racial, religious, and ethnic slurs in the 1987 mayoral campaign. (*American Jewish Committee*)

Alderman Edward R. Vrdolyak was a key opponent of Mayor Washington not only in "Council Wars" but also as a Solidarity party candidate for mayor in 1987.

Alderman Edward M. Burke, Vrdolyak's twin commander of the opposition "29 Bloc," which waged "Council Wars" against Mayor Washington.

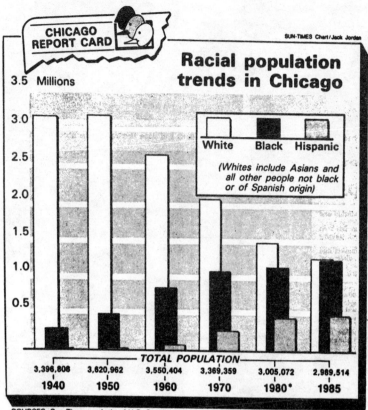

CHICAGO REPORT CARD

SUN-TIMES Chart/Jack Jordan

Racial population trends in Chicago

3.5 Millions

White Black Hispanic

(Whites include Asians and all other people not black or of Spanish origin)

TOTAL POPULATION					
3,396,808	3,620,962	3,550,404	3,369,359	3,005,072	2,989,514
1940	1950	1960	1970	1980*	1985

SOURCES: Sun-Times analysis of U.S. Census tracts for 1940-1960 figures. City of Chicago Dept. of Planning analysis of U.S. Census figures for 1970-1985 figures. *Asians represent 66,673 of the white population.

The great black migration from the South to Chicago stopped in about 1975, resulting in a near equilibrium between whites and blacks by 1985. Only the Hispanic community continues to grow in any appreciable numbers, suggesting that this group may hold the balance of power in Chicago's racial politics for the future.   *(Sun-Times chart, Jack Jordan)*

When it came to picking his park board, Mayor Washington chose (left to right) a City Hall loyalist, Jesse Madison; a professional feminist, Rebecca Sive; a black museum director, Margaret Burroughs; and a "limousine liberal" architect, Walter Netsch. (*Sun-Times*)

Washington greets the newest member of his team, Alderman Luis Gutierrez, as they celebrate the 26th Ward judge-ordered 1986 special election that gave Washington control of the Chicago City Council. (*Sun-Times*)

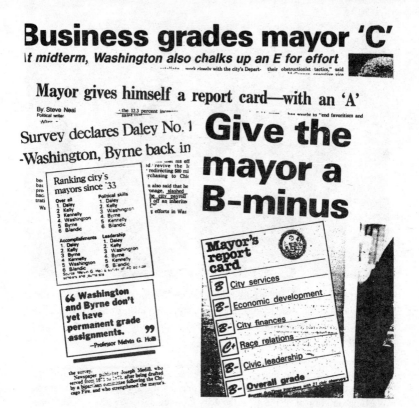

Business grades mayor 'C'

At midterm, Washington also chalks up an E for effort

Mayor gives himself a report card—with an 'A'

By Steve Neal
Political writer

Survey declares Daley No. 1 -Washington, Byrne back in

Give the mayor a B-minus

Ranking city's mayors since '33

Over all	Political skills
1. Daley	1. Daley
2. Kelly	2. Kelly
3. Kennelly	3. Washington
4. Washington	4. Byrne
5. Byrne	5. Kennelly
6. Bilandic	6. Bilandic

Accomplishments	Leadership
1. Daley	1. Daley
2. Kelly	2. Kelly
3. Byrne	3. Washington
4. Kennelly	4. Byrne
5. Washington	5. Kennelly
6. Bilandic	6. Bilandic

Source: Melvin G. Holli, a survey of 40 political scholars and journalists

66 Washington and Byrne don't yet have permanent grade assignments. 99
—Professor Melvin G. Holli

Mayor's report card

B	City services	
B-	Economic development	
B-	City finances	
C+	Race relations	
B-	Civic leadership	
B-	Overall grade	

Source: Survey of business executives with 21 civic observers

Mayor Washington's first year "report card," issued by civic leaders, business leaders, writers, academics, and political consultants, was a disappointing overall average grade of "B-minus." The mayor disagreed, giving himself an "A."

(HOLIME)

Washington answers questions from the press with his key political advisor and alter ego, Jacky Grimshaw, at his side. Grimshaw was considered by many to be the most politically savvy woman in Chicago politics. *(Sun-Times)*

Public opinion polls continued to pick up the mayor's poor job rating for most of his first term, 1983–1987. *(HOLIME)*

Washington, who once referred to himself as "a sepia Daley," loved his job as much as his illustrious predecessor had. "He salivates when he gets up in the morning," a close friend said, "looking for something political to do." Washington predicted that he would, like Daley, serve twenty years in that office.

(Sun-Times)

With State Senator Howard Carroll (right), Washington discusses a rash of anti-Semitic vandalism in the Rogers Park Jewish community. The liberal Jewish vote was crucial to Washington victories. *(Sun-Times)*

Press Secretary Alton Miller, amid a host of Washington allies and friends, sadly announces the death of Harold Washington at 1:30 P.M. on Wednesday, November 25, 1987. *(Sun-Times)*

Crowds gather quickly as news spreads throughout the city that Washington has been rushed to the emergency room of Northwestern Hospital.

(Sun-Times)

Washington's solemn funeral procession wends its way to the church for the final requiem service.   (*Sun-Times*)

Black Chicagoans, young and old, were deeply touched by the death of Chicago's first black mayor.   (*Sun-Times*)

Jesse Jackson, in a somber mood, eulogizes the dead mayor as Chicago's Cardinal Bernardin and Illinois Governor James Thompson listen.   (*Sun-Times*)

The deceased mayor lies in state at City Hall as tearful thousands pass to pay their last respects. Washington's death on the day before Thanksgiving cast a pall of gloom over Chicago's holiday weekend. *(Sun-Times)*

VIP mourners Detroit Mayor Coleman Young (top left), New York Mayor Edward Koch (center, overcome with grief), and New York Congressman Charles Rangel (lower right) at Washington's funeral service. *(Sun-Times)*

Both of Illinois's U.S. senators, Alan Dixon and Paul Simon, along with Congressmen Sidney Yates and Gus Savage (left to right), follow the program during the highly emotional funeral service. So many Chicago and out-of-town dignitaries attended the service that local admirers of the mayor were unable to get into the church. *(Sun-Times)*

Following Washington's burial, a huge public memorial service was held at the University of Illinois at Chicago's Pavilion. Unfortunately, it was turned into a political pep rally by many of the speakers, who hoped to name the next mayor. *(Sun-Times)*

Chicago's black political leaders hold hands as they mourn the fallen chief. Once Washington was buried, many of these same mourners would engage in a ferocious fight for succession to the mayor's chair. *(Sun-Times)*

A less than confident Alderman Eugene Sawyer seeks support of his council colleagues to be named acting mayor. Sawyer was picked to be acting mayor by a biracial council at 4 A.M., December 2, 1987, after a stormy night of mob scenes, shouting, and protests reminiscent of banana-republic politics.

(Sun-Times)

A weary and embattled acting mayor, Eugene Sawyer, flanked by corporation counsel Judson Miner, a former political opponent in the succession battle, takes charge of the Chicago City Council. *(Sun-Times)*

advisor Don Rose, "It's popular in the black community to beat up on the press," and so it won voting points with the mayor's core constituency. One of the mayor's allies explained that Washington "thinks the name-calling is useful to stir up the troops. It's 'us' against 'them'—black people against the press." Although the mayor's press secretary vehemently denied that, calling it a "damnable lie," nonetheless the "stir-up-the-troops" view was widely accepted as a rational explanation for the mayor's sometimes irrational-sounding attacks on foe and friend alike. There may have been another purpose served by Washington's attacks on the press: City Hall insiders claimed from time to time that the mayor had found the emotional panic button of a Chicago television newsman and that by dropping a few choice accusations of racism, he could send the reporter into a disorienting tizzy, which could sometimes squelch an unfavorable story. Not only was the mayor a "master manipulator," as Monroe Anderson suggested, but as Chicago journalist Steve Daley put it, the mayor's repeated charges that the media were unfair and "racist" had taken some of the sting out of their reporting and even "treed the press."[10]

Bloopers

Voluble and garrulous, Washington loved to talk almost as much as Hubert Humphrey did, but he lacked Hubert's gentle, small-town charm. Washington so delighted in using the language that he often crammed fifty-dollar words into two-dollar spaces. His gift of gab and tendency to shoot from the lip caused some lighter moments and bloopers. The mayor could also have his sillier spells and display an inordinate lack of perspective at times, as he did when his hand-picked candidate, Luis Gutierrez, won a 26th Ward run-off election for the city council in the spring of 1986. The story was buried somewhere in the innards of the newspapers because the Russian nuclear power plant disaster pushed most local stories off the front pages. The near meltdown was spewing volumes of dangerous radiation into the atmosphere and potentially endangering millions of lives in Western Europe and Scandinavia. In addition, the radiation clouds were expected to be over the United States within a week. No matter to Harold. He was outraged because his hand-picked Hispanic candidate's aldermanic victory had not made the front pages as the number-one news story of the day. To use one of his own favorite words regarding him, the mayor's perspective certainly appeared "myopic." But then, no one has claimed that Chicago politics breeds internationalists.

Because his entire career had been spent in the black community, the mayor sometimes had difficulty synchronizing his language to citywide multiethnic and multiracial audiences. The most egregious example was his 1983 campaign cry "It's our turn now," which played poorly among white ethnics. His poor knowledge of white ethnics extended to Hispanics, all of whom he lumped into the same category. He told an audience of Cuban businessmen that he was four-square behind affirmative action. It had apparently never occurred to him that Cubans, who are among the most prosperous, successful, and entrepreneurial of any immigrant group that has ever come to America (with median family incomes of $30,000 annually in Cook County) and are successful emigrés from communism and governmental meddling, would somehow not be attracted to his support of government-coerced quota hiring and affirmative action. On another occasion in 1983, he misfired when he told a Hispanic audience, "We're all niggers." Latinos "reacted negatively," according to his pollster Paul Maslin, and the mayor's racial characterization flopped badly. What Washington had meant to say was that blacks and Mexicans shared a common low socioeconomic status and thus should be brothers in arms politically; but his shorthand reference to a common "nigger" standing came off badly with that audience, for many of whom English was a second language.[11]

During a struggle with the U.S. Department of Housing and Urban Development over control of the Chicago Housing Authority, Washington insisted, "I am not a lump-lump . . . I am not going to sit there and let HUD or mud or anybody take over the CHA." Reporters and editors scurried to their dictionaries of black usages, vernacular language, and archaisms, but to no avail. It was simply a Washington coinage, and he was dubbed "Mayor Lump-Lump" for a few days thereafter. In a mayoral debate in 1987 the mayor used what a Chicago columnist thought was a strange new word, "poopery," in the phrase "a poopery of tax proposals." Washington's mispronunciation of the word "potpourri" as "poopery" brought down a rain of ridicule about gay bar washrooms, outhouses, and kitty litter boxes by columnist Mike Royko. "Potpourri" was dropped from the official campaign vocabular.[12]

But the mayor could be philosophical about his misses and hits, for he generally had more of the latter. One should also recognize that the mayor enjoyed the political fray; his face was often wreathed with smiles when he hurled a verbal missile at his political enemies and saw them squirm. His expressive face equally recorded the pain when a foe hit home with a harpoon of criticism. Pugnacious by nature, he loved to mix it up. "If I didn't have a political fight," Washington told WLS-TV, "I would have to go out and pick one." His carefully chosen metaphors from military combat and prize fighting underscored his combative nature. Among the city's contemporary mayors, Washington had broken a tradition. He was without peer as a master of bombast in the "smash-and-grab" style of politics.[13]

Campaign Conduct 1987

Campaign '87 witnessed a radical departure from Chicago's political past with the first-time entry of a new watchdog group to police the city's excessive and intemperate racial politicking. On the eve of the mayoral primary election in February, there was widespread fear that the city would repeat what the national press called in 1983 "Chicago's Ugly Racial Election." That campaign had unleased an overload of emotional appeals, racial code words, and ethnic slurs. In addition to "It's our turn now," there were "It's a racial thing, don't kid yourself " and "Ditch the bitch and vote for Rich" as well as "Epton! Epton! He's our man. We don't want no Af-ri-can!" Fears ran high for 1987. William Sampson, *Sun-Times* columnist and Northwestern University savant on racial matters, foresaw even more racial sloganeering when he said that Edward Vrdolyak's candidacy "has made Washington into the great black hope.... He will be saying, 'Vote for me because I'm black and whites are beating up on me.' " A Chicago *Defender* writer issued a frantic appeal: "Wake up, black Chicago! Listen to their war cries! Circle the wagons and brace yourself for the desperate all-out 'suicidal charge' of white ethnic Chicago in their last-ditch battle for City Hall." It went on to say, "Whites are dangerously desperate." Equally ominous were the words of Philip M. Hauser, eminent population expert and University of Chicago professor, who predicted "an even more intense election than the last one, with the possibility of violence...."[14] Yet experts can be wrong; their basis for prediction is what has happened in the past, but they don't know what is going to take place in the future.

Actually, the best predictor of the 1987 campaign was a person whom Washington called a "scurrilous little geek." Joe Novak came closer than anyone to describing in advance the character of the campaign. In a memorandum to his boss, Ed Vrdolyak, Novak predicted that racial issues would play less of a role in 1987 because "white fear is down" and "black enthusiasm has been tempered."[15] Novak had sensed early in mid-November 1986 that the upcoming campaign would not be a replay of the last mayoral election, with its fiery and hysterical code words and racial rhetoric.

Despite the heated exchanges and political acrimony discussed in the first section, the primary and general campaigns of 1987 were moderately quiet, almost civil in tone compared to the 1983 affair. Racial, ethnic, and religious slurs fell to a tolerable low. The civility of campaign '87 was a delightful relief. Helping to usher in the new civility was a group called CONDUCT, an acronym for Committee on Decent Unbiased Campaign Tactics. Co-founded by John McDermott, a former director of the Christian group Community Renewal Foundation, and the American Jewish Committee, it aimed to discourage the use of racial, ethnic, religious, and gender slurs and asked all candidates to pledge themselves to a "Code of Fair Practice." The press greeted the fledgling group with skepticism, calling the members "moonbeams" and sniffingly complaining about "word police" trying to "control the verbal crime rate." Yet CONDUCT soon proved its worth by calling fouls on both sides and dampening the smouldering appeals to race that lay just beneath the surface on both sides.

The most egregious racial blast in the campaign (as discussed in Chapter Four) came from Appellate Court Judge R. Eugene Pincham, who threatened blacks by saying that "any man south of Madison Street who casts a vote in the February 24 election, who doesn't cast a vote for Harold Washington, ought to be hung." CONDUCT issued a stinging censure of Pincham for his "demagogic appeals" and the "extreme and inflammatory" remarks that were "apparently calculated to intimidate black voters." Unhappy with the rebuke, Jesse Jackson threatened to found an all-black word police, but the idea never got off the ground. CONDUCT also censured or reprimanded three of the mayoral candidates: Jane Byrne was called on the carpet for a racially offensive remark about "Soul Coast to Gold Coast" and for a divisive television ad that paraphrased the infamous

Pincham remark; Candidate Vrdolyak was cuffed on the ear for an "unethical, irresponsible, and divisive" radio ad; and Harold Washington was rapped on the knuckles for his "anti-Semite" accusation. Ironically CONDUCT, which had been set up by liberal types to fight against 1983 campaign-style white racism, spent more effort in 1987 denouncing black racism. It issued thirteen reprimands involving charges rising directly from the mayoral campaign: nine fell on the Washington group, two on Jane Byrne, and two on the Vrdolyak camp. Republican mayoral candidate Donald Haider and Chicago First party's Thomas Hynes got a clean bill of health.[16]

Racial, ethnic, religious, and gender slurring dropped to a new low. John McDermott modestly said, "We're not saying this was solely due to CONDUCT," but added that they exerted a "kind of healthy pressure on the candidates that I think pushed them in the right direction." Though no exact statistical comparison to 1983 is possible, the general impression by city watchers and political junkies is that Chicago had a much calmer and quieter campaign in 1987. In fact, it was so quiet that Chicago *Tribune* columnist Mike Royko, in the closing weeks of the campaign, lamented "the lack of entertainment value in this election," and another major columnist, *Sun-Times* writer Basil Talbott, Jr. grumbled about the lack of "slur, insult, or bigoted remark" and the general drop in the city's verbal voltage rate.[17] With the help of CONDUCT, Chicago has passed an emotional and political watershed, and Campaign '87 seemed to signal the passing of another Chicago political tradition—the open and unabashed use of racial, ethnic, and religious slurs by political campaigners.

The Washington Administration and Labor

Another Chicago tradition that fell by the wayside after Daley's death was the intimate City Hall-Big Labor link that enabled labor to be one of the obvious and prominent clout players in Chicago politics. Washington helped end that cozy relationship of the Daley years, but he was aided and abetted by a real tradition smasher, Jane Byrne, and by a deindustrialization that was destroying factories and some of the power that unions drew from them.

The organized labor-City Hall relationship began back in the proletarian 1930s, but only after a bloody baptism in the Republic Steel strike of 1937, when Democratic Mayor Edward Kelly's police shot and beat up strikers in what is known as the infamous "Memorial Day Massacre." Inauspicious as that beginning was, Mayor Kelly and the city Democrats patched up their differences with labor and began what became almost a half-century honeymoon.[18] Organized labor got along well with party bosses such as Jacob Arvey, and later the reform mayor Martin H. Kennelly, and finally – famously – with an up-and-coming politician named Richard J. Daley. Mayor Daley brought organized labor into such an intimate working relationship with City Hall that it soon graduated to the upper case, "Big Labor." The American Federation of Labor and its skilled trades and crafts unions, often called the "aristocrats" of labor, received red carpet treatment from Daley, himself the son of a sheetmetal worker and union member.

Mayor Daley named his boyhood pal William Lee, then president of the Chicago Federation of Labor, chairman of the patronage-rich Chicago Park District. Others, such as Flat Janitors' Union leader William McFetridge, served on numerous commissions, where they protected organized labor's interests and acted as the eyes and ears of Daley, to whom they reported. Organized labor received from Daley what it wanted: no police strikebreaking as in 1937; a high "prevailing" wage for skilled craftsmen who worked for the city, along with fringe benefits and holidays denied their brothers in the private sector; no hostile legislation from the city council; and a downtown building boom set in motion by Daley which provided thousands of jobs for skilled craftsmen. Daley received in return no strikes, slow or no organizing of City Hall white-collar workers, and labor peace. The trust between Mayor Daley and Big Labor was symbolized by the phrase "handshake agreements," which was used to describe the unusually amicable relationship between the two.

Jane Byrne upset the applecart. Driven by cash-poor and high-inflation hard times, partly from necessity and partly by choice, Mayor Byrne threw out the "handshake agreements" and took on three costly public employee strikes. In December of her first year (1979) Byrne took on the transit workers, who were halting Loop-bound Christmas shoppers; in January it was the teachers' union that went out on strike; and in February the city's firemen, who had never struck before, walked out to gain the collective bargaining rights promised them by candidate Byrne in the campaign. She was running on a strike-a-month schedule. The firemen's strike was especially nasty and bitter: the mayor called in strikebreakers, some of whom were black, and the strikers calling Byrne a "union buster" and "Attila the Hen."[19] The union gravy train was sidetracked, the "handshake agreements" broken off, and the honeymoon with labor was over.

As a legislator, Harold Washington was considered a "friend" of labor—but spelled with a lower case "l" and not necessarily of the "aristocrats" of labor, the AFL craft unions with whom he was often at loggerheads over racial quotas. Mayor Washington faced a different labor situation from that of his predecessors because deindustrialization had rumbled through his city destroying factories and jobs. The rustbelt phenomenon had caused Chicago to lose factories at the rate of 100 to 200 per year for the past decade and a half—and more than 250,000 jobs. The blight did not stop during the Washington administration, when Chicago lost several hundred more plants.[20] In addition, two recessions, the persistence of medium to high levels of unemployment, and Mayor Byrne's humbling of the formerly proud firemen's union had diminished union expectations and taken some of the sting out of the threat of public employee strikes. Union chiefs had also become much more conscious of the fiscal limits of the city treasury. Thus, after 1983, Mayor Washington was dealing with downsized expectations by the unions and by everyone else, with the possible exception of his black movement supporters.

During his first term Mayor Washington talked openly about a number of legislative proposals that organized labor, and especially the craft unions, considered negatives: permitting modular prebuilt homes in place of expensive "stick-built" homes in the city; permitting the use of plastic plumbing in place of copper and lead, which would save rehabbers and citizens money but would cost plumbers jobs; permitting the use of plastic conduits for electrical work; and finally the administration stood behind jacking up the racial and minority quotas at Washburne Trade School to an astonishing three-fourths of all new enrollees. These were the negatives that had old-time labor leaders fuming.[21]

On the positive side, Washington promised collective bargaining and delivered on his promise, although it took a year and a half to hammer out agreements that extended the bargaining net over some 20,000 employees hitherto not covered. Professional bargaining between union representatives and equally hard-nosed city negotiators had replaced the old-boy network of handshakes and winks. Gone were the high-visibility appointments of labor big shots to agencies such as the Park Board. When it came time to choose his "parkers," Washington selected a wealthy "limousine liberal" architect, a professional feminist, and an Afro-American museum director; and he installed a black City Hall loyalist as his chief executive of the parks.

Other commissions and boards showed a similar conspicuous absence of big-labor names in big places. Jerry Harris, a keen student of labor history, went through the files of sixty city commissions and some 641 names of Washington appointees during the first two years of the administration and came up with a measly 31 appointments from organized labor, or fewer than 5 percent. And few were on mainstream boards. When asked about the matter in December 1987, Chicago Federation of Labor President Robert Healey could only point to one high-visibility job held by a labor representative. Asked about labor's low profile in the Washington administration, labor leader Edward Sadlowski, an industrial union leader known for his progressive and labor-left leanings, admitted to sometimes "being pissed off with Harold" over the mayor's failure to take action on matters close to the union. Yet on balance, Sadlowski expressed only mild disappointment, because the problems of the steelworkers were beyond the powers of any mayor to solve, and furthermore, Sadlowski added, having wrested collective bargaining for public employees was an important positive that outweighed many of the negatives.[22]

In summary, although Harold Washington did not establish personal, friendly, and cozy relations with Big Labor's top leaders and lavish on them publicly visible signs of their influence by appointments to boards and blue-ribbon commissions, as Daley had, he did expand collective bargaining rights to public employees as no other mayor had in the past. Unlike Byrne, he did not engage in strikebreaking nor did he oppose the formation of city workers' unions. On the other hand, after public unions were formed, Washington conducted hard-nosed bargaining with them in which he assumed the role of the employer; and in his last few months in office he took on a record-setting nineteen-day teachers' strike. Washington rejected Daley's "hands-on" policy of guiding the bargaining, personally entering into negotiations, and sometimes forcing a settlement. The new mayor followed a more laissez-faire approach; in fact, he was off on a Far East junket during the first strike, which Governor Thompson had to settle. But Washington took a stronger hand in the second strike: he remained in town and managed it by pulling strings from City Hall. The mayor's negotiators clearly prolonged the strike by trying to force on the teachers a contract that was not as good as the expiring one. The teachers' union won from the Washington school board only a small fraction of what it had hoped to achieve.

Thus Mayor Washington disappointed and pleased at the same time. His Mayor's Office of Employment Training, which retrained the unemployed for jobs, instructed trainees to expect fewer benefits and lower wages, while at the same time his professional collective bargainers were willing to bargain openly over how much less – or possibly more.[23] It is a mixed record when compared to the past: much better than Byrne's and not as good as Daley's – or perhaps better than Daley's, depending on one's point of view. Washington ended the folksy, highly personalized Big Labor-City Hall ties and modernized them with collective bargaining. At the same time, labor moved toward the back of the bus when it came to any public expression of its clout, and other more pressing causes, such as black empowerment, the women's movement, and minority representation, moved to the front. The public demotion of labor as a political force was a distinct break with Chicago's post-1937 political tradition.

Affirmative Action Patronage

But not all the mayoral traditions were junked in the post-Daley years; many have endured. The French have a saying, "plus ça change, plus c'est la meme chose" (meaning "the more things change, the more they are the same"). We think that has been the case with mayoral patronage, which is the ability of the mayor to reward his friends, punish his enemies, and put people loyal to him in positions of power. Despite the fact that civil service laws have been in effect for all of this century, patronage has never completely died in Chicago, as shown by the Kelly-Nash and Daley political machines. Although the same civil service laws and the more recent antipatronage court rulings weakened the new Mayor Washington's free hand in putting his own people in charge of City Hall, on the other hand, the first black mayor was strengthened by a new phenomenon, what we call in this book "affirmative action patronage."

Once in office, Mayor Washington delighted in performing repeatedly for newsmen and television audiences a reform skit that went something like this: He would look squarely at the camera and belt out: "Patronage is dead, dead, dead! I walked around its grave." Then in a squeaky falsetto voice the mayor would cry out: "Patronage, where are you? Patronage didn't answer. Do you know why patronage didn't answer? Because patronage is dead, dead, dead!"[24] Was patronage dead in Washington's first administration, or was it merely slumbering? Could Washington use the new "reform" programs to build up a body of stalwarts in the system who would function in something like the way old machine hacks did for Daley? We submit that this was not only theoretically possible but became part of regular practice after Washington took office in 1983 – albeit in the name of reform.

Although the Shakman decrees, which forbid wholesale firing and hiring for political reasons in Chicago, and the civil service system somewhat restricted the mayor's ability to put his people in place, the body of decrees, guidelines, and legislation that we call loosely "affirmative action" worked in the mayor's favor in building a loyal following, inside and outside the government. To begin with, civil service guidelines leave city administrators with a good deal of leeway in hiring and can be bent rather easily to the will of a strong executive. Firing those under civil service is more difficult, though not impossible. A position paper entitled "Patronage and Political Dismissals" was issued under the name of the mayor's chief of staff and city corporation counsel, James D. Montgomery, and prepared for presentation to the National Institute of Municipal Officers in October 1984. Although Montgomery denied being its author, this mayor's inner-office paper offered public administrators a how-to short course on political firing, a strategy on how to get around the civil service and court bans. For example, the paper said: "The public employer should never admit to discharging an employee solely for his or her political beliefs and should advise supervisors to keep quiet." Furthermore, if the public administrator was caught red-handed, the "Montgomery paper" counseled that he "should try to prove that the employee, who was discharged for his political beliefs, was a policy maker,"[25] because policy makers were not covered by civil service protection. Clearly, the mayor's top staff had put some thought into getting around civil service reform.

Affirmative action hiring, the use of quotas in promotions, contract set-asides, and preferential treatment of blacks and minorities, we suggest, enabled the mayor to reward his friends and punish his enemies in something akin to machine style. Affirmative action patronage worked like this: As the 1983 and 1987 mayoral election returns showed, about 85 percent of whites voted against Harold Washington and about 98 percent of blacks voted for him. Add the fact that the overwhelming recipients of administrative preferences, including affirmative action, quota promotions, and contract set-asides, were blacks. This translates into a situation where Washington could reward his friends and punish his enemies when he followed the body of decrees, court actions, and federal, city, and state guidelines loosely called affirmative action.

Harold Washington, in pursuing and pushing such policies, was behaving like an intelligent Bayesian (after Sir Thomas Bayes, the father of statistics); for he was obtaining what is very often complex information at a very low cost.[26] By merely knowing the race of the voter or seeker of a city job or a contract, Washington could be 98 percent certain that he had rewarded a "friend" and punished an "enemy" by giving preferential consideration to blacks over whites. As the election returns show, when he awarded a job or a contract to any black registered voter, he was 98 to 99 percent sure of rewarding a friend; conversely, when a qualified white was bypassed in a promotion procedure, or a white contractor or vendor was dropped from city business, the mayor was about 85 percent sure of punishing a political enemy—and abiding by the letter of the law at the same time. That is the political equivalence of alchemy in that it turns base metals into gold, or, at the very least the best thing since sliced bread for the black politico.

Thus, although the intent of affirmative action and its train of protections, preferences, and racial incentives may be called "reform," the effect could be very different. It is eminently clear that a mayor who is so inclined could use the system to punish his political enemies and reward his political friends by turning reform into redistributionism. This is more than simply an elegant political construct or a theoretical possibility; it is also an operational fact. As we have shown in Chapter Six, Washington gave nearly two-thirds of all the newly awarded top jobs in 1985 (officials and administrators) to blacks and only 24 percent to whites. In city contracts and purchases (see Chapter Six) Mayor Washington set aside 25 percent of all business exclusively for blacks and minorities and 5 percent for women; zealous application of such quotas had pushed that figure to nearly 35 percent by December 1986. Affirmative action was thereby turned into a friend of the mayor in power.

Washington had resourcefully turned the lemon of reform into the lemonade of "patronage," though he certainly never called it that. In unguarded moments, however, the mayor could be quite frank in equating affirmative action with patronage, as he was in November 1985, when he said: "It stuns me when I hear my Irish friends talk against affirmative action. How'd you get all those Irish firemen and Irish policemen? That was affirmative action." [27] Given a long tenure of twenty years, which Washington predicted he would serve, and the cumulative effect of affirmative action patronage applied year in and year out, it seems likely that a Harold Washington or another black mayor could install in power the same kind of body of stalwarts and loyalist hacks that Mayor Kelly did in his fourteen years and Mayor Daley in his twenty-one years in office. Affirmative action patronage may be the only new wrinkle or political innovation added to urban politics since Daley's demise. And thus the more things change, the more they are the same: rewarding your friends and punishing your enemies, the spoils system, endures now and is likely to endure in the future as a Chicago political tradition.

Corruption

Also enduring as a Chicago political tradition is municipal and City Hall corruption (discussed more fully in Chapter Two). To recapitulate briefly, like the Mayor Daley scandals of 1972-74, the "Operation Incubator" investigation of 1986-87 netted four of Mayor Washington's council supporters, the head of his revenue department, and an assistant for soliciting and taking bribes or other alleged misdeeds. As in the Daley case, Mayor Washington was pronounced innocent by the prosecutor of having any direct hand in the payoffs. Graft in politics seems to be especially resistant to these periodic cleanups, and it may be that no mayor can fully control it. As Republican candidate Donald Haider said repeatedly in the 1987 campaign: "Corruption in Chicago is endemic, and the job of the mayor is to make sure it doesn't become epidemic." [28]

Mayor Washington survived the widespread public exposure of administrative disarray, sloppy management, and mayoral inattentiveness, just as Mayor Daley had earlier survived the charge of public dereliction. In fact, during the very height of the storm over public corruption, in the spring of 1986, Washington helped carry the council special election for his allies and went on to comfortably win re-election in 1987. Daley, after his scandal did likewise, winning in 1975 the biggest re-election margin of his career. Corruption endured through the Washington years as a Chicago political tradition.

Mayoral Succession

Washington's death illustrated another page from the past in that, like Daley, he had made no provision for a successor. No ambitious understudy or political lieutenant was ready in the wings to take over, appointed and anointed by the chief to carry on. Both Daley and Washington were solo performers who towered above their followers like field marshals in an army of buck privates. Even at the end of his first term, Washington was openly boasting that he would be mayor for another twenty years, which would have enabled him to surpass his historic rival Daley, who served twenty-one. Neither gave any thought to a successor. The lack of forethought resulted in both cases in an interregnum, followed by a fierce battle for succession with plots, counterplots, bitter recriminations, and abortive coups in the grand tradition of banana republic politics. And in both cases, a less-than-consensus caretaker would be permitted to warm the throne while the cabalists vowed to pick the real mayor of Chicago at the next regular election. History may not repeat itself, as historians say, but in Chicago it certainly produces similar and analogous events.

Dead-end Job

In all of Chicago's mayoral history, from the beginning in 1837 to 1987, the office of mayor has never produced a U.S. president, a vice-president, a cabinet member, a U.S. ambassador, a Supreme Court justice, or even a U.S. senator. For most mayors it has been a terminal office, and for the four who died in office it was literally a "dead-end" job: two were assassinated, Carter Harrison and Anton J. Cermak, and two died of natural causes, Richard J. Daley and Harold Washington. Of the others, only one escaped the blight on upward mobility that plagues the office: Democratic mayor Edward J. Dunne (1905-06), because of a split in the Republican vote of 1912, climbed to the Illinois governor's chair. Harold Washington, like the vast majority of

Chicago mayors, would reach the political acme and the end of his career of upward striving in the office of mayor, confirming a long Chicago political tradition.

A Watershed in Chicago's History

Now that Mayor Harold Washington has passed from the political scene, we are beginning to see him in a clearer historical perspective. In the big picture, Washington's mayoralty was part of a historic watershed between 1979 and 1987, in which the city's political life was transformed as never before by five important changes. Washington was one of the primary beneficiaries and secondary causes of the flood tide of change in Chicago politics.

The first change is rather obvious but nonetheless significant: there was a switch in both gender and race at the pinnacle of Chicago's political system, the mayoralty. In 1979 Chicago elected its first female mayor, which made possible the election in 1983 of the city's first black mayor. One historic event flowed from another; as black city watcher Dempsey Travis so aptly observed at the time, "If a white woman, why not a black man?"[29] Byrne's election broke a 150-year Chicago tradition of electing mostly Anglo-Celtic white males to office.

The second significant change was the dissolution of partisan loyalties by Chicago voters. In the 1983 February mayoral primary, black voters overwhelmingly ignored the advice of the Democratic party and its chairman and voted for an outsider and a maverick, Harold Washington. In the general election that followed in April, white voters overwhelmingly ignored the advice of the Democratic party and voted for a maverick and an outsider, Republican Bernard Epton. Thus, as the late Milton Rakove pointed out, race has not only replaced ethnicity but also party loyalty, for voters identify less as Democrats and Republicans and more as blacks and whites.[30] Traditional ethnic and New Deal Democratic loyalty was on its last legs in Chicago.

The third point of interest is that Harold Washington ran and won on what many perceived to be an avowedly reformist platform. That in itself is not unprecedented, but one would have to go back to 1947 to find a card-carrying, blue-ribbon reformer running and winning under a reformist banner—in that year Martin Kennelly. Harold Washington's reform was not, however, the classic good government, civic uplift brand of reform that seeks efficiency, honesty, merit selection, low taxes, and the virtuous polity of chaste republican values. The heart of Washington's reform was really redistributionist. It sought to reallocate benefits, jobs, and contracts from one group to another—from the "haves" to the "have-nots." Its concerns about efficiency and low cost were minimal, as many insiders and the city's business behavior attest. Its primary goal, under the name of "fairness," was to redistribute the spoils of power to the "have-nots," who also happened to be its strongest supporters.

The fourth change is that the Chicago City Council has been transformed from a group of rubber-stamp robots of the Daley era into a deliberate and sometimes fractious assembly in the new era. In the best traditions of free assemblies, the council not only advanced its own programs but often debated, argued, and rejected the mayor's programs. The council, in short, behaved as its charter intended it to behave in a strong-council, weak-mayor government. Many Chicagoans mistakenly thought Chicago had weak-council, strong-mayor formulation of government because of the clout exercised by Mayor Daley in his time. The charter-intended condition prevailed for more than three and a half years of Washington's first term and changed only during the latter part of 1986, when a court redistricted the council, giving the mayor's faction twenty-five of the fifty seats and the mayor as presiding officer a tie-breaking twenty-sixth vote. The mayor's newly gained majority was a fragile one that lasted only about seventeen months. Compounding the problem of city governance is the fact that the Chicago delegation in the Illinois legislature was no longer united; it was divided into pro- and anti-Washington factions, and was the weakest Chicago delegation in Springfield that veterans could ever recall.

The fifth change is demographic and seismic in that it portends an uncertain and different future for Chicago. During the 1950s and 1960s, Chicago's black population increased by 200,000 to 300,000 newcomers per decade. In the 1970s, mass migration from the South stopped. The black population during the decennial period 1970 to 1980 increased by only 95,000, which is an average of 9,500 per year and, viewed over a population base of one million, can probably be accounted for mainly by natural population increase. Thus, as a historical convenience, we can say that the Southern black migration stopped in 1975. The result by the mid-1980s showed that Chicago was about 41 percent black, 42 percent white, and about 16 percent Hispanic, with the residue being other newcomers, including

Southeast Asians. The political implications of this stalled black migration and slow incremental increase suggest a possible political stalemate for Chicago into the foreseeable future, unless either blacks or whites can massively swing the Hispanic vote. But the "Hispanic balance wheel" hypothesis also has problems for Hispanics—for nationalistic and socioeconomic reasons. As their past voting behavior shows, Hispanics are a politically divided people, sometimes sharing only a common parent language. Furthermore, many are newcomers and thus below the level of local political consciousness, and large numbers are illegals not enfranchised to vote. Thus the "Hispanic balance wheel" theory of Chicago politics is problematic at best.

We have seen five significant changes that began in 1979, when Jane Byrne, a political lone wolf and an outsider, with the help of a snowstorm, knocked over the clout-rich Democratic machine and won the primary and then the general election. Her victory broke a kind of logjam of history (dammed up by twenty-one years of the Daley regime); after it followed a torrent, a veritable flood tide, of changes that forced many of the departures that we have canvassed. Again, it is worth emphasizing that Harold Washington *benefited* from these changes and then *contributed* some of his own. As a secondary cause, Washington helped accelerate the flow of change to an even faster pace. In addition to being symbolically and materially important to black people, Washington probably damaged the political machine irreparably: it is unlikely that any political organization will ever put a powerful Daley-style leader in office again. Harold Washington's election and first term closed a chapter in Chicago's history of powerful, clout-rich mayors running the city and thus ended another Chicago political tradition.

CHAPTER EIGHT

The Measure of the Man

MAYOR HAROLD WASHINGTON's first year in office, beginning in May 1983, was inauspicious by any historic measure of Chicago's mayors. No mayor in recent memory had such a bad start. Not Edward Kelly, Martin Kennelly, Richard Daley, or Michael Bilandic, or even Jane Byrne—none careened and skidded as badly off the political course as did Washington in the early months of his first term. Losing control of the council at the very first meeting, Washington gaveled the meeting to a close and stormed out, only to have his archnemesis Edward Vrdolyak take over as presiding officer and reorganize the committee structure of the legislative body to his liking. Worse yet, six months later the courts confirmed Washington's loss and Vrdolyak's takeover of the city council. A future black mayor, Eugene Sawyer, was appointed president protem by Vrdolyak. Few big-city mayors stumbled as badly as Washington did at his political debut as presiding officer of the council.

Grading the Mayor's First Year

Thus 1983-84 was not a banner year for the Washington administration. Two major municipal credit rating agencies gave the city a vote of no confidence. In March 1984 Moody's Investors Service dropped Chicago from a credit-worthy "Aa" to a lower "Baal." The other agency, Standard and Poors, had demoted Chicago in the credit markets the previous fall because, as vice-president Richard Larkin said, there was a "lack of cooperation needed to solve some of the city's fiscal problems." He added, "We were right last September to lower you from A-minus to BBB-plus."¹ A poor credit reputation for Chicago was not a good thing, because cities always run on money they do not have and depend on borrowing to meet operating costs. When credit ratings drop, it costs the taxpayers additional millions and also puts a chill into private investors.

But it was from the political front that the major perception of instability derived. Washington was losing most of the battles in "Council Wars." Not since 1931 had a mayor not had control of the all-important finance committee. And then in his weakened condition, Washington foolishly took on his foes in three high-visibility political battles, which he also lost. Outside the council, key defeats "had eclipsed the glow of victory" and dulled Washington's "hero status" among blacks, noted David Axelrod. Not only had he failed to expand his political base much beyond the black community, but he backed aldermanic ally Danny Davis in a losing battle against Congresswoman Cardiss Collins, supported Alderman Lawrence Bloom in a losing fight in the Democratic primary against Rich Daley for state's attorney, and finally, after boasting that he would oust Edward Vrdolyak from the chairmanship of the county-city Democratic party, he failed again. In addition, the mayor, at a tempestuous council session, lost his cool and threatened to punch Alderman Vrdolyak in the mouth. To add insult to injury, Chicagoan Jesse Jackson, inspired by Washington's upset victory, was making a run for the Democratic presidential nomination in 1984 and in the process bypassing Harold as Mr. Black Politician of the Year.²

On the administrative and managerial side of the ledger, the Washington record was mixed but nonetheless encouraging. In the plus column, the mayor in the first month symbolized the new austerity by eschewing the use of the city's luxury limousine and taking a 20 percent salary cut. By trimming some of the fat out of city departments and leaving vacant positions unfilled, he balanced the budget, as required by law. In June the mayor pleased reformers by signing the Shakman decrees, which banned political hiring and firing. Washington also took the unprecedented step of mandating a freedom-of-information executive order that opened up city records to public inspection. Blacks and other minorities were also being reassured repeatedly that they had a mayor who would listen to them, and increasing numbers were appointed to important and not-so-important jobs in City Hall. In addition, the mayor diverted some additional city funds to the neighborhoods and promised that more would follow. One of the positive results was that for the first time in nearly two decades, the "man on the fifth floor" had not been besieged, picketed, and taunted regularly by angry black protesters and community groups.

Less auspicious for the future was the mayor's anti-Loop campaign rhetoric, which promised to take development money away from downtown and shift it to the neighborhoods. "Non-downtown developments are more important than central area ones," declared one of Washington's position papers. This "scared the daylights out of many of Chicago's business leaders," observed one of Chicago's top business writers, R.C. Longworth, adding that they were the very ones "whose dollars were needed if the city is to grow." In addition, during the first year a vital north Loop development project faltered when a major hotel investor pulled out; and (as mentioned in an earlier chapter) the city's long-awaited and proposed new public library floundered, barely treading water for a lack of plans and funds; the Chicago Theater, an ornate movie palace from a bygone era that was valued by preservationists, was threatened by the wrecker's ball; and the Byrne plan to turn Navy Pier into a retail-recreation spa was killed by "Council Wars." And the developer's dream, the proposed World's Fair for Chicago in 1992, barely stayed afloat, with the mayor offering no words of encouragement. "A lot of projects are either on hold or falling off the edge," said urban expert Louis Masotti.[3]

The first year produced some pluses, but a bumper crop of complaints. Chicagoans love to grade all forms of entertainment—from movies to politicians. Like the Roman masses, they can be both generous and cruel at the same time, throwing out garlands of praise or signaling thumbs down to call in the lions. The grading exercise at the end of Washington's first year was especially elaborate, even for Chicago. The two major newspapers, especially the Chicago *Sun-Times*, put much money and reporting effort into pulse-taking: they impaneled experts, talked with politicians, both friend and foe, interviewed community leaders, and ran polls. The results showed some hits and some misses on the Washington record, and much unfulfilled expectation. The politically disaffected white ethnic communities on the Northwest and Southwest sides were decidely not enthusiastic about Washington's first year. The chairman of the Northwest Federation asserted that Washington had ignored the concerns of white ethnics and sought "revenge because we didn't vote for him." His southwest-side counterpart, Jean Mayer, charged that Washington was the author of his own council miseries for having "conducted such a polarizing campaign in the primary" that had turned off white voters; and now he was "governing from a position of vindictiveness and spite." As for grading him, "on a scale of one to ten," Mayer said, "I would give Washington a zero."

The Chicago League of Women Voters' council watcher Elinor Elam was considerably more charitable: she gave the mayor a "B" and qualified it by saying, "Maybe he didn't quite live up to the expectations of everyone." Also giving him a "B" was one of Washington's white allies, Alderman Lawrence Bloom, who added: "I think I expected something different. Perhaps I was naive." Bloom also complained about the new mayor's "cautious and secretive" ways that left his council supporters in the dark. "By nature, he trusts very few people," Bloom told his southside constituents. "These character traits permeate his performance in office and confound politicians – supporters and opponents alike." Two other white Washington loyalists, Aldermen Martin Oberman and David Orr, voiced concern about the mayor's parochial vision of his limited mission, saying that Washington had "to reach out more to the needs and interests of every alderman that supports him." Joining the litany of criticism of the mayor's monochromatic vision of his mission was the Chicago *Tribune*. Its editor, who had endorsed Washington's election a year earlier, now faulted the mayor for not "reaching out to expand his constituency" beyond his black base and for having "blamed" his "policy failures" on Council Wars.[4]

Council Wars, of course, was the stalemate occasioned by twenty-nine mainly white ethnic aldermen who opposed the mayor's mostly black bloc of twenty-one. The opposition bloc had sufficient votes to pass its own measures but not enough to override the mayor. The mayor could veto the opposition bloc, but he lacked sufficient votes to pass his own program. The result was the kind of political trench warfare that prompted the *Wall Street Journal* to call Chicago "Beirut on the lake." "This fight has polarized the entire city," agreed the mayor's friend, black alderman Clifford Kelley. From the other side, bloc leader Edward Vrdolyak admitted that the political slugfest had subtracted from governance: "So it has been a year of politics rather than substance. It's been rhetoric rather than deeds." The lack of strategic planning was disturbing to both friend and foe, for, as Vrdolyak put it, he could find no evidence of "long-range planning from the mayor." One of the mayor's white friends, Alderman Martin Oberman, could do no better, and noted a "lack of cohesion." He said, "A pattern is missing from the administration," adding that a "more systematic effort should be made to bring about the reforms the mayor is committed to." The mayor, in defense of his administration, said it was difficult to turn things around in one year, but he promised an economic development plan and improved administration.[5]

Confirming the testimony of political activists were the public opinion polls. The absence of glowing tributes by either black or white leaders for Washington's first year was confirmed by scientifically conducted surveys of the public by Gallup Associates for the Chicago *Sun-Times* and WMAQ-TV. A telephone poll of 1,000 randomly selected Chicago voters revealed that Washington's standing had been slipping since his win of a year before: only 44 percent of the city's voters said that they would like to see Washington run for re-election, and 46 percent said that he should not. Among black voters who had supported Washington the previous year at the 98 percent level, there was a significant drop of more than 20 percentage points in his rating: only 75 percent said they would like to see Chicago's first black mayor run for re-election. Among whites who said they had voted for the mayor, there was a precipitous plummet in the numbers: only 50 percent of them wanted to see him run again. A second term was opposed by even more, 60 percent, of the upscale and liberal lakeside voters (without whose vote there would have been no first black mayor in 1983). The contention that Washington had failed to enlarge his constituency beyond his mostly black base was believed by 58 percent of whites, who said that Washington had not tried hard enough to win white support for his policies. Blacks disagreed; only 14 percent faulted the mayor for not reaching out.[6]

On the general question of his performance in the job as mayor, Washington's percentage grades were mixed, with many of the negatives following racial lines. But there was surprising dissatisfaction expressed by black voters on a specific part of the Washington record. Almost one-half of white Chicagoans and more than one-third of blacks thought that the city had deteriorated since Washington took office. A widely voiced criticism was that Washington had accomplished very little: 62 percent of white voters said that Washington does not "get things done"; conversely, 70 percent of blacks said he did. On a long list of specific issues of governance, whites uniformly gave Washington grades in the 60-70 percentage range. Blacks gave the mayor fairly high marks on these issues, but not all. For example, some 58 percent of blacks rated the mayor "fair" to "poor" for not improving conditions in the Chicago Housing Authority, and they were about equally divided over whether Washington had maintained a good business climate to keep jobs in Chicago. On the issue of whether the new mayor had opened up city jobs to blacks and minorities, only 59 percent agreed that he had, while 30 percent said flatly that he had not. Whites, on the other hand, still fearful of Washington's "It's our turn now" campaign rhetoric, agreed by 75 percent that Washington "had opened up city jobs to blacks and minorities."[7]

Was Washington a "reformer," as he had touted himself during the campaign? Had he delivered on his reforms and healed the racial divisions that the campaign had engendered? Two of three blacks believed that Washington was trying to reform city government, whereas two of three whites felt that Washington "cares more about strengthening his political power than he does about reform." On the issue of racial healing, an astonishingly low 7 percent of whites and only 11 percent of blacks thought the city under Washington was "less divided racially" than under his predecessor. Some 45 and 30 percent of white and black respondents respectively perceived a *more* racially divided city, whereas about half of both races perceived "no difference."

The polls showed that Washington's debut was not a blue-ribbon year for the new mayor, nor did he compile the kind of record that he would like to present to the voters three years later. They also showed that the mayor had not won over any new support and that some of his old liberal support was slipping and some of his black support was softening.[8]

Letter Grades

On April 29, 1984, the Chicago *Sun-Times* issued a more formal "Mayor's report card" with both annotated and letter grades drawn from twenty-one community leaders, experts knowledgeable in civic affairs, and "respected authorities in various aspects of urban affairs." The mayor earned an overall composite grade of "B-minus," which was arrived at by averaging in the marks of all of the judges on five different dimensions of urban governance. In the various classes of governance, the mayor pulled individual marks ranging from "A" to "D." Civic Federation director Frank Coakley gave Washington a high mark for improved city services but rated him below average on economic development and civic leadership. Giving the first-year mayor a "D" in economic development was Thomas F. Roeser, City Club president, who complained that Washington was not interested in the kind of partnership Daley had with business. Alderman Martin Oberman rated the mayor a "B plus" in finance for cutting waste and trimming the city payroll. Also scoring Washington a "B" in finance was council opponent Roman C. Pucinski, who gave him a lower than average "D" in race relations for allegedly "throwing matches all over the place and hollering fire." Political consultant and public relations expert Don Rose was also unimpressed, giving Washington a "C-minus" on race and faulting the mayor for not reaching out to whites as a leader of good will. Hispanic Alderman Miguel Santiago issued "C" grades in all categories, but dropped the mayor to a "D" on race relations for "trying to play up to his own people and failing to relate to everyone." Southside businessman and author Dempsey Travis took issue with the hard graders, giving the mayor an "A" in race relations, adding, "I am not sure that anything he does is going to satisfy some white folks." When the year-end stock-taking was complete and all of the marks tallied, Mayor Washington went home with a first-year report card of one "B," three "B-minuses," and a "C-plus" – an overall grade point average that came out to "B-minus." Chicago business writer R. C. Longworth recorded in his journal the words of one of his graders: "The Washington administration reminds me of a freshman going off to college, who ends up burning the candle at both ends, does not get very good grades, and then settles down." [9]

Midterm Washington

In April 1985 the mayor was at the midpoint of his first four-year term, and Chicago again looked with interest to evaluate its first black mayor. The midterm grades were not much of an improvement on the mayor's freshman year in office. Many of the evaluators who were inclined to give the mayor the benefit of the doubt for his first-year showing now looked with a much more searching and critical eye to see what remediation the mayor had wrought with two years under his belt. They were essentially asking the Wendy's commercial's probing question

"Where's the beef?" and looking for performance instead of mere promise. Still, it was a messy time to hold the mayor to strict performance standards, because Washington was still stalemated in the seemingly endless Council Wars. A gridlocked mayor slugged it out with a muscle-bound ethnic majority, and the result came up the same every round: stalemate and no decision. Chicago newsman Thom Shanker aptly sized up the fight and the prospects for the city's favorite pugilist: "Washington is too weak to win, too strong to lose, and too stubborn to make a deal" with his aldermanic opponents.[10]

On the positive side of the ledger, the mayor was credited for an evenhanded delivery to both black and white wards of garbage service, curb and gutter repairs, and street resurfacing. Non-Chicagoans may find it astonishing that a politician could actually claim to be a reformer for picking up the garbage, an issue settled in most big cities seventy-five years ago during a reform binge called the Progressive Era. But Chicago had never really passed through the full regimen of civil service reform. Washington slimmed the bloated city payroll and retired much of the inherited city deficit. The number of mortgages obtained through city intervention for housing and home rehabbing increased to about 8,000, a figure surpassing that of his predecessor. The mayor also won high marks from those interested in truth in government with his continued support of his freedom-of-information executive order. Much of the administration's energy and effort had been directed to contract set-asides and racial and minority preferences; the mayor could point to large numbers of city jobs and contracts directed to his core constituency. Finally, the mayor had temporarily broken through the lines of his Council Wars opponents by getting a $1.25 billion airport expansion contract approved. To do so, Washington had to call in powerful elements of the business and labor communities to use the pressures of these interest groups to override the opposition 29-bloc. Unfortunately, that was Washington's only power play for the whole two years. For the most part the mayor was back on his heels playing defense or immobilized by a Chicago version of political trench warfare.

Harold Washington at midterm (1985) is not the Harold Washington one would hear about three years later at requiem time. In fact, most of his midterm reviews tended to be highly critical. Many of the same problems the mayor faced during his inaugural were still there two years later; some had become worse, and only a few had been improved on. The city's credit rating in the bond markets remained down, while property taxes had gone up; and the Washington administration had nearly lost $75 million in state transit subsidies through ineptness and last-minute tinkering. Washington's influence in both national Democratic party politics and at the state level had sagged to a new low for a Chicago mayor with the city's own legislative delegation divided, factionalized, and squabbling. Millions of dollars worth of uncollected city service fees and overparking fees continued to pile up.

The Chicago Housing Authority was lurching into its first full-fledged disaster under the mismanagement of Washington's friend Renault Robinson. On the school front, Washington had fired a fiercely independent black female superintendent, Ruth Love, and replaced her with a black male, Manford Byrd, who was believed to be more manageable by city hall directives. Crime, low reading scores, assaults on teachers and students, and high teenage pregnancy remained pretty much unchanged. The mayor had tried to lay off 500 police officers to save money; but the street gang shooting of a popular black high school basketball star had led to a firestorm of criticism, which sent the mayor into full retreat and to the restoration of the officers. The mayor had also been campaigning for an ethics ordinance from the council; but almost like a scene from comic opera, he failed to file his own ethics financial disclosure statement on time, enabling his council opponents to call for his removal as the state law provided. The mayor survived these "contretemps," as he called them, and had the state legislature change the law and diminish the penalty for being late. But such ineptness lent credence to the widely made charge that Washington ran a "haphazard" and "lackadaisical" administration.

Washington had done very little to broaden his base or conciliate his political enemies, and he continued to rely on his combative and abrasive legislative style. "Political confrontation is the meat of what this business is all about," he firmly asserted in April 1985. When chided for not keeping a promise, missing meetings, or appearing late, the mayor's favorite defense was to accuse his critics of "racism." Criticism that the "mayor didn't show up for some hotdog fest" he hotly dismissed as "racism— you're damn right it's racism."[11] He frequently resorted to his old campaign standby of "us versus them" with its racial overtones, which only heightened racial tension in the city. He also reneged on his campaign promise to sponsor home equity insurance for the white ethnic Northwest and Southwest sides, which his aides had taken to badmouthing as "insurance against niggers." Home equity supporters pointed out that such home ownership safety nets had stabilized a racially changing Oak Park (adjacent to one of Chicago's poorest black ghettos), stopped white flight, and turned Frank Lloyd Wright's racially uneasy village into a highly desirable integrated suburb.

Council Wars still remained at full throttle, and the administration's governance was erratic and haphazard. As Robert McClory observed: "Washington did not seem to realize that he could win without whites but he could not govern without whites." Sometimes the mayor retaliated against his white enemies in "childish" and nonreform ways, as McClory put it, such as withdrawing city support for a soccer field in foe Edward Vrdolyak's ward or firing Vrdolyak's brother Victor from his city job.[12] Furthermore, Washington's reform vows had been partly compromised by a series of transgressions where the chief of staff was caught soliciting favors from city vendors; the mayor had shifted lucrative bond attorney work to his political pals; he had sent court stenographic contracts to a campaign supporter; and finally he had tolerated a newsstand shakedown at O'Hare Airport that netted a black out-of-town contractor the prospect of a $1 million return for an investment of $100 – all done in the name of reform and affirmative action.

Preston Greene, who had "written enthusiastically" about the "national significance" of Washington's 1983 victory gloomily assailed the mayor at midterm for creating a "public image of aggressive, reactive negativism" by focusing "single-mindedly on the righteousness of his cause," a "reform-minded mayor bungling every initiative and squandering evansecent opportunities."[13] Northwestern University professor Donald Haider judged Washington's reforms "inscrutable to friend and foe alike" at midterm.

"Business grades mayor a 'C.' At midterm Washington also chalks up an 'E' for effort," announced the Chicago *Sun-Times* business section in a column by Graeme Brown. The business community saw the administration as mired in squabbling, continuing what it called "unconscionable waste": it had more employees than comparable cities and was paying city workers an average annual salary and benefits of $39,000 compared to the private sector's average of $29,000. Haider, in his pre-candidate days, predicted that the city would be bankrupt within five years unless significant spending cuts were made. The mayor's failure to lead with any kind of grand plan for economic expansion or development was souring the make-no-little plans school of Chicago business expansionists. Even friendly businessmen and campaign-backers, such as Soft Sheen Products' Edwin Gardner, said it was time for the mayor to get moving. Sam Mitchell, president of the Chicago Association of Commerce and Industry, summed it up by saying, "I think the business community just pushed the hold button on city government."[14]

Not surprisingly, the mayor disagreed, awarding himself an "A" report for midterm, said press secretary Alton Miller. The mayor claimed credit for Chicago's increase in retail sales, factories, and jobs, even though many economists saw them as part of the Reagan national economic recovery. Indeed, the Chicago figures lagged behind the national average. Washington claimed to have restored business confidence by opening up the bidding process and by installing ethical ways of doing city business. He also pointed out that he had diverted $80 million in city purchases to a "Buy Chicago" program and had slashed 4,000 jobs from the city payroll, along with having retired a $94 million debt from the previous administration. The mayor also reaffirmed that he had ended patronage hiring; at the same time, however, he wanted relief from the reform Shakman decrees and the right to hire more patronage employees at the "policy" level.[15]

The problems of the Washington administration at midterm were partly a result of the city council's having lurched into and bogged down in Council Wars, for which both the white ethnic bloc and the mayor could be held jointly accountable. But they were also a result of some serious internal problems with the mayor and his administration. Washington's entire career as an elected officeholder, an agitator, an activist, and a gadfly had not prepared him well for governing and administration. The lack of coherence and larger public vision beyond concern for his own core constituency, plus short-term, short-range tactical thinking, were responsible for some of the mess he faced at midterm. As one Deomcratic strategist put it: "Washington is used to ad libbing as he goes along. I don't get the sense they sit down and plan anything." Another critic saw it as "a seat of the pants style governing." The mayor was great on moral indignation and good on "insurgency in battling entrenched evil," but not in conciliating and governing. When push came to shove,

173

when it was time to make hard decisions, the mayor "invariably opted to solidify support among the blacks," asserted columnist Phil Lentz, as illustrated by his campaign promise of home equity insurance. When blacks complained, Washington quickly reversed his course and came down on the side of his core constituency. "That basic fact," declared Lentz, "and the fact that Washington won in 1983 without the white vote and thinks he can win again in 1987 without the white vote, underlies many of the strategies and policies of his administration." The mayor was widely perceived as directing a race-conscious administration.[16]

The problems of being disorganized, lacking a plan, and being reactive undercut the confidence of even friends of the administration. A cursory content analysis of the thousands of words in print assessing the administration at midterm would turn up over and over disturbing phrases such as "disorganized, haphazard, inept, can't deliver, doesn't know how to govern, lacking a cohesive strategy, can't mesh programs and philosophy," and the like. Even at the most elementary level the administration suffered in trying to shift the governance machine into gear. As one sympathetic observer put it, Washington suffered from the "Jimmy Carter syndrome—well-meaning, reform-oriented guys who can't find the levers of power to get anything done." "If city services suffered early in the mayor's administration, it was because people were just learning the ropes," council ally Lawrence Bloom asserted. "The mayor's admirable objective was to take on as many black managers as possible, but in some cases these people were in positions beyond their current capabilities." A member of Harold Washington's transition team told Sidney Lens of *Progressive* magazine that "Harold just doesn't know how to govern. He doesn't know how to assign work or keep in touch with his administration."

The reactive character of the first half of the administration was captured by a City Hall aide who said: "We've been firemen. We go around putting out fires the opposition sets and not starting any of our own." Even black leaders were disappointed with Washington's performance. Lu Palmer, the sparkplug who ignited the crusade that elected Washington, said that "some people on the street had unrealistic expectations. They thought once Harold was in, the jobs would flow. . . . Then they see him losing battles to the Eddies [Vrdolyak and Burke] and it hurts." Sidney Lens, the doyen of Chicago's left-wing causes since the

1930s, closed his assessment in the *Progressive* of Washington's first two years with his lamentation that the "Washington staff is not organized for a big breakthrough, and its ineptitude sometimes descends to surprising depths: Phone calls are not returned, letters go unanswered, the mayor misses meetings."[17]

An oft-repeated refrain in the chorus of criticism was that even Washington's supporters could not see any coherent plan for the city and no overall sense of direction from the top. "But so far as a cohesive, workable strategy on how to govern the city, he has done a poor job," said council friend Martin Oberman on the midterm Washington administration. "He has no plan for economic development, for creating the kind of atmosphere–good schools, good housing, reduced crime levels–that would attract new business and new jobs." Reformer Oberman added that Washington "had great opportunities but he didn't use them. He attacked people he didn't have to attack and made a bad situation worse."

After a sit-down interview with the mayor and a careful analysis of the administration at halftime, *Chicago* magazine writer Brian Kelly summed up the paradoxes that plagued the mayor: "He is a masterful politician who has, since his election, suffered numerous political defeats. He is a charismatic speaker who has been miserably inept at communicating his ideas to the city. He is an intelligent, some say brilliant, individual who has spent a lifetime in government, yet his administration is plagued with excessive disorganization. He is a person who lives and breathes public affairs yet leaves the impression that he is lax and unprepared." And the "final paradox," added Kelly, is that, "while even his supporters are expressing doubts about his administration, Harold Washington, at midpoint of his term, may be the most confident person in town." Kelly closed that plague of paradoxes with the observation that "while Mayor Washington may be vibrant his administration is not." As one City Hall staffer so aptly put it, "This is an administration that is desperately in need of some victories that will sell themselves to the public."[18]

Nor did the mayor do well in various measures of public opinion at midterm. A poll of forty knowledgeable political and urban experts drawn from academia, journalism, and civic leadership showed Washington ranking near the bottom of Chicago mayors since 1933 in "accomplishments," and near the middle in "leadership" and "political skills." Comparing him with all of Chicago's forty-one mayors elected since 1837, the experts ranked Washington out of the top ten, as number eleven – a notch above an ineffectual reformer named Martin Kennelly. Broader surveys of public opinion also lent little encouragement to the beleaguered administration. A public opinion poll released on the second anniversary of Washington's inauguration confirmed with a larger public what the critics had been saying and showed how little progress the mayor had made in winning over the voters. Given a choice between two candidates, the public chose the son of a former mayor, Rich Daley, over Washington, 49 percent to 43 percent. According to this Gallup Poll, Daley would have carried 68 percent of the white vote, 18 percent of the black vote, and 54 percent of the Hispanic vote were the election held then. But in a three-way race, which would split the white vote, Washington drew 36 percent to Rich Daley's 31 percent to Jane Byrne's 29 percent – with a few percentage point shifts, almost a copy of the 1983 primary election results. Not only had Washington made little progress with the city's pressing problems since taking office, but, as the polls showed, he had made no progress in winning new ground with the Chicago electorate, and that lack of progress was written large by the Gallup poll.[19]

Bashing Boss Daley

As the reader may have surmised, few big cities across the land are as fascinated as Chicago is in knowing the place of its mayors in history. Chicagoans love to apply a historical yardstick to see if the current incumbent measures up to what the citizens perceive to be their great mayors. Maybe Chicago lacks the eighteenth- and nineteenth-century slum buildings and livery stables to keep its preservationists happy and its historical appetite sated preserving the relics of yesteryear. But perhaps that lively historical interest is diverted to politics. In any event, the Chicago press and public enormously enjoy the process and engage in it with great gusto.

Washington demonstrated that he had quickly learned the game by issuing his own midterm report card in a preemptive strike against bad grades. Being the premier reader among Chicago's recent mayors, Washington was also very conscious of his place in history and fully cognizant that his reputation would be measured against that of Chicago's late Richard J. Daley (1955-1976). With an eye to dislodging Boss Daley from the winner's circle and shaping the writing of mayoral history, Washington began interjecting into his speeches a kind of subliminal drip-drip-drip about how bad his predecessor, Jane Byrne, and especially Daley had been. A line here, a paragraph there, sometimes tangentially and clumsily, sometimes artfully and mirthfully worked in, but always the same old drip-drip-drip of caustic corrosiveness: Daley the wicked boss; Daley the racist; Daley the oppressor. It was usually only an aside, sometimes only a one-liner, seldom a whole speech, but too continuous and regular to be passed off as mere speech filler.

It was, of course, to be expected that Washington, like other politicians, would take to blaming all of the city's shortcomings on his predecessors and taking credit for all of the good things. Yet Washington went much beyond that. In 1983 he set the official administrative line for the regard of Daley and all other Chicago mayors. When asked if he would incorporate the good qualities of past Chicago mayors into his administration, Washington, in what could have been mistaken for an apoplectic fit, roared back: "There are no good qualities of past mayors to be had. None! None ! None! I do not mourn at the bar of the late mayor [Daley]. . . . I have no regret at his leaving. He was a racist to the core, from head to toe, from hip to hip. He oppressed black people. . . . I give no hosannas to a racist nor do I appreciate or respect his son. . . . He is an insult to common sense and decency."[22] It was sometimes a tamer and sometimes a wilder version of this form of Daley-bashing that Harold dropped into his speeches around the city, to the press, civic groups, and university audiences, and to his core constituency.

How successful was Mayor Washington's campaign of disparagement? Not very. He failed to push the champ out of the winner's circle. A scientifically drawn random sample poll of 1,200 Chicagoans taken August 12-24, 1986 (three months after Washington had seized control of the city council) showed that 57 percent of whites and 58 percent of Hispanics said that they wished Richard J. Daley were mayor "today"; although a 52 percent majority of blacks disagreed, an amazing 36 percent of Washington's core constituency told Gallup Associates that they wished that Daley were still mayor. To Washington's consternation, the king of Chicago's political mountain had weathered the storm of negative rhetoric.

Year Four

In October 1986, in Washington's fourth year in office, the *Sun-Times* conducted another poll that showed the public grading the mayor "weak on job performance." The poll showed dramatically how the mayor had failed to expand beyond his core constituency and that 75 percent of whites gave him low grades, with "fair" to "poor" marks for his job as mayor. This figure was virtually unchanged since a 1984 poll. His high marks of "good" to "excellent" had improved somewhat among blacks: they went from 66 percent in April 1984 to 71 percent in 1986, a modest 5 percentage point gain. In seventeen specific job categories Mayor Washington was ranked by all Chicagoans above his all-category average in six areas and below average in eleven dimensions of governance, such as schools, crime, good business climate, attracting new jobs, eliminating patronage, avoiding corruption, merit contracts, keeping taxes down, and control of street gang crime. These were areas in which only 26 to 36 percent of Chicagoans thought that he was doing a good job. On the overall job performance question, 75 percent of whites gave the mayor low marks, checking off the "fair" to "poor" boxes, while 71 percent of blacks gave him high marks—from "good" to "excellent." The same political bipolar world that Washington had taken charge of in 1983 was still there in the final year of his first term.[24]

The mayor's response was to doubt the credibility of the polls. But in December, when Washington's re-election campaign was cranking up, the mayor's own pollster, Paul Maslin, gave him the bad news. There was a widespread public perception of poor job performance. Accordingly, Maslin advised Washington not to campaign on his own record but instead to attack the record of his major opponent, former mayor Jane Byrne. After a feint to accentuate the positive, the Washington camp launched into a stormy negative campaign against the former mayor in the final month of the campaign. Byrne had earlier responded in kind by releasing a blockbuster media stream of negativism that featured scary television shots of the Chicago lakefront with a Washington lightning bolt splitting the city into two halves, playing on the theme that Washington had racially divided the city. Donald Haider, the mostly ignored Republican contender, sized up the Washington-Byrne Democratic primary brawl by saying that the two were running for mayor on the basis of who had been the worse mayor. They were both right, Haider concluded. The negative job ratings and poor performance marks in the polls lent credence to Haider's assertion.

Chicagoans were hard graders. But they had to be, for if they had been anything less, the boodlers would have long ago run off with what was left of the city. As we can see, they did not succumb to liberal sentimentalism for the sake of the city's first black mayor. When it came to drawing the measure of the man, they were tough-minded and flinty-eyed but – as later events would show – always willing to be persuaded by better performance. Above all, Chicago demands winners, whether it is in sports or politics.

CHAPTER NINE

Requiem for a Heavyweight

WHEN HE DIED on November 25, 1987, of a massive heart attack, brought on by what the coroner called "morbid obesity," Harold Washington was grossly overweight. He weighed about 285 pounds, 100 pounds over what his 5 foot 10 inch frame was intended to carry, and his arteries were 95 percent blocked with fat. His heavyweight status was certainly physical, but there was growing evidence before his death that a new Harold Washington, a political heavyweight, was also emerging, a politician no longer content to play only to the "chitlins" circuit but angling for bigger citywide and multiracial venues.

The personal Washington remained something of an enigma. Chicago knew less about Harold Washington's private life than it did of any of its recent mayors. The private man was hard to fathom. Washington was uncooperative in revealing anything beyond what appeared in routine campaign biographies, in his stump speeches, or in his lavish public praise for his father. And the repeated praise of his father's responsible fatherhood seemed less revealing than didactic. It seemed aimed at young black males, many of whom were not home every night to share supper, as Roy Washington was with his children.

Washington's personal life, except for an occasional and sometimes inadvertent flash of insight that was captured in interviews, remained for the most part a blank page of Chicago history. This is apparently the way he wanted it. When asked by three Chicago reporters for an interview to reveal some of the inner man, Washington turned them aside with the phrase "no pay, no say." Very little of his personal lifestyle ever became public, although reporters learned that he apparently never watched television coverage of his term and that he favored black radio programs and listened to all-news station WBBM-AM. Aides said that during the week his fiancée, Mary Ella Smith, would stop by his office to tell him about something she had seen on television and that he might ask for tapes.

Surprisingly, little else leaked out about the mayor. We are told that he had stacks of books in his small apartment, but do not know if he was partial to the classics, political science, philosophy, or biography. His press secretary, Alton Miller, who had daily access to the mayor, said a day after Washington's death: "I couldn't tell you what he had for dinner, what books he read, or what if any—other than football games—television programs he watched." One of the few times that the unofficial Washington was captured was on a clandestine tape by patronage employee James "Skip" Burrell, who recorded a political bull session in the mayor's apartment. This is one of the few publicly revealing insights into the mayor behind the scenes. It showed that the mayor could swear like a dockwalloper, voice harsh opinions of many of his political allies behind their backs, trade off job promotions for political advantage like any Chicago politician, and that he liked to cook soul food and Aunt Jemima pancakes.[1]

Yet what made Washington tick on the personal side of his character was shrouded in privacy. After his death, the enigma became somewhat clearer, especially on the public side of the man. Wine, women, and song, or the love of money or family, seemed not to be a part of his life. In fact, the evidence suggests that there may not have been a personal Washington—only a public Washington and a political Washington. He was socialized in an eminently public lifestyle. Born and reared in the bosom of the political machine by a father who had been an itinerant preacher and a precinct captain, Harold took over his father's working life as a precinct captain after he died. He held a string of no-show or seldom-show patronage jobs and then made the leap to elective office. Other than boyhood interests in boxing and track, this lifelong public payroller did not hunt, fish, golf, play tennis or basketball, was not a fraternal lodgegoer, was not a member of a Great Books circle, did not tinker in the basement with carpentry or home projects, and was not a music buff. Apparently he did not collect stamps or chase women, as had other famous Democrats. A high school dropout, he married in 1942, was divorced a few years later, and had no children. His family members, including three full siblings and seven half brothers and sisters, all seemed remote.

Despite coming from a large extended family, Washington seemed to have few affectionate links to his kin. There is no record of his regularly attending family gatherings at Thanksgiving and Easter, playing Santa Claus to his nieces or nephews, or taking the initiative himself to call together family reunions. His half brother Ramon Price recalled once making elaborate preparations for a holiday dinner for Harold, only to have the mayor cancel at the last minute to attend to political business in his apartment. Harold's mooring to his family had been cut in 1981 after their mother died, Price recollected.[2] If it is true that the maternal tie lasted that long, it seems strange that Washington never mentioned his mother. The one woman in his public life was fiancée Mary Ella Smith. But even Ms. Smith, who suddenly materialized in the 1983 campaign, seemed to be a political convenience rather than a potential wife. She seemed to be part of the standard advice given to many an ambitious politician: lose 20 pounds, get a dog, and get married (or in Washington's case, engaged). More specifically, mean-spirited detractors suggested that Mary Ella may have been a convenient campaign stage prop to squelch nasty rumors of Washington's alleged homosexuality that circulated during the 1983 campaign.

The personal Washington was a cardboard figure; the real Washington was the public and political man. In a moment of self-transparent revelation, Washington stood in front of a campaign audience and said: "What you see is what you get." His vocation and his avocation were politics. Once "hooked by the habit," there was no quitting. As Washington so aptly put it, "Politics is like shooting pool or eating Cracker Jacks. Once you start you just can't stop."[3] "I was always involved in the political process," Washington told Dempsey Travis. "I actually worked in the precinct with my old man before I was fourteen years old. I used the help him pass out literature." Washington recalled that his "father discussed politics at the dinner table almost every night." Frequent visitors were old-time Chicago politicians such as William L. Dawson, Oscar DePriest, Mike Sneed, and as the mayor put it, "I was literally raised in a political atmosphere."

And it was the same for the adult Washington. "He loves his job as mayor," Travis testified at the second inauguration of Mayor Washington. "He salivates when he gets up in the morning looking for something political to do."[4]

The only reunions that one heard about were the informal snack-dinner confabs at which he and a few aides discussed politics. Deeply suspicious and distrustful, the mayor had few close friends. Trying to get to the inner core of Washington's life is like peeling an onion: the more you peel away, the less you have. There seemed to be no inner core, just the outer layers of the public man. Alderman Edward Vrdolyak, a shrewd judge of people, sized up Washington's character succinctly with his observation: "He was a political man. That was his life. He really didn't have a personal life, a family life. So all he had was politics. That's difficult. He didn't have to separate politics from his life because he only had politics."[5] Washington's friends did not dispute this assessment of the deceased mayor.

Harold Washington's death occasioned a puzzling reversal of judgment of his career as mayor of Chicago. If one reads the commentary, the tributes, the unreserved praise, and the efforts to beatify the mayor at the time of his death—only a year after those negative Gallup polls, the generally unsatisfactory job ratings, and the "B-minus" and "C" grades—one must ask, what happened? Had the mayor turned up the steam and pushed the ship of the city full speed ahead in a heroic effort to accomplish things in that year that he had not accomplished during the previous four years? Or were the extravagant tributes and heartfelt condolences simply liberal guilt, canned condolences, and a part of the requiem style of the Chicago political tradition?

The answer is yes to both questions. First, the issue of substantive change: the mayoral year of 1986-87 and the seven months of the second term were certainly a better time for Washington—not a Periclean age, but clearly better than his stormy, stumbling, and combative start. "After three and a half years he seems to have gotten the hang of it," concluded the Chicago *Sun-Times* reportorial team in a thirteen-part series assessing Washington. There were encouraging signs that the mayor had finally got his act together. He had taken over the city council in May 1986, the Parks District in July; and by then most of the city-run and city-connected agencies, such as the public schools, O'Hare Airport, the Chicago Housing Authority, and the Chicago Transit Authority, had long since been under his control. In fact, Harold could celebrate the 4th of July, 1986, for two reasons—the second being that it signaled his independence from the opposition council bloc. His enemies Burke and Vrdolyak were in retreat.[6] The mayor had about eight months before the primary and about ten before the general election to show what he could do while in full control.

There was some substantive basis for his improved press notices. By paring the payroll and raising taxes to a total of $364 million, the mayor had retired the inherited deficit, brought the city back to a sound financial footing, and restored the city's bond and credit rating to the "A" category with both major credit services. As noted earlier, he had also reduced the size of the garbage truck crews from an overstaffed four men to three. On the eve of the 1987 primary election, the mayor pushed an ethics ordinance through the city council—a feat in Chicago comparable to installing a Catholic confessional booth in the Kremlin. And finally, after years of delay, the mayor had found a key developer for the much-discussed north Loop hotel project and had made some minor repairs on Navy Pier to prevent its crumbling but had not produced a development plan for the padlocked Pier. He had also won approval for a $180 million sidewalk and street repaving project for the neighborhoods. These may have been his only concessions to the Chicago "builder mayor tradition." But in an obvious bow to the "show-and-tell" phase of the builder tradition, Washington greeted with glee the prospect of $180 million in street repairs, declaring: "This summer you are going to see cranes and bulldozers crawling all over the damn place." Washington would have something to show the voters by primary time: better streets, sidewalks, curbs, and gutters. Obviously, it was time for the mayor to strut his stuff; and finally there was something to strut.

The mayor had also brought under control a sometimes unruly and fever-pitched group of black nationalists, whose impolitic "Mau-Mau" rhetoric had been frightening white voters. Black activists "were victims of the movement they created," Edward Vrdoyak observed. "Harold controlled them, and if they differed with him on issues, they were caught up by their own rhetoric, that of being a traitor to the black constituency." Ironically, the mayor used the issue of black solidarity to silence some of the most excitable and inflammatory of the black chauvinists. Just as the Afro-nationalists had insisted on 100 percent voter loyalty from the black masses for black candidates and called those people "race traitors" who strayed from the party line, so would the mayor turn that two-edged sword of black solidarity on those feisty chauvinists when they got out of line and made excessive demands or criticism of him. When they bucked him, Washington would silence them by reminding them that criticism of the city's first black mayor was also "race treason."

"You could not, without some retribution, criticize Harold Washington. Harold was a kind of messiah," admitted one of the more flaming of the ultranationalists, radio show host Lu Palmer. "By pushing racial solidarity as we did with Harold's first election," lamented Palmer, "we may have contributed to that." Black people had lost their will to fight City Hall on issues, according to Palmer.[8] The mayor, being the clever tactician that he was, hung the black nationalists out to dry on their own clothesline, or, if one prefers, hoisted them on their flaming petards, when it suited his purposes to do so. This was on the credit side of the Washington ledger, especially for a mayor who had to answer to a multiethnic and multiracial city.

There were clearly some positives to be factored into the Washington record. Yet, by the most benign stretch of interpretation, the list of positives was nowhere a match for the negatives: the Chicago Housing Authority facing its worst crisis in fifty years; a school system that the U.S. Secretary of Education called the worst in the nation; high crime rates; a souring business climate; political corruption; and a messy administration that had backlogged an estimated hundreds of millions in accumulated and uncollected traffic tickets and other city fees. On this mountain of unresolved problems the positives did not make much of a dent.

There was widespread understanding by urban experts of the political necessity – and even some public tolerance – for the mayor's monochromatic vision of the public good, which generously translated into the need to satisfy his black constituency. But there was also unease, even among thoughtful liberals, over the fact that affirmative action had become the be-all and end-all of city policy, often to the exclusion of larger citywide and metropolitan-wide concerns.[9]

The New Washington

In a peculiar way, awareness of the mayor's less than citywide governance policies in his first term helps to explain some of the praise and requiem hyperbole after his death. The new initiatives and changes hinted at during his re-election campaign and during the beginning of his second term were a radical departure from the old Washington of the first administration.

Instead of rubbing salt into the wounds of the vanquished, as he had in 1983, Washington, in inaugurating his new term in 1987, spoke of the "new spirit of Chicago" and the "need to work together," and even went out of his way to compliment his hard-working predecessors who had helped build up the downtown area. He adroitly avoided "stomping" on his political foes, going so far as to excise a section of his written speech that cast aspersions on the Democratic machine. "He didn't challenge them to fight," noted aldermanic ally David Orr. "The mayor's message was we should lower our voices." A month earlier, in a short victory speech, Washington had foreshadowed the new unity theme: "We have an opportunity to wipe the slate clean and make a fresh start," and "we need to combine the talents of all of the people of Chicago to make it possible."[10]

Washington seemed to be genuinely (as opposed to rhetorically) reaching out toward opening a new chapter and aiming to make a fresh start. He took the first steps toward patching up his bad relations with business; he made a move toward seriousness in collecting unpaid millions in parking fees and other city fees (what would you expect, critics had grumbled during his first term, of a mayor who neglected to pay his own water, phone, and light bills and federal income taxes?[7]); he backed off mandatory linked development, which business saw as anti-growth; he also indicated a willingness to listen to business complaints about the city's heavy-handed intrusion into the private labor market by using the mayor's office as a hiring hall; and he had also eased off some politically unpopular tax measures.

Finally, on Wednesday, November 18, just seven days before his death, Washington made a generous gesture of peace toward white ethnics in the Democratic slating sessions. Some later discounted it as a "deathbed repentance," but that does not seem to be the case. There was no way of the mayor's knowing he would die the next week. He extended the olive branch in a way instantly understood by all Chicagoans. The mayor supported a multiracial slate of countywide candidates, including a former mayoral opponent and son of "Boss," Richard M. Daley for state's attorney; a Polish candidate, Aurelia Pucinski, daughter of one of his bitterest council opponents, for clerk of the circuit court;

and Carol Mosely Braun, a black, for recorder of deeds. This slate "tells people we've gone too far with this acrimony, this negativism, this inability to get along," Washington told the press. But even more important, the mayor warned the ultranationalist Afro wing of the Democratic Party, "If you don't support this ticket, you're no friend of mine." Calling it a "ticket made in heaven," the mayor issued marching orders to his mostly black male political legions to line up behind the multiracial and gender-diverse nominees.[11]

Some of the mayor's words need to be taken with a grain of salt and read as politician hyperbole; nonetheless, the important fact is that never in his first term had Washington taken such a promising step forward, indicating that he was prepared to become mayor for all of the people, including white ethnics and females. It was an existential moment, a flowering springtime for Democratic politics that came after a four-year winter of bitter wrangling and discontent.

By the autumn of his last year, Mayor Washington, now re-elected, had gotten over the disappointment of his poor showing with white voters. He had begun to smile again toward white ethnics. He no longer imagined (at least publicly) Klansmen in the ethnic lodges or saw businessmen as "pinstriped bigots." Washington seems to have begun to realize that bombast and *ad hominem*, the weapon of the political maverick and legislative gadfly, sometimes could do more harm than good when wielded by a politician who hoped to become a citywide leader and administrator. Washington had begun to move toward a "coalition of reality," as urban expert Edward Marciniak saw it, and away from "simply a movement of outsiders organized around their emotions and historic anger at the system."[12] It was all of these new directions and reaching out in the final few months that held such promise for a better second term, and not a list of tangible achievements, that brought forth the expressions of praise after his death.

Future Tense Mayor

Harold Washington's death on November 25, 1987, shocked the city of Chicago. The vigorous, combative, and seemingly robust mayor had shown no signs of ill health or slowing down. On the very morning of his death he was out of doors turning over shovels of dirt to mark the site of a new building. Richard J. Daley's death came similarly: on his fateful day he was on the

South Side dedicating a fieldhouse, even shooting a basketball or two at the hoop. Somewhat earlier in his last year, Washington had complained of chest pains and scheduled two stress tests; but he had failed to show up, dismissing the discomfort as flu symptoms. Suddenly, without warning, a few minutes before 11 A.M., the mayor slumped over his desk. Thinking that he was reaching for a dropped pencil, Washington's press secretary, Alton Miller, bent over to assist him, only to find that he was not breathing. The mayor was rushed away by ambulance, and heroic efforts were made to resuscitate him at Northwestern University Hospital, but to no avail. He was pronounced dead at about 1:30 P.M. His death came on Wednesday, the day before Thanksgiving, spreading a pall of gloom on that holiday weekend for thousands of Chicagoans.

The city went into a five-day period of mourning. Schools held special assemblies, the city's transit stations were draped in mourning colors, and with the mayor's body lying in state at City Hall, tens of thousands filed by in shocked and tearful reverence. VIP's and national politicians flew in by the hundreds, crowding out local people, to attend the elaborate and extended funeral services, including two hours of eulogies by politicians, preachers, and national leaders. Touching tributes were paid the fallen mayor, including a rhyming condolence by Hispanic alderman Jesus Garcia, which captured Washington's courting of Latino voters:

> You came to our community to help build the spirit of unity. . . .
> When others didn't care, you dared,
> To gain what was essential, you cultivated our potential.
> You made us see in 1983.
> We gained some more in 1984.
> We came alive in 1985. . . .
> And now that you are gone, we the people vow to stay strong.
> The unity of our coalition is a tribute to the Washington tradition. . . .
> Today, today in '87, we know that you're in heaven. Adios, amigo. Adios.[13]

That's about as close as politics ever gets to poetry in Chicago.

In a cold drizzle, tens of thousands of mostly black mourners lined the nine-mile-long funeral route to watch the mayor's cortege wend its way to Oak Woods Cemetery, where Washington was buried within a stone's throw of another Chicago spellbinder, Mayor William "Big Bill" Thompson. In addition, memorial services were held at many other churches and public facilities around the city, and all public attention seemed riveted on the sad requiem that marked the end of Chicago's first black mayoralty. Television, radio, and newspaper coverage was exceedingly thorough in covering every last detail of the last rites. The editor of the Chicago *Tribune* observed the next day that the last five days had been "without precedent in Chicago history. In all of its history, the city has never before said goodbye to one of its people with such prolonged stately pageantry and simple heartfelt grief from so many of its residents." Comparing Washington's burial to Martin Luther King's funeral, the editor concluded that "no other black leader in the nation has inspired such a farewell tribute."[14]

Mayor Future Tense Emerges

Beginning on the Wednesday night of Washington's death and extending for the next week and a half, into December, the city witnessed an outpouring of sympathy, superlative praise, and high-flying eulogy, along with elegant hosannas and angelic requiems intoned by VIP's, assorted politicians, and just plain Chicagoans. The rush to canonize the deceased Washington took the form of proposals to name in his honor a new library, a federal building, a junior college, possibly an expressway, and other suggestions—including renaming the airports, two yet-to-be-built stadiums, a county hospital, and possibly a southside black hospital. The list got so long that the Chicago *Tribune* called for "a moratorium on Harold Washington memorials."[15] Only days after his death, Washington, who had served for five years, had three institutions named in his honor—a junior college, a library, and a federal building—whereas the all-time champion officeholder of Chicago, Richard Daley, after twenty-one years at the city's helm, had only two namesake places, a junior college and a plaza.[2] Yet the historic meaning of the Washington years is not likely to be found in the heraldic, the hortatory, or in honorary tributes, no matter how lavishly bestowed.

Sizing up the meaning of the Washington mayoralty—engaging in much praise but also some serious evaluations—were the city's newspapers, radio stations, and television programs. Both major dailies put out special editions with entire sections devoted exclusively to Washington, including interviews with "the man on the street," VIP's, city watchers, and urban experts. It was from these elaborate, lengthy, and often thoughtful ruminations that mayor "future tense" emerged. Washington's "tangible record of accomplishments is a short list," the Chicago *Tribune* editor declared, calling the fallen mayor instead a "symbol" of success, adding that it was "impossible to know what he could have achieved" had he lived.[16]

Hope for the future became the dominant chord of the eulogies and evaluations of Washington. Most of the appraisal, like a fugue, began on a somber note but ended in the higher registers on a note of hope. It was almost formulaic, as if dozens of word processors of editors, reporters, and writers all had a file labeled "hope"–hope for a better tomorrow. All of them clicked into place at Washington's death and varied only slightly in their generous prognoses of a rosy future.

Optimism about a better tomorrow flowed. The mayor's relationship with business "was generally rocky," according to Ronald J. Gidwitz, chairman of Helene Curtis Industries; but at the time of his death, "Harold Washington. . . finally understood what it took to make this a more hospitable business climate." Hope for the future showed up as the main theme of many other Chicago business movers and shakers: Phil Delany of Harris Trust said, "If he had lived, the relationship would have shown great improvement." Philip Miller of Marshall Field Corporation said that Washington's "second term promised a significant change for the better." He "was closing the gap with business," said business writer Merrill Goozner; and according to another business leader, Washington had "started to really pull his act together" and was "beginning to solve some zoning concerns." What he was "on the verge of doing" was most important, according to journalist Robert Davis. Outside of reverential and pious platitudes, most of the assessments projected what observers thought would have happened or possibly should have happened in a second term. The language all pointed to the future, filled as it was with phrases such as "it was just a beginning. . .," "his administration was embryonic in nature. . .," "he was just emerging. . .," "just starting to develop. . .," "many hoped. . .," "he would start moving the city forward. . .," "had he lived, relations with business would have shown great improvement. . .," and so forth.[17]

It was not only the business community that hoped for a better second term. The political realm was also filled with the springtime of hope for a better tomorrow under a new Washington at the helm. It was the future-tense mayor that Chicago writer M. W. Newmann described as "reaching out for ethnic Chicago"—but obviously not quite reaching it yet. The future was where former mayor Michael Bilandic and white councilman Roman Pucinski saw hope. The latter said that Washington was "just starting to develop a new line of communication with various ethnic groups in Chicago." Mary Gonzales-Koenig, executive director of the Spanish Coalition for Jobs, said that Hispanics "were not that pleased" with his first term but were "looking forward" to a better second term. The Chicago *Tribune* editor summed up the Harold Washington story as a "dream" not yet realized.[18]

Not all of the feelings were pietistic and reverential. In one southside white ethnic tavern on the funeral day the viewers switched over the TV channel from Washington's last rites to reruns of Betty Boop cartoons. When Washington's death was announced on Wednesday over the public address system of a private school, the fourth graders and others broke out into cheers. Just as Washington had said that he did "not mourn at the bar of the late Mayor Daley," so these ethnic kin of Daley did not mourn at the bar of the late Mayor Washington. They were not necessarily mean-spirited youngsters, but simply reflected the sentiments of their parents about the mayor. Another southsider said that they didn't want to see him die but would rather have voted him out of the office. "He wasn't exactly our mayor," offered a Chicago public school teacher. "He was never mayor of the whole city." That line of assessment, though subdued for the occasion, must also be factored into any stock-taking of the Washington legacy, for it was a widespread view that was broadly shared among the approximately 85 percent of whites who voted against Washington twice.[19]

Although the evidence is only fragmentary and suggestive that Washington would have worked out better relations with white Chicago, evidence is abundant and overflowing of his warm and passionate political love affair with black Chicago. Northsider N.K. Dutt declared: "I realized we had full protection and an equal chance in this city" after he was elected. There was voluminous testimony to that effect on radio, television, and in the press, all of which was encapsulated by Dan Wilson's remark:

"He really cared about black people." "Losing our mayor is like losing a folk hero," lamented a southside waiter. Rev. George Clements, a prominent priest and black educator, argued that Washington will be remembered for "being a source of true authentic racial pride to black people."[20]

Washington had made a profound impression on his core constituency, black Chicago. Blacks moved from the periphery to the center of politics, and Washington permanently changed the nature of race relations in the city. His "greatest accomplishment," according to *Illinois Issues* columnist Ed McManus, was simply that he had won and had become the first black mayor of Chicago, and that his election "told every boy and girl in the ghetto" that people with black skins "can achieve political power in our society." The future-tense mayor had found his niche in Chicago history. At death's door, he had offered the promise of becoming mayor of all of the city. In that sense, the denouement was not unlike John F. Kennedy's mythic Camelot, the unwritten epic of what-might-have-been. "He will be in the history books, because if George Washington was the father of his country," declared *Sun-Times* writer M. W. Newman, "Harold Washington in less than five years became the father of his city—or at least that part of it that elected him."[21] On that triumphant accolade a clear consensus had emerged.

Postscript

Yet politics Chicago-style is no respector of the death of the mighty and powerful. The political show must go on. Before Washington's body had been lowered into its final resting place, the black power seekers and mini-power wielders were gathered at O'Hare Airport in a secret meeting with Rev. Jesse Jackson, who had just jetted in from the Persian Gulf—a world-class trouble spot where the civil rights leader had been pursuing his presidential ambitions. Because Jackson has never held elective office, his meddling in local Democratic politics was not appreciated by some important black—and many white—leaders, who thought of him as a "political ambulance chaser." Caballing with the reverend were the alleged legitimate claimants to the Washington reform heritage; they were drawing lots for the fallen mayor's power and sharpening their knives for the inner palace struggle to follow.

A so-called memorial for Washington, which had been orchestrated by Jackson, turned into a heated, passion-filled political pep rally for Jackson's favorite mayoral successor, Alderman Timothy Evans. Opposing Evans was another black alderman, Eugene Sawyer, who had the support of the white ethnic bloc. Black columnist Vernon Jarrett lost his cool at the University of Illinois at Chicago Pavilion conclave and screamed at the audience to treat those "black enemies [of Jackson and Evans] like you treat members of the Ku Klux Klan." A no less emotional Hispanic alderman, Luis Gutierrez, threatened: "We will surround City Hall because it is ours. We are not giving up City Hall. . . . Tomorrow we have destiny in our hands. Let's not give up the throne."[22]

And surround the Hall they did. When it came time for the council to pick the next acting mayor, thousands gathered around City Hall, closing the streets and chanting, "Sawyer, Sawyer you can't hide / You're committing suicide." The alternative shout was "Uncle Tom Sawyer, Uncle Tom Sawyer!" When the doors of City Hall opened, the Jackson-Evans crowd rushed in carrying placards and hurling rhetorical threats at anyone who dared wander from the Jackson-Evans line.[23] Eight of the ten aldermen who reported death threats were opposed by the Jackson-Evans party. Black Alderman William C. Henry, the point man for the Sawyer candidacy, was told by the Marquette Police District to wear a bulletproof vest to City Hall. "My life has been threatened," Alderwoman Anna Langford protested in a dramatic television appearance. "I have been cursed. My office has been picketed. Is this what Mayor Washington stood for? . . . died for?"[24]

The succession to Washington's chair was fought out mostly in the back rooms, but also in the City Hall lobby and the council gallery, which was packed in advance by Jackson-Evans partisans. Hooting and jeering derisively, the Jackson-Evans clique held dollar bills aloft, shouting, "No deals! No deals!" They cursed Sawyer and made occasional allusions to the biblical Judas. Two fevered partisans were caught throwing pieces of silver (probably quarters) at white and black supporters of Sawyer, and they had to be ejected by the police. Their enemy was the growing black-white coalition supporting Sawyer, which was composed of many political foes of the late mayor. All of this melee was broadcast live on television; an astonishing 480,000 households stayed up until at least 2:00 A.M. to watch the proceedings, according to the A.C. Nielsen rating service. To viewers outside Chicago, it looked like a banana-republic coup being staged by a group of tipsy bit-part actors straight from enacting a shaky version of the passion play, with the language of Golgotha and Judas's betrayal still on their lips.

Despite the political histrionics, the putative Jackson-Evans group lost the all-night battle in a 29-19 council vote, taken at 4:01 in the morning. They were beaten by the new coalition, composed of twenty-three white and six black aldermen, who named the new mayor. "The successor would almost have to be black," white alderman Roman Pucinski advised. "We talked with our constituents and most of them agreed that there would be a strong reaction if the City Council tried to change the complexion of the mayor's office." The new acting mayor was Eugene Sawyer, a soft-spoken black conciliator (so soft-spoken, in fact, that the press took to calling him "Mr. Mumbles" a few days later). A former alderman, Sawyer had worked both sides of the street, machine and reform, and was acceptable to the ethnics and the Democratic regulars. The prognosis for the new leader, according to Sophie of Kuczak's Deli in the old Polish section, was that Sawyer is "going to be a little more tolerant. He's going to play ball more with these [white] guys than Evans would."[25] Acting Mayor Sawyer would fill out that part of Washington's unexpired term that passed before the next election.

This was dynasty politics, Chicago-style, similar to the Daley interregnum eleven years earlier. There was just a different cast of characters, more melodrama, and the benefit of round-the-clock and into-early-morning-hours television coverage. Some called it the "living room coup," which was similar to the Vietnamese War in that people could participate vicariously and watch it comfortably from the sidelines in their living rooms. The Washington era had officially come to an end.

Notes

Notes to Chapter 1

1. See John D. Buenker, "Edward F. Dunne: The Limits of Municipal Reform"; John R. Schmidt, "William E. Dever: A Chicago Political Fable"; Melvin G. Holli, "Jane M. Byrne: To Think the Unthinkable and Do the Undoable," in *The Mayors: The Chicago Political Tradition*, Paul M. Green and Melvin G. Holli, eds. (Carbondale, IL, 1987), 33ff., 82ff., 172ff.

2. John Camper, Cheryl Devall, and John Kass, "The Road to City Hall," Chicago *Tribune Magazine* (November 16, 1968), 12ff.; Dempsey Travis, *An Autobiography of Black Politics* (Chicago: Urban Research Press, 1987), 477-500; Florence H. Levinsohn, *Harold Washington: A Political Biography* (Chicago: Chicago Review Press, 1983), 39ff.

3. Doris Graber, "Media Magic: Fashioning Characters for the 1983 Mayoral Race," in *The Making of the Mayor: Chicago 1983*, Melvin G. Holli and Paul M. Green, eds (Grand Rapids, 1984), 70.

4. Dennis Byrne, "Images Not Issues May Sway Voters," Chicago *Sun-Times*, February 20, 1983; see also Susan J. Holli, "Combative Communicating in Chicago: The Paradigm and Campaign of 1983" (unpublished B.A. paper, University of Iowa, 1986.)

5. TV advertisements shown on WBBM-TV, Chicago, December 1982 through February 1983; Paul M. Green, "The 1983 Chicago Democratic Mayoral Primary," in *The Making of the Mayor: Chicago 1983*, 25.

6. Rick Soll, "Sawyer Still Stunned by Byrne Loss," Chicago *Sun-Times*, April 3, 1983.

7. Chicago *Sun-Times*, February 20, 1983.

8. Richard Day, "Polling in the 1983 Mayoral Election," in *The Making of the Mayor: Chicago 1983*, 92f.; Carol Oppenheim interview of Jane Byrne, Chicago *Tribune*, May 6, 1983.

9. Interviews with Bernard Epton, Chicago, July 10 and August 14, 1983.

10. *Ibid.*

11. Paul M. Green, "Chicago Election: The Numbers and the Implications," *Illinois Issues*, 13 f.

12. Byrne, "Images not Issues Sway Voters," Chicago *Sun-Times*, Feb. 20, 1983.

13. Green, "Chicago Election," 15.

14. Graber, "Media Magic," 73; Don Rose, "How the 1983 Election Was Won," in *The Making of the Mayor: Chicago 1983*, 119-20.

15. Green, "Chicago Election," 13f.

16. William C. McCready, "White Ethnic Vote for Washington: An unsung story that provides hope," Chicago *Sun-Times*, April 27, 1983; Paul M. Green, "The 1983 Chicago Democratic Mayoral Primary, 17f.; Don Rose, "How the 1983 Election Was Won"; Paul Kleppner, *Chicago Divided: The Making of a Black Mayor* (DeKalb, IL, 1985), 186f.; Charles Branham, "Why Washington Really Won: The Historical Roots of Contemporary Black Politics in Chicago" (unpublished paper, University of Illinois at Chicago, 1985).

Notes to Chapter 2

1. Bernard Judge, "Suspected of Mole Scam," Chicago *Sun-Times*, January 26, 1986; Thomas Burton and John Camper, "City Reeling," Chicago *Tribune* January 7, 1986.

2. John Camper, "City Hall Probe Puts Squeeze on Washington's Inner Circle," Chicago *Tribune*, February 21, 1986.

3. John Camper and John Kass, "Scandals Get Too Big for Mayor to Ignore," Chicago *Tribune*, February 9, 1986; Dean Baquet and James Strong, "City Counsel Quits," Chicago *Tribune*, February 20, 1986; Kelley quoted in D. Baquet and Bob Wiedrich, "Lobbyist . . . ," Chicago *Tribune*, April 6, 1986.

4. Douglas Frantz, "McClain Used Contract Clout," Chicago *Tribune*, January 28, 1986; Mark Eissman, "McClain Helped Officials Get Wind of His Windfall," Chicago *Tribune*, February 28, 1986.

5. Washington quoted in Dean Baquet and Thomas Burton, "Mayor Drops Hot Potato, McClain," Chicago *Tribune*, February 8, 1986; Philip Wattley and Dave Schneidman, "McClain Arrest on DUI Charge," Chicago *Tribune*, March 4, 1986; John Kass, "McClain Says He Was Robbed," Chicago *Tribune*, March 25, 1986; McClain quoted in John Kass, "Judge Orders McClain To Pay," Chicago *Tribune*, April 22, 1986.

6. John Kass and John Camper, "Scandal Gets Too Big For Mayor to Ignore," Chicago *Tribune*, February 9, 1986; Editorial, Chicago *Tribune*, January 24, 1986; John Camper, "Mayor Suggests FBI Plotted City Setup," Chicago *Tribune*, February 11, 1986; Washington quoted in Douglas Frantz, "City Hall Inquiry," Chicago *Tribune*, February 24,

1986. Former reform alderman and then city council parliamentarian Leon Despres declared flatly that Washington's attempt to smear the FBI with racism "was a mistake" and probably done in the heat of the moment (interview with Leon Despres, Chicago, November 9, 1987).

7. Leon Despres cited in Eugene Kennedy, *Himself: The Life and Times of Richard J. Daley* (New York, 1978), 265; William Singer quoted in Len O'Connor, *Clout: Mayor Daley and His City* (Chicago, 1975), 252.

8. Interview with Leon Despres, Chicago, November 9, 1987; interview with Martin Oberman, November 28, 1986.

9. Similarly, some community groups who had been vehement opponents of previous administrations had been "bought out" and, in the words of an ethics report, "refused to challenge the city when it was in the best interests of their neighborhoods to do so" (Jean Butzen, Jerome Franzel, Diane Kallenbach, Charles LeHew, Arthur Lyons, "An Overview of the Costs and Consequences of Corruption: A Report to the Chicago Ethics Committee, June 3, 1987," Center for Urban Affairs, Northwestern University).

10. Don Benedict, "A Summit Meeting on Corruption," Chicago *Tribune*, April 8, 1986. It almost seemed as though social theorist Robert Michel's "Iron Law of Oligarchy" was operating in Chicago municipal politics. The Iron Law held that social movements like "reform" "perished" the moment "reformers" triumphed. The new oligarchies would place political survival above all else, including reform ideologies. See Robert Michels, *Political Parties: A Sociological Study of the Oligarchial Tendencies of Modern Democracy* (New York, 1962), 18, 19, 333f.

11. Dean Baquet and Thomas Burton, "A Backstage Drama of Clout," Chicago *Tribune*, October 26, 1986; "A Report Card from Mr. Sullivan," Chicago *Tribune*, October 27, 1986.

12. Burke poll cited in Steve Neal, "Poll Shows Byrne Has Edge," Chicago *Tribune*, May 12, 1986; Penn Schoen in S. Neal, "Vrdolyak Bid Help to Mayor," Chicago *Tribune*, November 18, 1986; Gallup poll printed in William Braden, "Mayor Leads in Poll," Chicago *Sun-Times*, September 7, 1986.

13. Maurice Possley and David Axelrod, "Court Orders New Map for City Wards," Chicago *Tribune*, May 18, 1984.

14. *Mars Ketchum*, et al. (plaintiffs-appellants) *v. Jane M. Byrne, et al.*, U.S. Court of Appeals, Seventh Circuit, decided May 17, 1985.

15. *Ibid.*; Possley and Axelrod, "Court Orders New Map for City Wards."

16. David Axelrod, "New Ward Map Sets Up Struggle," Chicago *Tribune*, May 20, 1985; Editorial, "Remapping a Chasm," Chicago *Tribune*, May 23, 1984.

17. Robert Davis and Cheryl Duvall, "Remap Puts Survivors to Test," Chicago *Tribune*, February 17, 1986.

18. *Mars Ketchum, et al. v. City Council of the City of Chicago*, U.S. District Court, Judge Charles R. Norgle, December 27, 1985; *Mars Ketchum et al. vs. City Council of the City of Chicago and John P. Daley, et al.*, U.S. District Court, Charles R. Norgle, December 30, 1985; interview with Alderman Edward M. Burke, October 20, 1987, Chicago.

19. John Camper, "Mayor and Vrdolyak Show Their Muscle," Chicago *Tribune*, March 20, 1986; Jerry Thornton and Charles Mount, "Write-ins May Force Runoff In 26th Ward," Chicago *Tribune* April 4, 1986.

20. Robert Davis, "Mayor Feels the Power Shifting His Way, "Chicago *Tribune*, April 30, 1986; "Chicago Week in Review," WTTW-TV, May 1, 1986.

21. Washington quoted in Tom Fitzpatrick, "Arrogance Taints Washington Victory," Chicago *Sun-Times*, May 11, 1986. Examples of Washington's political maladroitness can be seen in the mayor's attitude toward the politically vanquished.

22. City of Chicago Council Chambers, May 9, 1986.

23. Basil Talbott, Jr., "Mayor feels the power," Chicago *Sun-Times*, May 11, 1986.

24. Tom Fitzpatrick, "Arrogance Taints Washington Victory," Chicago *Sun-Times*, May 11, 1986.

25. John Kass and John Camper, "Mayor Victory Enrages Kelly," Chicago *Tribune*, July 4, 1986.

26. WBBM-TV News, July 24, 1986.

27. Manuel Galvan and Jack Houston, "Mayor Cries Foul Play on Petitions," Chicago *Tribune*, August 21, 1986; WBBM- TV News, August 21, 1986.

28. WLS-TV News, August 2, 1986.

29. WLS-TV News, August 21, 1986.

30. "Mayor Charges 50% of Petitions are Fraudulent," Chicago *Sun-Times*, August 26, 1986.

31. News "retrospective," WBBM-TV, November 1, 1986.

32. Mark Brown, "Referendum KOd," Chicago *Sun-Times*, September 3, 1986.

33. Robert Davis and Charles Mount, "Referendum Ruling to Mayor," Chicago *Tribune*, September 17, 1986.

34. Michael Briggs and Mark Brown, "High Court Rejects Mayoral Referendum," Chicago *Sun-Times*, October 2, 1986; Joseph Tybor, "Ambiguity Killed Referendum," Chicago *Tribune*, November 1, 1986.

Notes to Chapter 3

1. Chicago *Sun-Times*, July 17, 1985. For the Byrne mayoralty, see Melvin G. Holli, "To Think the Unthinkable and Do the Undoable," *The Mayor*, pp. 172ff.

2. Personal interview, November, 1986.

3. Chicago *Tribune*, December 28, 1985.
4. Personal interview (individual wishes to remain anonymous).
5. Chicago *Sun-Times*, August 14, 1986.
6. Chicago *Sun-Times*, September 25, 1986.
7. *Crains Chicago Business*, August 4, 1986.
8. Chicago *Tribune*, November 19, 1986.
9. Chicago *Tribune*, November 7, 1986.
10. Chicago *Tribune*, November 13, 1986.
11. Chicago *Sun-Times*, November 12, 1986.
12. Personal interview with Donald Haider, June 23, 1987.
13. Chicago *Tribune*, December 16, 1986.
14. *Ibid.*
15. Chicago *Sun-Times*, December 27, 1986.
16. Personal interview (individual wishes to remain anonymous).

Notes to Chapter 4

1. Chicago *Sun-Times,* January 19, 1987.
2. Chicago *Tribune*, January 18, 1987.
3. Chicago *Sun-Times*, January 21, 1987.
4. *Ibid.*
5. Chicago *Tribune*, January 6, 1987.
6. Chicago *Sun-Times*, January 23, 1987.
7. Chicago *Tribune*, February 1, 1987.
8. Chicago *Sun-Times*, January 27, 1987.
9. Chicago *Tribune*, February 1, 1987.
10. Chicago *Tribune*, January 28, 1987.
11. Chicago *Sun-Times*, February 1, 1987.
12. Chicago *Sun-Times*, February 2, 1987.
13. Personal interview with John Halpin, May 22, 1987.
14. *Ibid.*
15. Byrne speech, Conrad Hilton Hotel, February, 1987.
16. Chicago *Tribune*, February 16, 1987.
17. Chicago *Sun-Times*, February 23, 1987.
18. Chicago *Tribune*, February 16, 1987.
19. Chicago *Sun-Times*, February 6, 1987.
20. Chicago *Tribune*, February 8, 1987.
21. Personal interview, February 24, 1987.
22. Personal interview, February 24, 1987.
23. Personal interview, February 24, 1987.
24. Personal interview, February 24, 1987.

Notes to Chapter 5

1. Chicago *Sun-Times*, February 26, 1987.
2. Chicago *Tribune*, February 26, 1987.
3. *Ibid.*
4. Chicago *Sun-Times*, February 27, 1987.

5. Chicago *Sun-Times*, March 12, 1987.
6. *Ibid.*
7. Chicago *Tribune*, March 11, 1987.
8. Chicago *Tribune*, March 16, 1987.
9. Personal interview.
10. Chicago *Tribune*, March 19, 1987.
11. Chicago *Sun-Times*, March 31, 1987.
12. Chicago *Sun-Times*, March 19, 1987.
13. Chicago *Sun-Times*, March 24, 1987.
14. Chicago *Sun-Times*, March 23, 1987.
15. *Ibid.*
16. Chicago *Sun-Times*, March 25, 1987.
17. Chicago *Tribune*, March 27, 1987.
18. Personal interview, August, 1987.
19. Chicago *Sun-Times*, February 28, 1987.
20. Chicago *Tribune*, March 9, 1987.
21. Personal interview, April, 1987.
22. Chicago *Tribune*, April 8, 1987.
23. Chicago *Sun-Times*, April 1, 1987.
24. Personal interview with Donne Trotter, June, 1987.

Notes to Chapter 6

1. H. Paul Friesma, "Black Control of Central Cities: The Hollow Prize," *Journal of the American Institute of Planners*, XXXV (March 1969), 75.

2. "Do Black Mayors Make a Difference?" *Ebony*, 39 (August 1984), 84-86; "Why Black Mayors Are More Than Symbolic Figures," *Black Enterprise*, 12 (January 1982), 7; "New Hurdles for Developers," Chicago *Tribune*, November 1, 1985.

3. Peter K. Eisinger, *Black Employment in City Government, 1973-1980* (Washington, D.C., 1983), 6-9; *U.S. Census* Subject Reports, PC 2-F, 2-4. Eisinger's data does not include part-time workers or policy and patronage personnel who were appointed by black mayors and were likely to be mostly black. According to the 1970 U.S. Census, the median age of blacks was 22, whereas the median age of Irish-Americans and Italian-Americans was 36, Polish-Americans 39, and Russian-Americans, 45 (*U.S. Census 1970*, Subject Reports, PC 2-F, 2-4).

4. John Schrag, "Minorities Getting More State Jobs but Fewer Top Posts," Chicago *Reporter*, XV (November 1986), 14.

5. Devereux Bowly, Jr., *The Poorhouse: Subsidized Housing in Chicago, 1895-1976* (Southern Illinois University Press, 1978), 78-79; see also Louis Masotti's comments on Washington's charges in William Braden, "Mayor Daley Remembered," Special Reprint Chicago *Sun-Times* (December 1986), 14.

6. *Official Report of the Task Force on Affirmative Action*, City of Chicago, December, 1985, 1, 2. Pierre deVise has argued that a disproportionate number (more than 1/3) of the patronage workers hired in the 1970s were also black. DeVise, "The Color Gap in Chicago Employment," Chicago *Tribune*, January 28, 1984. One of the better and more reliable measures of the available work force by race, gender, and ethnicity is a measure called "external work force." Because the "external work force" responds to the profit motive and efficiency, it is probably a better measure of the available and qualified natural level of employment than is a politically driven work force such as city payroll.

7. *Official Report of the Task Force on Affirmative Action*, City of Chicago, December, 1985, 1-2.

8. Ronni Scheir and Laura Washington, "Byrne's Record on Race," Chicago *Reporter*, XI (September 1982), 3.

9. Robert Davis, "Byrne's Equality Attack Backfires," Chicago *Tribune*, January 21, 1987; Ann Marie Lipinski and Mark Eissman, "City's Women Workers Stand By Their Man," Chicago *Tribune*, January 22, 1987.

10. Washington quoted in Mark Brown and Harry Golden, Jr., "Byrne, Mayor Feud Over Gender Gap," Chicago *Sun-Times*, January 21, 1987, and Davis, "Byrne's Equality Attack Backfires."

11. Pierre deVise, "Mayor Washington's Second Term: Dividing the Spoils," Chicago Regional Inventory Paper, no. II, 1-8; Barry Cronin, "City's Black Hiring Called Mockery," Chicago *Tribune*, May 25, 1987; James Strong, "Mayor Calls DeVise Report Plain Junk," Chicago *Tribune*, May 27, 1987; Harry Golden, Jr., "Mayor Belittles DeVise Report," Chicago *Sun-Times*, May 27, 1987.

12. "A professor discovers human nature," Chicago *Tribune*, May 29, 1987.

13. Pierre deVise, "Chicago After Harold," Chicago Regional Inventory Paper, no. II, 93 (December 1987), 4, 5, 13.

14. Pierre deVise, "Wrongheaded Racial Studies," Chicago *Tribune*, October 2, 1986.

15. City of Chicago Personnel Office, "Total Applicant Pool, April, 1983-December, 1986," with race and ethnic totals.

16. McClain quoted in John Kass and Dean Baquet, "Mayor's Friends Seek City Minority Contracts," Chicago *Tribune*, November 1, 1985; James H. Lowry and Associates, *Study of Minority and Women Owned Business Enterprise Procurement Programs for the City of Chicago* (March 27, 1985), 3:12, 7:3 [hereafter cited as Lowry Report].

17. Lowry Report, 4:2; Mayor Harold Washington's "Executive Order 85-2, April 3, 1985; interview with deputy commissioner of purchasing, McNair Grant, July 1, 1987.

18. "MBE/WBE Business Enterprise Reports," December 1986, Department of Purchasing, City of Chicago; Manuel Galvan, "Mayor Goes to Bat for Affirmative Action," Chicago *Tribune*, May 30, 1987.

19. Gary Washburn, "Skies Not Friendly to Blacks: Collins," Chicago *Tribune*, March 3, 1987.

20. Sherman Miller, "Affirmative Action: Blacks & Jews," Chicago *Defender*, February 11, 1987.

21. Arthur Okun, *Equality and Efficiency: The Big Tradeoff* (Washington, D.C., 1975), vii, 90.

22. Interviews with City of Chicago deputy commissioner of personnel Samuel Ackerman, December 10, 1986 and January 15, 1987.

23. Okun, *Equality and Efficiency*, 120. A not very successful effort to challenge Okun's thesis can be seen in the revival of a 1950s notion that desegregation will bring economic benefits for all by releasing "now suppressed capacities for initiative in black communities." The authors approve of "reverse discrimination," saying, "somebody's rights will have to be sacrificed" (meaning whites) for a greater good. Alan B. Anderson and George W. Pickering, *Confronting the Color Line: The Broken Promise of the Civil Rights Movement in Chicago* (Athens, GA., 1986), 227, 418, 419.

Notes to Chapter 7

1. Interview with Robert Mier, March 31, 1986, Chicago; Jane Byrne quoted in Mark Brown, "Byrne's Tour Challenges Mayor's Progress," Chicago *Sun-Times*, January 23, 1987; see also special reprint, "Mayor Washington's Chicago," Chicago *Sun-Times*, October 12, 1986.

2. See Douglas Bukowski, "Big Bill Thompson: the Model Politican," in *The Mayors: the Chicago Political Tradition*, Green and Holli, eds., 61f.; Herman Kogan and Lloyd Wendt, *Big Bill of Chicago* (Indianapolis, 1953).

3. Robert McClory, "Up From Obscurity: Harold Washington," in *The Making of the Mayor, Chicago 1983*, Holli and Green, eds., 3, 5, 10; Florence H. Levinsohn, *Harold Washington: A Political Biography* (Chicago, 1983), 186; William Braden, "Songs of Laughter Temper the Tears," Chicago *Sun-Times*, Dec. 1, 1987. Washington quoted in M. W. Newman, "Racial Politics in Chicago," Chicago *Sun-Times*, November 23, 1986; media advisor cited in Ray Hanania, "Candidates...," Chicago *Sun-Times*, March 16, 1987.

4. Steve Neal, "Harold Washington, Master of Invective," Chicago *Tribune*, August 31, 1986 and "Fight's Over, but Mayor's Cheap Shots Aren't," Chicago *Sun-Times*, March 30, 1987; Washington speech at "Future of Chicago" series, February 21, 1987, University of Illinois at Chicago; Editorial, "The big losers in the petition fight," Chicago *Tribune*, August 27, 1986; replay of Washington interview on WBBM-TV, November 25, 1987; Harry Golden, Jr., "Mayor Happy Foes Got Blast," Chicago *Sun-Times*, September 9, 1986; John Kass and Manuel

Galvan, "Washington Takes Message," Chicago *Tribune*, February 18, 1987; Mark Zambrano, "Mayor Turns Up Heat," Chicago *Tribune*, August 31, 1986; Steve Johnson, "Washington, A Master of the Quick Quip," Chicago *Tribune*, November 29, 1987; "Inc.," Chicago *Tribune*, November 26, 1987.

5. Daniel Egler and Mitchel Locin, "Mayor Has Words for Thompson," Chicago *Tribune*, October 26, 1986; Ray Hanania, "Mayor Takes it Back, Jim is No Nincompoop," Chicago *Sun-Times*, November 7, 1986; Governor Thompson's eulogy at Washington funeral, WBBM-TV news, November 30, 1987

6. WBBM-TV news, January 26, 1987; Neal, "Washington, Master of Invective"; John Camper, Cheryl Devall, and John Kass, "The Road to City Hall," Chicago *Tribune Magazine*, November 16, 1986; Mitchell Locin and Manuel Galvan, "Foes Try to Get Race out of Mud," Chicago *Tribune*, March 29, 1987; Washington describes Tillman in "Mayor Secretly Taped," Chicago *Tribune*, February 20, 1985.

7. Neal, "Washington, Master of Invective"; Jim Merriner, "Mayor Styles Complex Image," September 3, 1986, and "Mayor Raps Shameful Journalism," October 17, 1986, Chicago *Sun-Times*; Ann M. Lipinski and Dean Baquet, "Washington Views the Press," Chicago *Tribune*, December 14, 1986; editorial, "A true confession," Chicago *Tribune*, June 27, 1984; Monroe Anderson cited in "The Media and the Mayor: Round II," February 11, 1987 at University of Illinois at Chicago; "The Media and the Mayor," WBBM-TV, November 26, 1987; Tom Fitzpatrick, "Ganging up on Byrne," Chicago *Sun-Times*, December 15, 1986.

8. Interview with member of Mayor's cabinet, December 10, 1987; Harry Golden, Jr. and Mark Brown, "Byrne Brushes," Chicago *Sun-Times*, February 21, 1987; Mark Brown and Don Terry, "Byrne Tunes out her Own Debate," Chicago *Tribune*, February 16, 1987; Steve Neal, "Harold Washington, Master of Invective."

9. R. Bruce Dold and Robert Davis, "Campaign . . . ," Chicago *Tribune*, March 24, 1987; "Lighten Up, Harold," Chicago *Reader*, April 3, 1987; "Inc.," Chicago *Tribune*, May 7, 1986.

10. Steve Neal, "Washington, Byrne agree on Distrust," Chicago *Tribune*, February 18, 1987; Ann M. Lipinski and Dean Baquet, "Washington Views the Press," Chicago *Tribune*, December 14, 1986; Steve Daley, "Stay Tuned to Mayor," Chicago *Tribune*, October 21, 1986.

11. Camper, Devall, and Kass, "The Road to City Hall"; Washington quoted in Thomas E. Cavanagh, *Race and Political Strategy: A Roundtable* (Washington, D.C., 1983), 40; Ben Jarovsky and Eduardo Camacho, *Race and Politics in Chicago* (Chicago, 1987), 59f.

12. Mike Royko, "A Word About Debate 'Poopery,'" Chicago *Tribune*, April 2, 1987; see also Raymond Coffey, "The Mayor and his People Have Found a New Scapegoat," Chicago *Tribune*, August 2,

1986; "Mayor Lump Lump's Last Stand," Chicago *Tribune*, July 29, 1987.

13. WLS-TV news, November 12, 1983.

14. Hauser and Sampson quoted in M.W. Newman, "Racial Politics," Chicago *Sun-Times*, November 23, 1986; Anderson Thompson cited in Chicago *Defender*, January 8, 1987; Orfield cited in Stanley Ziemba, "Experts Give Black Mayors Good Marks," Chicago *Tribune*, February 25, 1983.

15. Steve Neal, "Vrdolyak Targets Little Guy," Chicago *Tribune*, November 11, 1987.

16. Interview with John McDermott, November 19, 1987; Nancy Isserman's CONDUCT press releases and "Numerical Summary of Complaints"; John Camper, "Campaign Watchdogs Merit a Good Conduct Medal," Chicago *Tribune*, April 28, 1987; Paul Tarini, "High Profile Helps CONDUCT Keep Mayor's Race Fair," *Heritage* (Spring 1987), 4-5; John A. McDermott to Edward R. Vrdolyak, Letter of Censure, April 2, 1987, CONDUCT files.

17. Interview with McDermott, November 19, 1987; Mike Royko, "Ho-hum Election Needs Hynes Exit," Chicago *Tribune*, March 20, 1987; Basil Talbott, Jr., "Hardly a Bite for Racial Watchdogs," Chicago *Sun-Times*, March 22, 1987; Nancy Isserman and Jan Czarnik, "CONDUCT Staff Report on the 1987 Primary and General Elections in Chicago," August 1987.

18. Roger Biles, *Big City Boss In Depression and War: Mayor Edward J. Kelly of Chicago* (DeKalb, 1984), 62-65.

19. Melvin G. Holli, "Jane Byrne: To Think the Unthinkable and Do the Undoable," 174-177; for labor influence, see Michael Kilian, Connie Fletcher and F. Richard Ciccone, *Who Runs Chicago?* (New York, 1979), 235-247.

20. Interview with Edward Sadlowski, December 16, 1987, Chicago; R.C. Longworth, "Factory Flight Most Deadly Blight," Chicago *Tribune*, December 16, 1987.

21. Interview with Daniel Lydon, executive secretary of the Plumbers Council, December 17, 1987, Chicago.

22. Jerry Harris, "Labor's Influence in the Harold Washington Administration" (M.A. thesis, University of Illinois at Chicago, 1987); interview with Chicago Federation of Labor president Robert Healey, December 16, 1987; interview with Edward Sadlowkski, December 16, 1987; Basil Talbott, Jr., "Labor Nearly Locked Out of City Politics," Chicago *Sun-Times*, September 6, 1987; Edward A. Marciniak, *Washburne Trade School* (Chicago, 1986), 59-60.

23. Interview with Edward Sadlowski, December 16, 1987, Chicago; interview with Robert Healey, December 17, 1987, Chicago. The authors would like to thank Professor William Ademan, vice-president of the Illinois Labor History Society, for a critical reading of this

section. He bears, of course, no responsibility for whatever errors may occur herein.

24. Washington quoted on Walter Jacobson's "Commentary," WBBM-Tv, Chicago, April 6, 1984.

25. Montgomery position paper quoted in Maurice Possley, "Never Admit Political Firing," Chicago *Tribune*, February 26, 1985.

26. Water E. Williams, "The Intelligent Bayesian," Chicago *Sun-Times*, November 9, 1986.

27. Washington quoted in Dean Baquet, "Mayor scores coup . . . ," Chicago *Tribune*, November 24, 1985.

28. For one variant of Donald Haider on corruption, see Jim Merriner, "Reform a Hit and Miss Effort," Chicago *Sun-Times*, September 10, 1986.

29. Dempsey Travis quoted on WBBM-TV news, May 4, 1987.

30. Milton Rakove, "Observations and Reflections on the Current and Future Directions of the Chicago Democratic Machine," *The Making of the Mayor, Chicago 1983*, 127f.

Notes to Chapter 8

1. John McCarron and David Axelrod, "City Council Wars Shake Financial Footing," Chicago *Tribune*, May 27, 1984.

2. David Axelrod, "Key Defeats Eclipsed the Glow of Victory," Chicago *Tribune*, April 29, 1985.

3. R.C. Longworth, "Holding Actions," Chicago *Tribune Magazine*, April 15, 1984; Masotti quoted in John McCarron, "Chicago's Status on the Skids," Chicago *Tribune*, April 15, 1984.

4. The community organizers are quoted in Thom Shanker and Jean Davidson, "Mayor's Year 1 a Mixed Bag," Chicago *Tribune*, April 13, 1984; Elam quoted in T. Shanker, "New Era at City Hall," Chicago *Tribune*, January 1, 1984; Editorial, Chicago *Tribune*, April 29, 1984.

5. Aldermen quoted in Thom Shanker, "New Era at City Hall"; see also Martin Oberman interview, November 26, 1986; Harry Golden, Jr., "Washington Cites his Performance," Chicago *Sun-Times*, April 30, 1984.

6. William Braden, "Poll: City Split Over Mayor's Second Term," Chicago *Sun-Times*, April 29, 1984.

7. William Braden, "How the Mayor Rates on the Job," Chicago *Sun-Times*, April 30, 1984.

8. William Braden, "Racial Split on Mayor's Reforms," Chicago *Sun-Times*, May 1, 1984.

9. Harry Golden, Jr. and Jim Merriner, "Give the Mayor a B-minus," Chicago *Sun-Times*, April 29, 1984; Longworth, "Holding Actions."

10. T. Shanker, "Washington, Mayor's First Year," Chicago *Tribune*, April 29 1984.

11. Washington quoted in Philip Lentz, "Assessing the Mayor at Midterm," Chicago *Tribune*, April 7, 1985. For Renault Robinson's

mismanagement of the CHA, see Gregory Squires, Larry Bennett, Kathleen McCourt, and Philip Nyden, *Chicago, Race, Class, and the Response to Urban Decline* (Philadelphia, 1987), 116.

12. Interviews with proponents and opponents of home equity insurance at public meeting, October 29, 1987, Chicago; see also *Report of the Guaranteed Home Equity Research Project* (Chicago Neighborhood Organizing Project, 1987, Chicago); Robert McClory, "Washington at Midterm: A Look at the Record," *Illionis Issues*, (January 1985): 22, 23.

13. Preston Greene, "A Short and Unhappy Reign," Chicago *Tribune*, February 1, 1985.

14. Graeme Brown, "Business Grades Mayor 'C'," Chicago *Sun-Times*, April 28, 1985.

15. Steve Neal, "Mayor Gives Himself a Report Card – With an 'A'," Chicago *Tribune*, April 28, 1985.

16. Philip Lentz, "Assessing the Mayor at Midterm," Chicago *Tribune*, April 7, 1985; on home equity insurance, see also "Color Line," *Chicago* magazine (October 1987), 14, 16, and "Carter Slammed for Home Equity Flip-Flop," *Southwest News Herald*, July 23, 1987.

17. Bloom cited in John Camper, "The mayor and the record," Chicago *Tribune*, April 27, 1986; Sidney Lens, "A Mayor's Dilemma," *Progressive* 49 (June 1984): 18, 22; Palmer quoted in Brian Kelly, "Harold Washington: The Balancing Act," *Chicago* magazine (April 1985): 183, 206.

18. Oberman quoted in Lens, "A Mayor's Dilemma," 18; Brian Kelly, "Harold Washington: The Balancing Act," 180. See also R. McClory, "Washington at Midterm," *Illinois Issues* (January 1985):24.

19. Melvin G. Holli, "Ranking Chicago's Mayors" in *The Mayors*, 204-206; William Braden, "Daley Edges Washington," Chicago *Sun-Times*, April 28, 1985.

Notes to Chapter 9

1. Miller quoted in Hanke Gratteau, "Aide Offers Glimpse of the Private Mayor," Chicago *Sun-Times*, November 30, 1987; see also Dempsey Travis on WBBM-TV news, May 4, 1987; and for Washington's praise of his father, see Travis, *An Autobiography of Black Politics* (Chicago, 1987), 468, 477; for James Burrell secret tape, see Michael Sneed, "Mayor Secretly Taped," Chicago *Tribune*, February 20, 1985.

2. Telephone interview with Ramon Price, January 27, 1988.

3. Quoted in *The Making of the Mayor, Chicago 1983*, 3.

4. Washington quoted in Travis, *An Autobiography*, 468; see also WBBM-TV news, "Inauguration," May 4, 1987.

5. John Camper and John Kass, "Private Man with a Public Life," Chicago *Tribune*, November 26, 1987

6. "Washington's Chicago: A Critical Examination," Chicago *Sun-Times* special reprint, November 1986.

7. John Camper, "The Mayor and the Record," Chicago *Tribune*, April 27, 1986.

8. Vrdolyak and Palmer quoted in John Kass and John Camper, "Coalition That Kept the City Together," Chicago *Tribune*, November 29, 1987.

9. Interview with Alderman Martin Oberman, November 28, 1986; Dean Baquet, "One cheer for the Washington administration," Chicago *Tribune*, April 27, 1986; Tracey Robinson, "Future Uncertain for Washburne," Chicago *Sun-Times*, August 31, 1987.

10. Washington and Orr quoted on WBBM-TV news, April 7, May 4, 1987.

11. WBBM-TV news, November 18, 1987: Thomas Hardy, "Mayor Keeps Byrne Off Democrat Slate," Chicago *Tribune*, November 19, 1987.

12. Dr. Edward Marciniak quoted in "Meeting on the Implications of Recent Events in City Hall," December 4, 1987, letter to advisory committee, Illinois Ethnic Consultation.

13. "He was Our Beacon of Hope," Chicago *Sun-Times*, December 1, 1987.

14. "Pageantry and Politics Chicago style," Chicago *Tribune*, December 1, 1987.

15. "Please, a Moratorium on Memorials," Chicago *Tribune*, December 23, 1987.

16. Chicago *Tribune*, November 26, 1987.

17. Business leaders quoted in Merrill Goozner, "Business leaders," Chicago *Tribune*, November 29, 1987; Robert Davis, "Black Leader, on Verge of Dream," Chicago *Tribune*, November 26, 1987; see also Editorial, Chicago *Tribune*, November 26, 1987.

18. Pucinski and Gonzales quoted in Don Terry and Mark Brown, "Mayor is Hailed," Chicago *Sun-Times*, November 27, 1987; M.W. Newman, "The man who made a difference," Chicago *Sun-Times*, November 29, 1987; Editorial, Chicago *Tribune*, November 26, 1987.

19. Thomas Hardy, "Just When Peace Seemed at Hand," Chicago *Tribune*, November 29, 1987; Barbara Brotman, "It's No Big Deal in Vrdolyak's Ward," Chicago *Tribune*, December 1, 1987.

20. Testimonials quoted in Robert Davis, "Black Leader on Verge of Dream"; P. Reardon, "Death Ended a Budding Friendship," Chicago *Tribune*, November 29, 1987; Jerry Thornton and Cheryl Devall, "It's Like Losing a Black Folk Hero," Chicago *Tribune*, November 26, 1987; Bruce Dold and Mitchell Locin, "Contenders Courting Jackson," Chicago *Tribune*, November 28, 1987.

21. M.W. Newman, "A Man who Made a Difference," Chicago *Sun-Times*, November 29, 1987; Ed McManus, "Harold Washington," *Illinois Issues*, 14 (January 1988): 33.

22. John Kass and Mitchell Norris, "Service Becomes Rally for Evans," Chicago *Tribune*, December 1, 1987; "Evans Backers Seek Rally to Stop Sawyer," Chicago *Sun-Times*, December 1, 1987.

23. Larry Close and M. Iherjirika," Thousands Jam City Hall," Chicago *Sun-Times*, December 3, 1987.

24. Anna Langford quoted on WMAQ-TV news, November 26, 1987.

25. Lynda Gorov, "Long night Was Hard to Stomach," and Robert Feder, "480,000 homes Maintained a TV Vigilance," in Chicago *Sun-Times*, December 3, 1987; Pucinski and Kuczak quoted in "Fallout Burns, Soothes Sawyer Backers," Chicago *Tribune*, December 7, 1987.

Index